CONFESSING CHRIST IN A POST-HOLOCAUST WORLD

CONFESSING CHRIST IN A POST-HOLOCAUST WORLD

A Midrashic Experiment

Henry F. Knight
Foreword by Zev Garber

PUBLISHERS
Eugene, Oregon

Wipf and Stock Publishers
199 W 8th Ave, Suite 3
Eugene, OR 97401

Confessing Christ in a Post-Holocaust World:
A Midrash Experiment
By Henry F. Knight
Originally published in hard cover by Greenwood Press,
an imprint of Greenwood Publishing Group, Inc., Westport, CT.
ISBN: 1-59752-628-2

Copyright © 2000 by Henry F. Knight.

Paperback edition by arrangement with Greenwood Publishing Group, Inc.
All rights reserved.

No part of this book may be reproduced or transmitted in any form
or by any means electronic or mechanical including photocopying,
reprinting, or on any information storage or retrieval system, without
permission in writing from Greenwood Publishing Group.

www.greenwood.com

Copyright Acknowledgments

The author and publisher gratefully acknowledge permission to use the following material:

Unless otherwise noted, all biblical quotations are from The New Revised Standard Version of the Bible © 1989, Division of Christian Education of the National Council of Churches of Christ in the United States of America.

Earlier versions of chapter 1 appeared as "Meeting Jacob at the Jabbok: Wrestling with the Text" in *Journal of Ecumenical Studies* 29, no. 3–4 (Summer-Fall 1992): 451–460; and with further expansion as "Wrestling with Two Texts: A Post-Shoah Encounter" in *Shofar* 15, no. 1 (Fall 1996): 54–79. Reprinted with permission of *Journal of Ecumenical Studies* and *Shofar*.

An earlier version of chapter 3 appeared as "The Transfigured Face of Post-Shoah Faith: Critical Encounters with Root Experiences" in *Encounter* 58, no. 2 (Spring 1997): 125–149. Reprinted with permission of Christian Theological Seminary.

An earlier version of chapter 4 appeared as "The Burning Bush in the Shadows of Auschwitz: A Post-Shoah Return to Holy Ground" in *Quarterly Review* 19, no. 2 (Summer 1999): 167–194. Reprinted with permission of *Quarterly Review* and United Methodist Publishing House.

For Pam

From the Psalms I have learned to pray:

*May the words of my mouth and the meditation of my heart
be acceptable in your sight, O Lord,
my rock and my redeemer.*
(Psalm 19)

From Irving Greenberg I have learned to add:

May they be credible in the presence of the burning children.
("Cloud of Smoke, Pillar of Fire")

Contents

Series Foreword *by Carol Rittner and John K. Roth*	xi
Foreword *by Zev Garber*	xiii
Acknowledgments	xix
Introduction: A Midrashic Experiment in Post-Shoah Faithfulness	xxiii
1 Facing the Night—Wrestling with the Text: Meeting Jacob at the Jabbok and Jesus in Gethsemane	1
2 Looking Back at Sodom with Abraham and Jesus: The Search for Hospitality and Justice in the Face of Destruction	39
3 The Transfigured Face of Post-Shoah Faith: Critical Encounters with Root Experiences	63
4 From the Bush to the Vineyard (and Back): A Post-Shoah Return to Holy Ground	85
5 Can These Bones Live?: From the Valley of Dry Bones to an Opened Tomb and Beyond	123

6	Looking Back over the Journey: Theological Implications for Post-Shoah Faithfulness	155
7	The Return to *PaRDeS*: A Concluding Midrash	173

Selected Bibliography   175

Index   181

Series Foreword
Carol Rittner and John K. Roth

The Holocaust did not end when the Allies liberated the Jewish survivors from Nazi Germany's killing centers and concentration camps in 1945. The consequences of that catastrophic event still shadow the world's moral, political, and religious life.

The Christianity and the Holocaust—Core Issues series explores Christian complicity, indifference, resistance, rescue, and other responses to the Holocaust. Concentrating on core issues such as the Christian roots of antisemitism, the roles played by Christian individuals and groups during the Holocaust, and the institutional reactions of Christians after Auschwitz, the series has a historical focus but addresses current concerns as well.

While many of the series' authors are well known, established Holocaust scholars, the series also features younger writers who will become leaders in the next generation of Holocaust scholarship. As all of the authors study the Holocaust's history, they also assess its impact on Christianity and its implications for the future of the Christian tradition.

In distinctive ways, Henry F. Knight embodies the aims of this Greenwood Press series. Deeply immersed and well versed in Holocaust studies, Knight's dual role as university chaplain and professor of religion at The University of Tulsa situates him especially well to examine the institutional reactions of Christians after Auschwitz, assess the Holocaust's impact on Christianity, and explore its implications for the future of the Christian tradition.

Christianity alone did not cause the Holocaust, but without Christianity's turning against the Jewish tradition, the Holocaust would scarcely have been imaginable. Ably expressed in the chapters of this book, Knight's conviction is that if post-Holocaust Christianity is to have anything worthwhile and credible to say, it must honestly confront Christianity's complicity in the Holocaust and also return repentantly to Christianity's Jewish roots. This work, Knight affirms, cannot be done by Christians acting in isolation from Jews or Jewish interpretations of Scripture. Nor can it be done, Knight's subtitle suggests, apart from Christians' "confessing Christ in a post-Holocaust world." In Knight's view, one way the needed work should be started and persistently pursued, for the sake of Christians and Jews alike, is through what he calls "a midrashic experiment."

Knight carries out this experiment in dialogue with two Jewish partners, Zev Garber and Steven Jacobs, as well as with James F. Moore, a fellow Christian. This team-work has made Knight and his colleagues leaders in interfaith midrashic interpretation, which features close, sensitive, constructive, and paired readings of key texts from the Hebrew Bible and the Christian New Testament. In the pages that follow, Knight's voice is prominent, but it is nuanced by the voices of his partners in study and conversation. He reads the biblical texts with Christian perspectives on both of these religious traditions.

Knight calls his midrashic approach "threshold thinking." It wrestles with biblical stories—they involve familiar figures such as Abraham, Jacob, and Jesus. Sometimes Knight retells the stories in ways that reveal unnoticed perspectives or unexpected prospects; always he explores the issues they raise and especially the questions they provoke after Auschwitz. The result is a post-Holocaust vision that sincerely values Jewish tradition and profoundly reaffirms a way of life that can restore credibility to Christianity. Both strands of Knight's effort encourage the healing hospitality that the world so much needs.

Foreword

Zev Garber

In an attempt to bridge the alienation between Church and Synagogue, I suggest a triple prescription: (1) Church leaders must take seriously the fruits of Judaic scholarship, particularly the Bible and rabbinics, and incorporate them in confessing, preaching, and teaching Christ in a post-Holocaust world; (2) dialogue between Christian and Jew is a proven way to contain talking badly about the other by learning from each other, that positive, constructive words of healing tend to convert yesterday's "teaching of contempt" into today's "theology of reconciliation"; and (3) never again proclaim core Christian dogma (Easter faith) and dicta (Jesus is Lord; "all [are] one in Christ Jesus"; etc.) unaffected by Auschwitz whose symbol is neither the Star of David nor the cross of Christ but the chimney of the crematoria. Henry F. Knight reflects on all three recommendations in his attempt to reconstruct a post-Shoah Christian theology rooted in Hebrew and Christian Scripture and nurtured "in the midrashic framework of Jewish/Hebraic hermeneutics." That is to say, by focusing on rabbinic beliefs and hermeneutics, the author correctly recovers the oral traditions preceding and following from the Jesus way. Ultimately, what the volume shows is the reshaping of a Christian point of view (abstract, universal) to incorporate rabbinic interpretation of the Bible (particular, contextual) in reading and understanding the moral and spiritual message of Jesus then and now.

MIDRASH: THE WORD AND THE WAY

What is rabbinic midrash? Midrash is biblical inquiry, an attempt to explain the biblical text in as many ways as seemed possible to the inquiring mind of the Jewish sage. Thus midrash has a variety of interpretations and includes compilations and collections of scriptural exegesis, sermons, and nonlegal discussion. The genius of midrash lies in its *aggadah* (nonlegal ethical and hermeneutical pronouncements peppered with philosophic wisdom and a vast amount of folk tradition), although parts of midrash are legal and very close to the halakhah of the Talmud. In present usage, midrash may also describe the process in which a contemporary relates directly to the Bible and offers existential observations juxtaposed to the text that may or may not be consistent with the accepted classical interpretation found in the Midrash, Talmud, or Codes. Unfamiliarity with the midrashic way can pose serious problems for those who seek the foundation of rabbinic Judaism, the particular Judaic system with which the life and teaching of Jesus are associated, in whose image normative Judaism is shaped, and what its theology can and cannot do in explaining the effect of the worst catastrophe in Jewish history on the faith of Israel, the Shoah.

Rabbinic midrash is not only a "how to swim" in the Sea of the Talmud but also an invitation to learn and understand the religious thought patterns and emotional tone of the rabbis in their quest for truth and life. In addition, the term suggests a holistic approach: examining specific data in the setting of life, embracing ideas, rituals, and rabbinic methodology through the prism of selectivity. This in turn leads to the midrashic worldview that integrates data within self-contained literary constructions that enables one to raise questions of form and source criticism, transmission, redaction, and so on, in accordance with the history of the *Gattungen* (text types) and grounded in the way of Torah.

An illustration is in order. Three times the Pentateuch mentions the legislation of *Lex Talionis* (Law of Retaliation; "eye for an eye"): the penalty for causing a pregnant bystander to miscarry when two individuals fight (Exod 21:23–25); the case of one maiming another (Lev. 24:19–20); and the punishment meted out to one who gives false testimony (Deut. 19:18–21). Although the law of "measure for measure" existed in the Ancient Near East, there is little evidence that the Torah carried out this legislation literally, except in the case of willful murder (e.g., Gen. 9:8; Num. 35:31). "Life for life" in cases of nonhomicidal intention and "eye for eye" when physical injuries are not fatal are seen as the legal terms for fair compensation. Thus, equitable monetary compensation is understood by the sages in the case of a pregnant woman who loses (fetal) life ("You shall give life for life," Exod. 21:23) and when animal life is forfeited (Lev. 19:18). Indeed, the midrash in the Torah casts aside all doubts as to the intent of the Hebrew *Lex Talionis*: "And he that kills a beast shall make it good, and he that kills a man shall be put to death" (Lev. 24:21).

Rejecting the literal application of *Lex Talionis*, hopefully, puts an end to the mean-spirited charge in Christian supersessionism that Judaism is "strict justice." Rather, in the midrashic understanding, the law of *'ayin tahat 'ayin* advocates remedial justice for the guilty and just concern for the injured. Not "Law of Retaliation" but "Law of Retribution." Nevertheless, the strict language of the Torah's "eye for an eye" sends forth a strong message. There is no remuneration in the world that can properly compensate serious enslavement, injury, victimization, or death.

The sages taught that God is in the details of Torah, Talmud, and Midrash. But whither the "in search of" the historical Jesus? Are there enough readers of serious quests to make it other than an exercise in primitive Christian mythologies or an invitation to the ongoing scholarly debate on "Who do people say that I am?" and the origins of the Christian movement? Are scholars who maintain that Jesus and teachings about him were created by different Christian communities for different agendas, in response to the trend of culture and taste characteristic of the social and political events of that era, tone-deaf to the sounds of the pew and marketplace that seek the truth about the Word in the traditional gospels of faith?

I ask these questions because they hum in the air around this study by Knight, who proposes a setting in the life of Jesus beyond the pale authorized by Christian orthodoxy. His book is determined to go its own way and gives little comfort to the reader who sees the Greek idiom as the medium in which the Second Testament is conveyed and who sees that Hellenistic Christianity, which handed on this tradition, also formed it. Knight is a keen observer of the passages, parables, and parabolic actions of Jesus. He points to specific narratives within the matrix of Torah and first-century Palestinian Judaism, thereby promulgating a Christian midrash—the book's implicit subtext.

DIALOGUE MATTERS

Dialogue gives insight to the temper of our age and to the temper of our own religion. Dialogue matters go beyond acquiring bits of information to a critical exchange of ideas and experience. It matters seriously in the four sequential steps of a learning exchange: *confrontation*, where the participant experiences the idea superficially; *analysis*, where the participant seriously probes the occasion or text in light of previous experience and knowledge; *interaction*, where the participant's mutual or reciprocal communication with others helps him or her benefit from their feelings, ideas, and experiences with the reality under discussion; and *internalization*, where by turning the new experience and sharing of ideas upon oneself the participant reacts meaningfully to the new reality as it relates to him or her as an individual and as a member of society.

Coincidentally, Knight climbs the four-step ladder of learning when his hermeneutical moments ascend and descend into *PaRDeS*. Namely, in focusing on *peshat*, he confronts Scriptures in its received, plain meaning; by interacting with the text, he is digging into *remez*, scriptural understanding bordering on the allegorical and philosophical, and *derash*, extracting inherent meaning via homiletics; and by seeking the *sod*, he encounters inner and mystical meanings existentially understood and applied. His approach makes an interesting contrast to that taken by proponents of Rational Christology regarding the proper context in which to mourn the Innocent and the Innocents of Calvary and Auschwitz.

Indeed, dialogical exchange has all the possibilities and dangers inherent in any real communication. On the one hand, dialogue can extend one's experience at the most profound level of his or her religious sensitivity. On the other hand, it can devaluate one's past attitude and ideas and develop a new orientation of what it means to be human. Comparisons are inevitable, and this may lead to a spiritual death and rebirth. That is to say, the old meaning and orientation may have to disintegrate while a new one emerges. Clearly, an imagery of deconstruction before creation.

This may well explain the Christian "Transfigured Face" in Henry "Hank" Knight's midrashic response to the Shoah. Succinctly put, the Shoah has destroyed Christian innocence. Whether or not there is a direct link between 2,000 years of Christian supersessionist teaching and the Shoah, the murder of millions of Jews in the heart of Christendom cannot be denied. As stated, the culpability of Christian teaching in fostering cultural and religionist anti-Judaism in doctrine and dogma must be confronted. To love the Lord Jesus Christ and to walk in his footsteps cannot be out of step with the Jewish victims of Hitler's inferno. Then and only then can the post-Auschwitz Christian understand and hopefully respond to Jesus' agonizing question at the cross.

WRESTLING WITH NIGHT/KNIGHT

Echoing the double entendre characteristic of midrash, Hank's journey into night is also a journey into Knight. He wrestles with Jacob at the Jabbok and with Jesus at Gethsemane; asks with Abraham and his Seed, "[S]hall not the Judge of all the earth do justly?"; examines Torah at Sinai and the Teaching's reconfiguration at the Transfiguration; hears the call of vocation and mission at the bush and in the vineyard; and travels from the valley of the bones to the empty tomb and beyond. He moves through the texts and other material confidently and enthusiastically, pausing whenever he wishes to illustrate a lesson, taking what appears to be a detour until we are brought back to the true course, enhanced by the sights we have seen, perfectly confident that we have been in an unusual midrashic experience. That is to say, against the dominance of Shoah before us and behind us, the

Christian confesses and the Jew professes: God lives. Dialogue matters. As a Jew in dialogue with Hank Knight, I am pleased to say:

Rabbi Eliezer ben Hyrcanus said: He [Jacob of Kefar Sikhnim] said a word of *minut* ["heresy"; read, "Here, Say"] in the name of Yeshua ben Pantira [Jesus], and it gave me pleasure. (*Tosefta Hullin* 2:24)

Acknowledgments

The work reflected in this volume began in earnest over fifteen years ago. Haunted by the complicity of my own tradition, I could not shake the issues raised by the Shoah, with regard to both the content of Christian theology as well as the form in which it was pursued. Eventually, I discovered not only the promise of midrash for incorporating the kinds of fundamental questions I had but also the integrity that midrash retained as an overlooked strand in biblical hermeneutics. Quite simply, midrash provided a critical style of being faithful that had the capacity to advance Christian theology in necessary directions while at the same time remaining accountable to the traditions it challenged. Throughout these reflections, I have tried to be attentive to the difference between adding midrash as a previously overlooked or misunderstood genre to be used in decoding the true or original meaning of a text and actually attempting to do theology midrashically. To do otherwise would violate the character of midrash. In other words, a different kind of critical engagement is called for and, with it, the development of a distinctive voice, which can be at once playful and serious as it engages the most harrowing concerns. Although I am still learning, I pray I have represented my sources faithfully and given sound expression to the theological voice of midrash.

As with most scholars, I have many people to thank, not only for the writing of this manuscript but for supporting me through the years in the "looking back" that permeates this kind of work. Like many, I begin with Elie Wiesel, whose written works penetrated my heart and whose friendship and encouragement led me to risk sharing my work in this area with others. Likewise, I cannot proceed far along the way without identifying Franklin Littell, whose powerful book *The Crucifixion of the Jews* shook me to the core many years ago. Later, through his friendship and mentoring, and that of his wife Marcie, I have found myself drawn deeper and deeper into a community of scholars whose impact is now beyond measure: the Annual Scholars' Conference on the Holocaust and the Churches. I cannot begin to identify all of them, yet they have all contributed significantly to what I have attempted here. I am particularly in debt to three of them, however, who in 1993 joined me in what has become an ongoing project of doing post-Shoah midrash together. They are James Moore, Zev Garber, and Steven Jacobs. They have shared in this dialogue profoundly, reading and responding to drafts, sharing panels, and offering their reflections to the process. Two others who briefly participated in our dialogue left their mark as well: Joseph Edelheit and Rachel Brenner. Leonard Grob of Fairleigh Dickinson University, with whom I co-chair the Pastora Goldner Holocaust Symposium, deserves a special thanks as well. The list of colleagues continues, including Hugh Burtner, Bob Fowler, and Fred Blumer at Baldwin-Wallace College and John Bowlin, Jane Ackerman, Jacob Howland, and James Ronda at The University of Tulsa. I also owe Keith Ward of Oxford University a debt of thanks. When he was a visiting professor at The University of Tulsa, we had several extended conversations that were helpful in completing this project. And I cannot overlook the support of John Roth and Carol Rittner, who encouraged me to press on with this project and to draw these reflections into a larger whole. I am in their debt.

I also wish to thank the editors of several journals for their support of my work: Nancy Krody at *JES*, Clark Williamson of *Encounter*, and Sharon Hels of *Quarterly Review*. And what more can I say to thank my colleagues Zev Garber and Jim Moore for their work with the special edition of *Shofar*? Previous versions of several of the chapters in this volume have appeared in their pages. More specifically, chapter 1 has appeared in earlier drafts in *Shofar* and in the *Journal of Ecumenical Studies*. An earlier version of chapter 4 was published in *Encounter*, and the first part of chapter 5 appeared in *Quarterly Review*. Lastly, I am pleased to acknowledge the support and patience of Elisabetta Linton at Greenwood Publishing. I am in her debt for believing in this project.

At the personal level, I must thank a number of people for the time and opportunity to write: Robert H. Donaldson and Robert W. Lawless, the past and current presidents of The University of Tulsa; the late Robert and Josephine Sharp, whose generous gift of the Sharp Chapel Endowment has underwritten my work at the university and the Sharp Summer Colloquia at Wroxton College in Oxfordshire, England, where major portions of this volume were polished and pared; and Nicholas Baldwin, the director of Wroxton College. Over the course of three different visits, I have been able to write major portions of this material while in residence at Wroxton Abbey with my Tulsa colleagues. And last, but not least, I want to thank my family, who have endured the absences when I have been away writing and put up with me when I have been preoccupied at home with these concerns. I cannot imagine undertaking a project like this one without their support. To Paul and Laura, my children: Besides expressing my love and appreciation to you, I can only add my hope that this book will make some difference for you and your generation. And to Pam, my wife, who has participated in the birth of so much of what I have tried to share here: This book is for you.

Introduction: A Midrashic Experiment in Post-Shoah Faithfulness

How shall Jews and Christians engage each other and themselves as people of contending faith traditions in our post-Shoah world? This volume identifies one promising path for such confessional work from the Christian side of the dilemma. Finding help in the midrashic framework of Jewish/Hebraic hermeneutics, this project seeks out critical vantage points for confronting and correcting Christian supersessionism and its accompanying traditions of contempt, which have become problematic legacies of shame for post-Shoah disciples of Jesus.

The reflection begins within the framework of biblical narrative, posing the driving question of otherness and its problematic of betrayal and reconciliation by reentering the conflicted world of Jacob and his struggles with his significant and signifying others: his brother, his mother, his father, himself, and God. Before turning to a similar story of anguished wrestling in Christian Scripture, a critically reflective turn is made, calling attention to the interpretive framework and rhythm that are being followed in this work. In the midst of often anguished searching, the confessional self joins others in looking back at the anguish and the interpretive frame that give one's life perspective and meaning. This hermeneutical pause, as it were, allows the midrashic approach being followed in this work to be encountered and examined within the rhythm and spirit of the critical encounter that midrash fosters. With this subtext in view, the biblical narrative is reentered midrashically in search of meaning and perspective on our troubled time as well as with regard to crucial, though often troubling, texts.

Midrashically speaking, the reader is invited to face the long and historic night of the Shoah in terms of two biblical nights of torment and anguish: Jacob at the Jabbok and Jesus in Gethsemane. The wrestling continues with subsequent encounters wherein the Shoah is faced in and through the figures of Scripture. The issues of memory, mission, and hospitality are entered through the story of Sodom (and Gomorrah) as related first through the eyes of Abraham and then through the brief, but telling, glance of Jesus. Our midrashic journey next poses the question of relating to its own root experiences, in effect, doubling back on the orienting power of Sinai in critical fashion. After the Shoah, how does Sinai inform and sustain life? After the Shoah, how does Jesus appear and instruct post-Shoah faith? How does a midrashic return to Ezekiel's valley of dry bones and Jesus' opened and empty tomb affect how he is seen and followed? More specifically, the divine question posed in the text to Ezekiel, "Can these bones live?" is put to Israel's story of restoration and hope along with the Christian narration of resurrection.

Throughout, key passages from the Gospel of Matthew are paired with appropriate ones from the Tanakh, the Jewish Bible. The logic of the pairing is midrashic, as is their critical treatment. However, a few preparatory remarks about my adoption and use of midrash are in order before proceeding any further—enough, that is, for preliminary orientation but not enough to change the hermeneutical thrust of the work itself.[1] While the first chapter will explain it in more detail, midrash is a form of Jewish interpretation that, as a Christian interpreter, I have tried to recover in spirit and form without reducing it to caricature or usurping it as my own. Indeed, what I have undertaken is a project best described as midrashic in style and form as well as attitude but not, in itself, midrash. In other words, as a post-Shoah form of interpretation, I am seeking to recover an overlooked and misunderstood way of interpreting the narrated world of past and present that restores the place of the missing, signifying others—Jews, in my Christian hermeneutic. The approach is intended to be restorative, not supersessionist. Consequently, the differentiation between midrashic and midrash is vital. The hermeneutics of midrash, however much I am influenced by them, remain other to me—significantly and signifyingly other and yet, nonetheless, other. Moreover, that issue, how to relate to otherness, runs throughout this work and its concerns as a guiding theme.

As one might expect, there are important others whose presence can and should be overheard in my text. As an experiment in midrash, such a work actually requires their presence. They share the wrestling with these texts, literally and figuratively. Many of them are present in quotes and other scholarly references acknowledged in endnotes. A small group of them[2] are actually dialogue partners in a self-consciously constructed post-Shoah project of Jewish and Christian theologians doing this kind of midrashic work together. To these colleagues and friends, I am indebted more than I can fully represent or perhaps even recognize. They are acknowledged where I can see their explicit influence. Nonetheless, they are present throughout this work and in the ways I have learned to approach these matters with them. Consequently, while this particular midrashic experiment is only one voice along what I am convinced is the appropriate confessional path for me to walk after Auschwitz, there are immediate echoes resonating with the text while I work—whether I am literally in their presence or not. Their styles and preoccupations often diverge from mine. But the hermeneutical experiment is shared, nonetheless, as it should be in our post-Shoah times. Consequently, as these reflections unfold, the reader should presume a larger community of interpreters to whom this work is accountable as well as a smaller group of significant others with whom this project has emerged as a witness to post-Shoah faithfulness in troubled and troubling times.

The volume moves toward conclusion with a final, critical look back to identify the various theological implications that grow out of this approach. In faithfulness to the midrashic framework and its rhythm of engagement and response, the world of the text is once again reentered by way of a concluding, but unfinished, Christian midrash meant to demonstrate faithfulness to the victims of Auschwitz as well as to the confessional heart of the Christian story.

NOTES

1. A more Enlightenment style of critical abstraction is developed in the endnotes. The critical voice of midrash is inter- and intratextual; consequently, it is only briefly introduced, allowing the selected texts to lead the way forward.

2. The principal conversation partners are James F. Moore, Zev Garber, and Steven Jacobs. We have been joined in public presentations at the Annual Scholars' Conference on the Holocaust and the Churches by Rachel Brenner and Joseph Edelheit as well. Our work in the context of post-Shoah, Christian-Jewish dialogue can be examined in a special edition of *Shofar: Jewish-Christian Dialogue After the Shoah*, vol. 15, No. 1 (Fall 1996).

1

Facing the Night—Wrestling with the Text: Meeting Jacob at the Jabbok and Jesus in Gethsemane

Genesis 32:22–32 and Matthew 26:36–46

What might Jews and Christians discover if they met over a shared biblical text in an honest and forthright attempt to interpret a text each honored as the Word of God? What might they discover if they moved to more problematic ground, namely, a text that for one was sacred and paradigmatic and for the other historically and existentially problematic? We begin by examining these interrelated questions, focusing on two key biblical texts: Genesis 32:22–32 and Matthew 26:36–46. In the first case, Abraham's grandchildren Jacob and Esau are preparing to meet in the context of a twenty-year estrangement. Jacob has displaced his older, twin sibling, taking his birthright and blessing. The night before their historic encounter, Jacob wrestles with a mysterious unnamed figure.[1] Reflecting on this text, the Jabbok story is reentered, and the dynamics that Jacob faced are explored. In the second case, the story of Gethsemane is explored, focusing on Jesus' night of wrestling and its meaning for contemporary Christians and Jews as they ask how this central story for Christians has been affected by what happened during yet another night, the long night of destruction called the Shoah. What follows is written in a single voice in this encounter—a Christian one—and is offered, where it begins, at the threshold of the Jabbok, self-consciously on the post-Shoah side of the history of Jewish-Christian relations.

MEETING JACOB AT THE JABBOK

Facing the Text

Who was the *ish*, the one with whom Jacob wrestled during the night at the Jabbok? With whom (or what) did Jacob wrestle on the banks of the Jabbok? Was it the guardian angel of Esau, as the sage R. Hama b. R. Hanina has suggested?[2] Was it Esau, the estranged brother, sneaking into the camp under the cover of darkness? Was it fear personified? Was it guilt? Was the stranger the haunting and stalking shadow of Jacob's father, Isaac? Was the stranger God? Was the *ish* Jacob himself, that is, the other side or sides of Jacob?[3] Who was encountered that night? What was encountered that night?

At the Jabbok, Jacob prepared for meeting his estranged brother on the following day. He sent his family across the river, out of harm's way, and prepared to wait and rest. But nightfall brought no rest. Instead, it brought struggle. An unnamed stranger, an *ish* (literally, a man), came and wrestled with Jacob through the night, putting his hip out of joint in the struggle. When dawn approached, the assailant asked Jacob to let go. Jacob resisted, demanding to be blessed in return. So the figure asked for Jacob's name, which Jacob offered freely. At that point, Jacob received a new name, Israel, meaning, according to the text, that Jacob had striven with God and with human beings and had prevailed. Jacob, now Israel, held his grip long enough to ask for the name of the one with whom he struggled. But Jacob received no name, only a question, asking Jacob why he wanted to know. Jacob's question was met by another question that forced Jacob to search more deeply within himself asking: Why did he want or need to know? Once more, Jacob had to face himself, even as he faced the *ish*, in that returning question. There the encounter ended, and the stranger blessed Jacob.

Whatever else happened that night, Jacob struggled with his own identity and legacy. Wiesel in his commentary on the story contends that Jacob wrestled with himself, the other Jacob, hidden from view: weak, vulnerable, and dependent on his mother Rebecca. According to Wiesel, this Jacob fearfully anticipated the morning encounter with Esau. Surely then, whatever else Jacob wrestled with that night, it included, even if it was not limited to, the legacy and identity he brought to that riverbank. In other words, Jacob wrestled with *a lifetime in one night*.

The Unnamed Other

Jacob asked for the intruder's name. Instead he received a question: "Why do you want to know?" Jacob's request was returned to him, and then he received a blessing. What happened in between? Did the returned question become the occasion for further wrestling? Perhaps Jacob, then, inquired more deeply about his own motives in the encounter: Why did he want to know the intruder's name? Did he want to control the *ish*, which he would be able to do if he learned the name? Did he want to master the encounter and the one whom he encountered? Was he playing a power game of mastery and deceit even in the wrestling? Did Jacob care about the stranger's reality or simply his own welfare? Perhaps all these options fit. Or perhaps the question was ironic, in effect, asking Jacob, "Do you really need to ask? Certainly, you know whom you have encountered!" The reader can only wonder. Nothing more was said between them, at least nothing recorded in the text. The story reports only that afterward Jacob named the place *Penuel/Peniel*, the face of God.

Why name this place the face of God? The story says because in that place Jacob met God face to face and lived. Surely that implies that God was the assailant. However, the word used for the assailant was *ish*, man, and is not a name used for God. Neither was the word *malak*, meaning messenger or angel, used, although that word is used in other texts that interpret or refer to this one (e.g., Hos. 12:5), lending increased ambiguity to the encounter and its interpretation. Given what the text reports, then, why name the place *Penuel/Peniel* (face of God)?

First, the story describes a change. The old Jacob—who was the trickster, the deceiver, the supplanter—that one might have stolen the chance to name the other, just like he once usurped his brother's birthright. Up to this point in the story, the text even relates that Jacob had come hoping to placate his brother and redirect Esau's anger—especially after years of fearing reprisal, even death (Gen. 32:20). In this episode, however, Jacob respected the limit. Jacob was satisfied not having the name of the other and yet, somehow, knowing in the encounter that he had been wrestling with God as well as with his past, his trickery, his pain, his deception, his shame. So he named the place, the encounter, *not the one encountered*. He left what or whom he encountered open and rich: never just God, or just the past or just fear or just shame. And yet never without any of them.

Jacob had encountered, among other things, a legacy of shame and fear, and *in all that*, he encountered God as well. They went together, inseparably. The struggle with everything he encountered brought change and a new name, a new identity—though not without cost. Whatever else Jacob encountered that night, it included the history he brought to the riverbank and the consequences of facing that history. So Jacob named the place, that is, the encounter, not the one encountered.

The Limp

The story says that Jacob's thigh was put out of joint. The wound was physical and permanent. Thereafter, he would walk with a limp. For a tradition that speaks of the way of right living as *halakhah*, to be permanently hindered in one's walking could never mean just a simple physical wounding. The linguistic echoes penetrate far deeper. Right living, *halakhah*, is literally derived from the verb *to go* or *to walk*. The lingering limp of Jacob could not have been just in his legs. It would have reached to every fiber of his identity as he stood before God, now as the "Godwrestler."[4] Jacob was marked by the wrestling and by what he had encountered in the struggle—the shame and fear, as well as by everything else he confronted that night. The limp was, and remained, psychic and spiritual as well as physical. His "walk" thereafter would reflect his struggle.

As Jacob left the banks of the Jabbok to face his brother, he brought with him his shame, his fear, his remorse, *and* his strength—all in a new name and in a new configuration. His encounter with Esau would not be without shame. Neither would it be without everything else. That night, that place in his life he named *Penuel/Peniel*—because there, in that place, Jacob had met God, face to face, as he faced himself, and faced up to his fears as well as his shame: the lifetime he brought to that riverbank. Whatever else Jacob wrestled with that night, it included his legacy of shame. Similarly, the wound he bore thereafter, his limp, was bound to what he faced that night. Jacob would wrestle with that legacy, along with everything else, the rest of his life. That night he learned he could and that doing so was how he must live thereafter.

A Tragic and Shameful Parody

The legacy of displacement and shame borne by Jacob vis-à-vis his brother Esau is not unlike that borne by sensitive Christians setting out to meet their Jewish siblings in the late twentieth century. Yet the journey to this modern Jabbok is a fearful and ironic twist to Jacob's story—indeed, it is a tragic parody. This encounter takes place on the other side of another night, not unlike Jacob's first night of wrestling. This time, however, the displacement is borne by those who have tried to usurp the place of Jacob in history, stealing birthright and name, as well as blaming the victim for the loss of sacred identity. After Auschwitz, any meeting between Christians and Jews over the biblical story of Jacob at the Jabbok calls forth an awareness of this other historical text and invites further wrestling with the issue of shame and the lifetimes brought to such an encounter.

The dynamics of displacement reach deep into the historic identity of Christianity and penetrate the story Christians tell in describing their place in history as God's people. Paul van Buren has put the issue concisely: "[I]n the Church's story the Jewish people was displaced by the Church as the sole legitimate representative—and successor—of Israel."[5] Other theologians, like Rosemary Radford Reuther and Gregory Baum from the Roman Catholic side and Clark Williamson, a Protestant representative following in the spirit of James Parkes, contend that the adversarial treatment of Israel is rooted in the sacred story of Scripture itself, not just in the story of the Church. Reuther identifies this legacy as the "left hand of Christology,"[6] whereas Williamson characterizes the canonical image of Jewish life as a caricature rooted in the early conflict between Church and Synagogue and in need of "ideological critique."[7] Van Buren clarifies what is at stake: "If the ... story did not lead directly to the Shoah, it surely provided a suitable climate for the development of modern antisemitism; and when the Shoah did come, the traditional way of telling the story offered little resistance to it."[8] He adds, "[W]hat is at stake is nothing less than the Christian story."[9] The point: Christians with no direct linkage to what happened in Nazi Germany, even those born after the Shoah, share responsibility for *how* they claim their identity even if they have no direct responsibility for the displacement or theft of identity the story they tell conveys. The issue is bound to identity and not simply to behavior (though for some it may include behavior). Consequently, what must be faced is shame as distinguished from guilt.

Shame is not the same phenomenon as guilt. Guilt has to do with behavior. Guilt is rooted in something someone does to another that violates the covenantal fabric of his or her shared life. Shame, on the other hand, is rooted in being, in who people are, not what people do. Shame is an expression of identity, not behavior. To be sure, shame and guilt are often related, and one can give expression to the other, but the distinction is essential.[10] For example, even if someone has not committed an act that violates the covenantal bonds shared with another, he or she can participate in an identity that denies another's full participation in community or even provides a foundation for the act of violation itself. The displacement theology on which Christians have been nurtured for centuries is just that sort of identity-related phenomenon. The displacement need not be a behavior consciously engaged in by Christians vis-à-vis Jews; it is *in* and passed on *by* the story that tells Christians who they are. Unless this identity-bearing narrative is transformed, the violence it breeds will remain in utero, ready to be reborn in another generation. And without shame, it can go unchecked.

In this way, shame is deeper than betrayal, at least the way many people think of betrayal. For much of what has happened in the shameful history of the Church's relationship to the Synagogue grew out of fidelity to a triumphalistic mission that sought to convert and finally to eliminate the disconfirming[11] identity of Jewish siblings. Yet in a more critical way, this, too, is betrayal—betrayal of the covenantal intention of creation that Christian traditions tragically distorted in the very expression of that intention.

Facing Shame without Being Ashamed

When fully faced and forthrightly acknowledged, shame can lead to the kind of wrestling described in this Genesis text. It can wound as well as transform. It can be a deep, identity-penetrating struggle that brings an entire lifetime into the conflict. Such struggle should not be avoided. A lengthy and convoluted history must be faced, rethought, and even transformed. In the case of the Shoah, Christians must face not simply what was done during 1933–1945; they must also confront a long history of contempt that led to the twelve years of terror dictated by Hitler. Christians must grapple with how they name themselves and their world, asking, What is it about how Christians inhabit the world that can lead to such hatred and contempt? How has the Christian identity, in the way it has traditionally embodied its confessional claims about being God's people, led to the betrayal of its covenantal partnership with the Jewish people and with God? In the shadows of Auschwitz, Christians must confront the legacy that fed the fires of the Shoah, a legacy of supplanting, of claiming a blessing that rightfully belonged to an older sibling. It is one thing to be included in another's blessing, as Paul, for example, sought to extend God's covenantal embrace of life to Gentiles through Jesus.[12] It is quite another matter to usurp that blessing as one's own, forgetting or ignoring the original inclusion on which any claim to the blessing can be based.

How, then, might Jews and Christians engage each other as they meet at the Jabbok a generation after the Shoah? Clearly, shame will be a component of their conversation. But dialogue built only on shame is built on an inadequate foundation. To be sure, shame is a necessary aspect of such a meeting. However, if only the shame is faced, particularly by Christians, their displacing identity claims remain in place. Christians have learned to identify themselves *over against* Jews in ways that feed antisemitism and contempt and that, after doing their violence, then lead to shame. For example, shame, of course, can lead to repentance. Such has been the prophetic call of responsible Christians wrestling with these matters. But what is meant or addressed by such a call for repentance? If repentance leads only to a shame-based quality in Jewish-Christian interaction, then Jewish partners in such activity will surely be uncomfortable, if not suspicious. The foundation for engagement, then, would be negative and unequal, even paternalistic. What must happen is for the shame to be confronted, as shame, with its identity-bound source likewise confronted and transformed, in repentance.

Repentance is not just an inward attitude of regret brought on by guilt or shame or both. Neither is it simply an act of soul-searching contrition. Repentance is a turning from sin, a reorientation of a person's identity, even a community's identity, from sin to life—more specifically, the covenantal fabric of life to which Jews and Christians are committed as the divine intention of creation. There is, of course, an inward moment of recognition and acknowledgment, which is essential to the act of repentance. For Jacob, it involved facing his identity as the supplanter, the "heel-sneak, heel-holder" (*Yaakov*) [13] when he wrestled with the *ish*. For Christians, facing their shame involves naming the source of their shame as forthrightly as they can and acknowledging what has been problematic in their own identity before God and their Jewish siblings. This acknowledgment, however, is only the first moment in a bold yet vulnerable confession. The second moment involves reframing the way Christians express their relationship with God to include God's continuing relationship with Jews, thereby showing a new face to an estranged sibling. In addition, this confessional task must address what it means for each community to be included in the covenantal purposes embraced by God. Christians, together with Jews, must contend not only with shame but also with how to articulate some form of common ground for including one another and their claims as people of God.

How Christians engage Jews and confront their tangled history has implications beyond their own interfaith encounter despite the particularity of the issues they face. Western Christians do not carry a legacy of shame and mixed blessings with regard to Jews only. For example: White, middle-class American males carry a similar legacy in their relationships with women, African Americans, and Native Americans. Those relationships include dimensions of shame that they dare not avoid. Consequently, as white, male, Euro-American Christians learn to face the shame in their faith identities with regard to Jews, they will be called to continue wrestling with shame in other aspects of who they are. Wrestling with their own personal and cultural texts will take them to the Jabbok again and again as they meet African American and Native American brothers and sisters as well as their own Euro-American sisters. Over and over, they will discover they know more than they wish to know about mixed blessings. And as children of Abraham, Jacob's story will continue to hold them accountable.

Any call to repentance that faces such legacies must confront shame as well as guilt—and sometimes shame even when no guilt is experienced. Never again can responsible people of faith accept, for themselves, an unchecked naïveté as an acceptable quality for their lives. By facing the shame and wrestling with the identity issues generating it, responsible persons of faith can learn to face their shame without remaining ashamed. They can break the cycle of shame and transform its source as they discover, perhaps more often than they wish, new ways of naming their relationship with God and their siblings. In the end, this is the hope of sharing such a journey to the Jabbok.

Wrestling with Intimacy

As we ponder the implications of this story, we should not overlook the way in which the metaphor of wrestling, often associated with competition, can invite further reflection on relationships and intimacy. We should not forget that the wrestling in this story began in the womb between twins. The closest of siblings struggled from the beginning with their essential relatedness. They competed for what the other had. They played one parent off against the other even as their parents played them off against each other. Indeed, throughout their lives, they were unable to reconcile their ties to one another. Moreover, though literally created in each other's image, they were unable to see their mutually reflected self in the other. Instead, they, like the narrator, saw each other in distinctly unrelated fashion. Each was the other's opposite. Yet in their difference they never recognized that which they shared. What more intimate relationship can two people have than sharing the same literal origin as twins? They bear each other's image and reveal in their mutual reflection a reality everyone shares—that all human beings, no matter how distinct, how different, bear one another's image even as they/we bear the image of God. Yet Jacob and Esau are troubled with their relationship. Indeed, there is no intimacy shared between them. Instead, there is great enmity. The nighttime encounter between Jacob and the unidentified *ish* must also include Jacob's problematic relationship with his twin and their absence of intimacy. Relationship, the very essence of which is embodied in their lives, is denied in such fashion that exile is the consequence for Jacob and a defining characteristic of his life. At the Jabbok, Jacob wrestles with that exile and his estrangements from relationship and intimacy in his life.

Any recovery of the covenantal legacy that is Jacob's heritage requires confronting this dimension in his life. As he does, he incorporates the perils as well as the promise of intimate companionship with an estranged sibling. And he does so now by choice. He holds on. He does not let go. He insists on being blessed by the one he so embraces. The struggle is not easy; indeed, it is costly. And the relationship changes in the process, as well as Jacob.

Wrestling itself is an interesting metaphor that we should not overlook. One cannot wrestle with another without touching and being touched by that other. Certainly it implies struggle, even conflict, and often a contest. Yet always, it carries a level of familiarity and closeness that other forms of contention do not. Indeed, except for the contention, wrestling would resemble lovemaking more than any other interpersonal activity.

An Unfinished Encounter

In the end, this encounter with Jacob, just as Jacob's encounter with his sibling, remains unfinished. The tale unfolds in the biblical text with Jacob (still identified as Jacob and not yet as Israel) confronting Esau the next morning. Eventually they embrace, weeping (Gen. 33:4). Some would thereby conclude the two were reconciled. Yet, as the tale continues, a painful distance remains between the two siblings. They do not unite in a shared journey even though Esau invites his brother to accompany him to Seir. For whatever reason, Jacob does not accept his brother's invitation to go with him there. Instead, Jacob promises to come later—a promise he never keeps. Why? What still separates Jacob and Esau? However much Jacob has faced himself and his past (including his relationship with his brother, father, mother, and God), he has more to face with Esau. After their tearful embrace, Jacob and Esau remain significantly other. Their journeys lead in different directions: Jacob eventually to Bethel; Esau to Seir. And yet their otherness, because it is familial, remains covenantal. Nonetheless, the biblical tradition leaves the subsequent relationship between Jacob and Esau unspecified and therefore open to interpretation, except to identify Esau with Edom and, thereby, with a long tale of enmity and violence. Later commentaries fill in the open places by identifying Rome with Esau/Edom. The point: Though perhaps reconciled in one sense, the distance and conflict between these two siblings remain; their story is, indeed, unfinished.

Any contemporary encounter with Jacob and his story remains similarly incomplete. Jews and Christians, however much they may meet and embrace, even while weeping, still find themselves confronting the distance between themselves and the tangled history that describes how that history has come to be. At the core of Jacob's wrestling was a mixed legacy that included the burden of shame. To be sure, there was guilt, too, for all he did. Yet deeper still, was the reality (along with his awareness of it) that he was weak, indecisive, and capable of deceiving those he loved. The shame fed the guilt and the fear, whereas the fear and the guilt fed the shame. Likewise, Christians wrestling with who they are in the shadows cast by their legacy of displacement also encounter shame. The task before them, as it was before Jacob, is to confront the shame, wrestle with it, and even demand from the wrestling (if not the shame itself) a blessing and a transformed identity.

Still, the wrestling does not end. Further struggle follows, particularly if Christians and Jews choose to face each other over confessional ground they *do not* share, as is the case that will be considered in the text from Matthew. Portraying Jesus' anguish in Gethsemane, it recalls another nighttime encounter that for Christians is paradigmatic but that for Jews can be thoroughly problematic. Like the episode at the Jabbok, this story focuses on a deep existential struggle, filled with questions of fidelity and vocation. Like the Jabbok, Gethsemane is approached with fear and trembling—though for very different reasons for Jews than for Christians.

WRESTLING WITH THE TEXT

However, before moving from the Jabbok to Gethsemane, it may be wise to pause and consider the kind of interpretive path being followed here. Actually, it is reflected in the very story just recounted and explored. That is, we have been wrestling with the text, much like Jacob wrestled with the *ish* (the intimate other[s] in his life) whom he faced in the night at the Jabbok. In many ways, we contend with the text, in its otherness and with the other within us that it calls forth and forces us to face. Just as Jacob did not let go of his unknown assailant, we have not released the text from our grip. Likewise, we have insisted that it bless us in our wrestling, just as Jacob insisted in his encounter. And just as Jacob had to face up to much in his life that he brought to his struggle, we must face up to much in our legacy with our biblical siblings as we struggle with this text. In other words, we have been wrestling with the text, a signifying, if not significant, other in our lives.

Wrestling with the biblical text is not new. Indeed, it has a distinctive tradition of its own associated with the term *midrash*. Derived from the verb *derash* (to seek or ask), the word literally means "from seeking" and more generally interpretation. Its Greek equivalent, *exegesis*, which is also taken over into English, similarly means the interpretation of a text. Still, because midrash can be a slippery term, its definition is not so simple. As Jacob Neusner points out, midrash can refer to interpretation in a generic sense as well as to a compilation of interpretation and/or a process of interpretation.[14] Geoffrey Hartman refers to midrash as a "type of discourse with its own rules and historical development,"[15] combining Neusner's distinction between compilation and process. Regardless, both Neusner and Hartman explain that midrash in its more specific usage is understood within a framework of the kind of interpretation undertaken by the sages of ancient Judaism known as rabbis and compiled in a body of literature known by the designation Midrash. Moreover, the compilation that Neusner identifies can refer to the collected body of commentary as well as to the discrete units within it. Furthermore, each individual commentary stands by itself in relation to the passage being interpreted as simply another interpretation offered as one among many readings of the text in question. Our interpretive path in this book winds along the way of midrash as process, but not without attending to its classical context. Indeed, when one enters the domain of midrash, one enters the domain of the rabbis. Consequently, our work is undertaken in dialogue with the compilation of their work as well as within the guiding wisdom of their way of wrestling with the text.

The Midrashic Way

Generally speaking, midrash is a style of interpretation that leverages the text in question by reference to similarly constituted texts in the canon. As Hartman explains, "[T]hrough [one] text, other texts speak."[16] In fact, in one text there are echoes (what Hartman calls a kind of "frictionality") of other texts, traces of other stories that in the way they are incorporated offer subtle comparisons and contrasts and thereby invite commentary and critique. Obviously, such an approach requires a thoroughgoing knowledge of the full canon in significant depth. With primacy accorded the text, attention is given to even the smallest detail, present or missing in it. Each and every text is taken with utmost seriousness. Nothing is overlooked, whether it is an obscure matter of grammar, metaphorical word-play (which is legion), a still-present orality lingering in the background of the text, or traces of other texts incorporated in another. Full attention is given even the open spaces where information is missing (with midrash often supplying a missing voice).

As Hartman explains, the biblical text is "stacked" with layers of meaning that require unpacking. Words are so used and arranged that their etymological roots are still showing, which internal word-play often accentuates, drawing attention to itself and calling forth nuanced response.[17] Interpretation is called forth by the text with the recognition that even in its silence an oral character is still present and evocative of the kind of interpretation appropriate to such a dimension within the recorded text. That is, the text is heard as it is read, even if it is not actually vocalized in the process.

In attending to the subtleties of the text, midrash unfolds as a method of correlation, prophetically oriented from the text toward the present and parabolically reading the same text in the light of the present situation. Neusner distinguishes these qualities, identifying three kinds of discourse that he designates as paraphrase (interpreting by retelling the text with fresh word choices, filling in missing information, extending the story and the text as received to connect with lived experience), prophecy (reading contemporary experience and usually some problematic piece of it through the interpretive lens of the text), and parable (reading the text as a densely packed, meaning-laden entity capable of sustaining multiple readings and interpretations). His differentiation is heuristic, with midrash unfolding in a richly textured method of correlation in which a text may be addressed parabolically, applied prophetically, and rendered in paraphrase even in a single reading.[18] In other words, midrash is an interpretive prism that mediates between the text and the contemporary world, "equally and reciprocally invoking the one as a metaphor for the other."[19] Neusner explains this as a constant interplay between Scripture and everyday life that "holds together two competing truths, first, the authority of Scripture, and, second, that equally ineluctable freedom of interpretation implicit in the conviction that Scripture speaks now, not only then."[20] Midrash is a method of correlation in which the biblical text provides a prism for viewing the contemporary world, whereas the contemporary situation provides an equally important lens for interacting with the scriptural text.[21] Holding these two critically interactive tasks together is an abiding confidence that the covenantal partnership and the story mediated in and by Scripture continues to unfold in the lived reality of the present.

In midrash, the interpretive act takes on added significance as a partner in the revelatory significance of Scripture/Torah. While midrash distinguishes between Revelation and its interpretation, it recognizes and gives itself to a complex interdependence between them.[22] The story mediated by the text unfolds in the interpretive act as a living and ever-unfolding story that instructs and further discloses reality. In other words, meaning does not reside simply in the text to be released by interpreters. Rather, meaning unfolds (like the story) interactively in the midrashic process.

Midrash also recognizes the plural voice of the text. Whether it is a silent but nonetheless still present oral quality of a text or the echoes of other texts incorporated in the narration of the one before the reader/hearer, the midrashist (*darshan*) attends to the multivalent quality of the text, working parabolically with the layers of meaning embedded in it. In fact, the compilations referred to as midrash (e.g., Midrash Rabbah) render this multivocal plurality in its very format, following the sequence of the biblical text with sometimes conflicting readings recorded sequentially and introduced simply as "another interpretation" (*dabar aher*) with no attempt to reconcile their differences of interpretation. Very specific rhetorical strategies grow out of this parabolic approach to the text. Recognizing that the text preserves a silent orality and that scribes added the vocalizations of vowel sounds later, interpreters are attentive to possible alternative readings to words when given similar sounding but substantively different words. Likewise, present circumstances call forth the need for rereadings that these rhetorical devices permit. The midrashist uses the word phrases *al tiqre . . . elah* (do not read . . . but) and *kivyakhol* (as it were) to signal two of these critical turns.

In this fashion, midrash is a creative approach to textual interpretation. However, its innovation is not without boundaries. At every step, the text is honored in its specificity as that to which midrash is accountable. As well, the openness affirmed in the plurality of its meanings is monitored by a community of interpreters (past and present) who hold individual readers and their *midrashim* accountable to the perduring community and its living story.[23] Indeed, there is an implicit epistemology at work here. Neither subjectivist nor objectivist, midrashic knowing is truly interactive, between interpreter and text, each of which participates in an authorizing community of interpreters similarly engaged with one another. Together they constitute an interactive ecology of meaning within the living and unfolding world of the text. Unfortunately, however, as feminist theologians and biblical scholars have pointed out, patriarchy pervades the biblical world and the authorizing, interpretive community of Jews and Christians. This is demonstrably true of classical midrash. Still, following its hermeneutical path, we can look for ways the story as mediated by midrash can "criticize and correct itself from within."[24]

PaRDeS—The World of the Text

Michael Fishbane offers a modern rendering of the midrashic project designating the interactive layers of meaning with which the interpreter wrestles. In a creative reconsideration of the medieval hermeneutical differentiation of the four essential levels of interpretation, he proposes to re-read, in midrashic fashion, its layered hermeneutic—in effect, saying, Do not read *PaRDeS* (the world of the text) in the medieval manner but in this way (*al tiqre PaRDeS . . . elah . . .*). He explains:

> [*PaRDeS* is] an acronym for *Peshat*, the literal meaning; *Remez*, the allegorical meaning; *Derash*, the tropological and moral meanings; and *Sod*, the mystical meaning. The eternal nature of Scripture reveals itself here as a well of living waters, releasing different and simultaneous dimensions of its words to all hearers at all times.
>
> My concern is . . . to reframe modern text study through the schemata of sacred learning—wherein each level of interpretation requires a different orientation to the text and discloses different dimensions of truth. The integrity of the text is thus the fullness of these possibilities, even as it is the integrity of the reader to mediate this fulfillment.[25]

Fishbane further distinguishes the levels and dimensions designated by *PaRDeS*. The first level, *peshat*, the plain sense or literal meaning of the text, constitutes its "thisness." Presenting itself to the reader, the *peshat* is the givenness of the text that resists the reader and every interpretation. The *peshat* is the text in its otherness, giving itself to interpretation but not giving itself over to the interpreter without remainder. Midrash, by holding itself accountable to *peshat*, honors the discrete otherness of the text and recognizes its integrity and that of the interpreter in the dialogue of interpretation. Thus, the text is approached by an approximation in which the text retains its otherness as the abiding limit of interpretation. The second level, *remez*, the allegorical dimension, unfolds by means of information and understandings that are external to the text. For example, information about historical conditions gleaned from historicocritical research provides necessary context and correction to material treated in the text. Likewise, questions and conditions from experience place limits and burdens on how one approaches and reads the text. Such material is correlated with the text, enlarging the world portrayed in the text as well as the experience addressed by the text. Without *remez*, *peshat* remains flat. Together, they relate with *remez*, giving life to the text like the oral to the written Torah. The third level, *derash*, "focuses on the positional and intrinsic matter of the text."[26] Among tropological concerns, Fishbane identifies root or word structure, editorial structure, and motif structure.[27] Within the moral sphere, he notes the referential character of the text. That is, the text is oriented "for the sake of life."[28] It "directs attention to the effect that [its] words may have upon us and our being in the world."[29] *Derash* digs into textual matters to discover nuance and depth hidden in the plain sight of what is written as well as in the interstices between the actual words of the text. The final level, *sod*, represents the eternal or mystical dimension of the text in which each new reading expands and extends the reality mediated in and through the text in ongoing fashion. *Sod* represents a spiritual openness and humility with regard to the living and unfolding revelation mediated in and through midrash's interpretive partnership with the text.[30]

PaRDeS also provides an allegorical prism for rendering the differentiated moments of midrash.[31] The interpretive action begins with facing the text. Initially, the reader or interpreter begins with a simple encounter with the plain meaning of the text, its *peshat*. Recognizing the text as other, the interpreter begins coming to terms with it. In so doing, he or she turns to the work of others, consulting tradition and the expertise of scholars in gleaning insight from previous encounters with the text. This interaction prepares for the analytical probing of the text in a close examination of its roots, structures, and connotations. The text is turned and turned again, to explore previously unrecognized facets and implications. Wrestling with the text in this manner, the midrashist, like Jacob with the *ish*, seeks a blessing from the encounter. The interpreter thereby seeks to incorporate the text in his or her lived experience, at the same time stepping more fully into the world of the text. Importantly, integration proceeds as an inward as well as an outward act. Eventually, the *peshat* reasserts itself, drawing the interpreter into renewed encounter wherein the text resists being controlled by the interpreter. In this fashion, *peshat* faces the reader/hearer, asserting its givenness and remaining other in relation to the interpreter.

It is more than coincidental that the acronym formed by the essential components of this hermeneutic constitute the Hebrew word *pardes*, which means "orchard" and from which we derive the word *paradise*. On our side of creation, it is the garden of delight to which we can return in study and covenantal fidelity. To shift metaphors, it is the world of the text, rendered by it but not restricted to it. As French philosopher Paul Ricoeur points out, "It is not the text which is sacred" but that which gives rise to the text and to which the text bears witness.[32] Midrash inhabits that narrated[33] world in the doing of its interpretive work. Indeed, as the word midrash suggests, especially when linked with the acronym *PaRDeS*, that work is the digging, cultivation, and care of the narrative garden of Scripture and its encompassing world.

According to Ricoeur, biblical poetics is not closed in on itself, but opens out to the world in multidimensional ways—cosmic, ethical, and political as well as existential and hermeneutical. When followed to the end, this dynamic leads to a partnership between God and God's people and the rest of humanity in what Ricoeur calls a poetics of politics—or what I prefer calling a covenantal partnership.[34] Furthermore, the world of the text is not restricted or reduced to a private mystical or spiritualized world. Rather, it is the reconfigured, even transfigured, world in which we ordinarily dwell, made new with its hidden treasures now revealed in the light of our engagement with the text.

While Ricoeur's analysis of the interpretive world of the text is helpful, it falls short of all that midrash intends. Where he speaks of the world of the text as the world in front of the text (what Neusner describes as the focus of prophetic activity), midrash also includes the multivalent world within and behind the text that it discloses and makes available for hermeneutical indwelling (what Neusner indicates being addressed by parabolic activity). Yet Ricoeur is partly correct in asserting that the biblical text is not self-referential. For the world of the text is the corporate memory of a people *through which* they view their past and orient themselves for life in the present, ready to step out into the future responsibly. In other words, the midrashic world of the text, its *PaRDeS*, is all that Ricoeur describes yet more, recognizing that what he calls the overarching, encompassing story that narrates the world of the text unfolds in a dynamic, open manner both in front of *and* within the text as a prism through which life is perceived and served.[35] Moreover, the world mediated by the text, while it is narrated, is more than narrative—even in the sense of an overarching one, for it includes the reality of covenantal obligation that is pre/proscribed in law (*halakhah*). The covenantal reality of obligation transcends and stands apart from the stories and even the metastory in which it is embedded. In other words, *PaRDeS* can be identified with the covenantal garden of life that is intended and described in narrative (*aggadah*) and prescribed in law (*halakhah*). With this friendly, but essential, qualification in place, Ricoeur's description of this metastory remains instructive regarding its application to the interpretive work of midrash:

Dietrich Ritschl summarizes [the] role of the encompassing story as generating partnership by describing the partnership itself as a confluence of stories. . . . .

Ritschl does justice to [the] enigmatic character of the overarching story by calling it a metastory. By that he means two things: first, it does not have the structure of the self-contained stories that we tell because it is an open or ongoing story; and second, it can be told *only through* [italics added for emphasis] the stories collected and gathered within its range. In that sense, besides the detail stories, it is, as such, an unspeakable story. There are stories of the exodus, of the passion, and even fragmentary stories such as the story of Joseph or that of Peter's betrayal. But the story of the partnership between God and Israel is, as such, not only open and ongoing but also unfathomable and unspeakable.[36]

The narrated world of Scripture is not subsumed under a simple narrative plot. Rather, it is complexly punctuated by contrasting and sometimes fragmented stories as well as other internal ambiguities. As well, it not only describes the partnership between God and Israel; it mediates it. Hence, the partnership itself is conveyed along with its story. Within the world of the text, Ricoeur specifically identifies three levels of discourse: myth, wisdom, and gnosis. Regarding the first two levels, he explains that while myth gives pattern, meaning, and order by providing a life-encompassing framework of orientation, wisdom builds on that framework, speculating and exploring those aspects of life that the mythic narrative fails either to address or to handle adequately. To use Ricoeur's shorthand: "Myth narrates, wisdom argues,"[37] guarding narrative from a seductive drift toward triumphalism.[38] In other words, the logic of midrash captures an important dynamic that Ricoeur could, but does not, extend to midrash. In a sense, then, midrash combines myth and wisdom, as well as the partnership they portray, embracing each in the way it embodies the latter, wrestling, as it were, with the text.

Through a creative, inter- and intratextual[39] rhetoric, midrash establishes an orienting framework that is at once critical and confessional. That is, the critical voice of midrash is rooted in the encompassing story and its world that the text mediates with its leverage secured by that world in one of two ways. In the dimension of *derash*, leverage is provided by other biblical texts offering contrasting perspectives to the one proffered by the text at hand. In addition, thoughtful distance from the text can be provided by the other scriptural structures and motifs that constitute this dimension of midrashic interpretation. Of course, the obligations articulated in *halakhah* also provide covenantal orientation in this regard.

Critical perspective can also be derived from outside the text (but not necessarily from the encompassing story and its covenantal obligations)—in a fashion that Fishbane associates with the dimension of *remez*. In this latter case, the reader, trusting his place in the vineyard of *PaRDeS*, exercises readerly resistance to the text, often playfully, in the name of the reality the text serves. Indeed, as if to signal other readers, the midrashist prefaces his or her critical interaction with the text with Hebrew word phrases *al tiqre . . . elah* (do not read [this] *but* [that]) and *kivyakhol* (as it were, or if one may suppose). In either case, the text, as received, is retained with an alternative reading offered for consideration. The critical leverage for this resistance to the text is brought to the text by the reader, but its source is typically the extratextual reference to which the verse in question speaks. As Fishbane explains, the *al tiqre . . . elah* and *kivyakhol* formulations indicate a way of reading the text in which the reader becomes the master of the text and its theology while also acknowledging the independent and abiding authority of the text.[40] In other words, this extrabiblical exegesis avoids the charge of eisegesis (imposing an external meaning on a text or reading an imposed meaning into the text) by retaining the text as received at the same time it offers an alternative way of perceiving it (*kivyakhol* adding a figurative twist in a textually playful manner, *al tiqre* offering an assertive challenge to the text in the light of articulated extratextual reasons).

Indeed, a distinctive feature of midrash is its capacity to generate the externally rooted critique that it weaves (often playfully) into the story or prescribed obligations (often by way of an expanded text, i.e., paraphrase) that the text mediates. The *al tiqre* strategy proceeds by directly confronting a problematic aspect of a received text, challenging it with "Do not read [this] but [that]." In this case, the text is not exegetically revised but reread in a self-conscious act of hermeneutical resistance. However, the *kivyakhol* strategy, often directly linked to the *al tiqre* hermeneutic, is not so much a readerly challenge as a creative maneuver to render an alternative hearing of the text as a figurative twist hitherto not associated with the text. In other words, subtlety and nuance are artfully and often playfully added and punctuated with the rhetorical aside "as it were" or "if one may suppose." Although the *al tiqre* and *kivyakhol* strategies are revisionist, they retain an important conservative component. While these strategies stand apart from the text, they stand within the narrated world mediated by the text, much the same way Torah stands in life-giving relation to each text. We can describe this dynamic with our own midrashic twist. If we do not read (*al tiqre*) PaRDeS according to its medieval formulation, but (*elah*) in the fashion we have been helped to identify by Fishbane, then we can designate the narrated world (of story and law) that the critical activity of midrash discloses, *kivyakhol*, as PaRDeS.

With this understanding, let us return once again to the world of the text. The internal, critical dimension of intertextuality, *derash*, may be illustrated by comparing the scriptural garden of *PaRDeS* to the topographical metaphor of the Promised Land. In a very literal sense, the Land of Promise from which the biblical text arises is roughly textured terrain and punctuated by hills and mountains. The text can be likened to a mountain rising up from Galilee. From it, one can view neighboring peaks, and valleys, and from the neighboring peaks one can look back to gain perspective on the vantage point from which one has just moved. Or to put the matter midrashically, we can read the text, *kivyakhol*, as if it were a mountain top that provides perspective on the terrain surrounding and including it (much like Sinai and Zion provide the overarching vantage point for seeing the full lay of the land called Israel).

A POST-SHOAH FRAMEWORK AND STRATEGY

According to Emil Fackenheim, midrash is the most appropriate framework for Jews to respond to the Shoah and still be able to affirm their identity as Jews.[41] With midrash, lived experience is not predigested nor domesticated before being incorporated into midrashic reflection. That is, midrash is a truly dialogical method of correlation that stubbornly permits (often at great confessional risk) the full weight of reality to come to bear on the witness of Scripture and tradition. In other words, the Shoah, with all its radical implications, can be admitted into the framework of midrash as the midrashist with equal stubbornness refuses to give up on the tradition's capacity to address the reorienting reality of the Shoah.[42] For example, biblical texts that express extreme suffering and oppression can be reread in the light of the Shoah; texts that report mass destruction can be revisited in the reporting of what happened in the Shoah, including new qualifications and disclaimers (in the manner of *al tiqre* and *kivyakhol*). The overarching story and world of covenantal partnership that individual texts mediate can even be revisited and revised in the light of what the Shoah discloses about the divine-human relationship. And not surprisingly, midrashic paraphrase can even render the fundamental threat the Shoah poses to the confessional story of covenant life and its world of obligation. This openness—what we might call its midrashic flexibility—allows for the incorporation of the most radical questions, even those that question the very logic of the text giving them voice.[43]

Midrash is able to take Irving Greenberg's assertion that the Shoah is a reorienting event with utmost seriousness. It provides a confessionally rooted embrace of the critical life that allows the shadow of the Shoah to be fully confronted without reducing it to theologically manageable terms in the process. Christians who recognize the covenantal crisis occasioned by the Shoah are similarly challenged to incorporate this reorienting character and its impact on their confessional identities. Midrash, with its method of correlation, unlike most Christian models, gives respected weight to the questions generated by the world external to the biblical story. The Shoah is thereby allowed its fully radical and challenging presence. Hence, the midrashic option offers guidance for Christians as well.

And yet there is a significant danger in any Christian adaptation of this midrashic voice: The very problem that tempted, seduced, and eventually haunted Jacob lingers in post-Shoah shadows with haunting implications. Any adoption and adaptation of a midrashic approach must confront the possibility of methodological and structural supersessionism,[44] avoid the attempt to make midrash other than what it is—a Jewish hermeneutic, as well as acknowledge and respect its Jewish otherness (i.e., its *peshat*) including the full scope of Torah, especially its halakhic realm of law and obligation.[45] Nonetheless, otherness can lead to increased responsibility and call forth growth, especially when it is incorporated as respect for a significant and signifying other. In this spirit, dialogue can proceed, and an appropriate post-Shoah hermeneutic can emerge and perhaps lead to healing between estranged siblings.

With this important caution, this midrashic experiment can proceed. From its method to its playful madness, the midrashic way followed here is a Christian theological adaptation. While it seeks to be fully informed by its Jewish roots, as long as it serves Christian theology, it can never be more than a greatly and gratefully indebted approximation with multifold accountability to:

1. the Jewish community of midrashic scholars (past and present);
2. Jewish and Christian Shoah scholars (especially my colleagues in this study);[46]
3. Holocaust survivors;
4. the Christian confessional community (which I represent and serve as a pastor and theologian).

In a complex and interactive mix they render confirmation or rejection of this work regarding its authenticity in each of its spheres. Does it (do I) come to terms with the Shoah, with Jewish otherness, with my own Christian identity, and that of the people and tradition I represent and serve? Like midrashic authority, it will be thoroughly communal. To be sure, that commentary remains open.

The midrashic dynamic, at least as I have come to terms with it, may be represented with the following diagram:

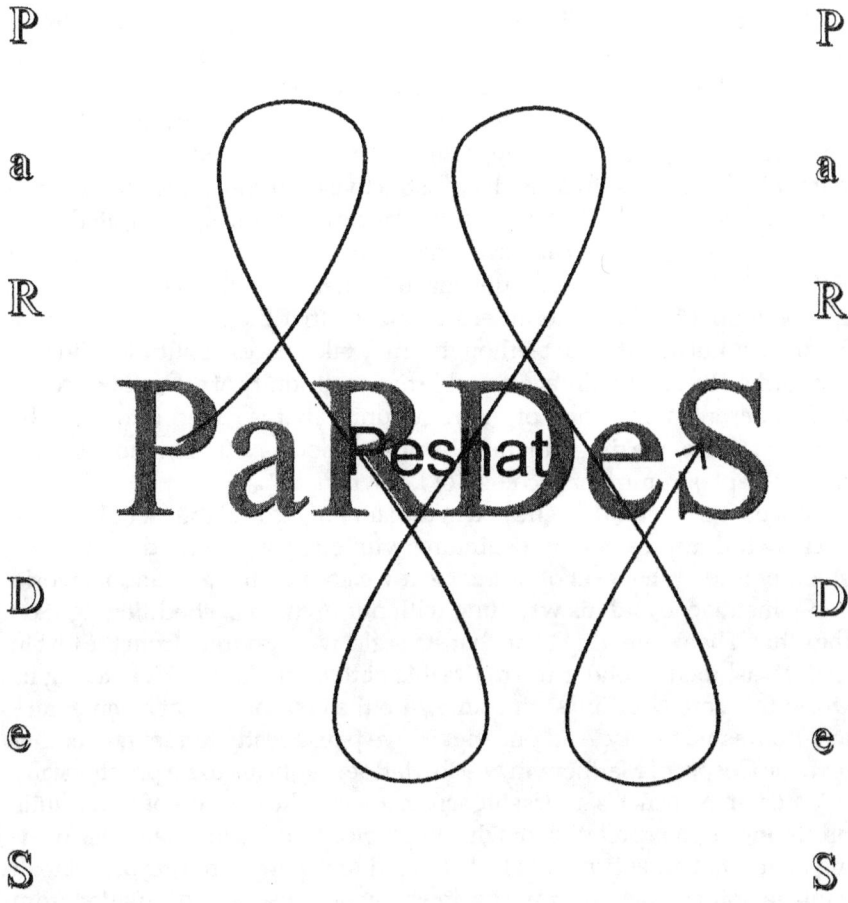

Each arc represents a critical turn, with one external to the text and the other internal to it. Each, of course, participates in the background and foreground that it mediates, *PaRDes*. That is, the text's horizon of interpretation draws upon what the interpreter brings to the text as well as what one discovers (uncovering and recovering) there. Together, the world of the text, its *PaRDeS*, unfolds in its multifaceted reality. As the vertically rendered borders of the diagram indicate, while *PaRDes* provides the horizons of meaning in front of and behind the text, *PaRDeS* is also disclosed through or mediated by the text. In other words, the text is embedded in its narrated world at the same time its *PaRDeS* requires and is accountable to the text. Furthermore, the ongoing movement is parabolic, figuratively though not graphically, as it discloses the world within and in front of the text. The unfolding and accumulative connections (*sod*) mark the return to *peshat* as the midrashic movement pushes forward and thereby extends the story. As the interpreter brings the insights of the first critical movement with him or her into the interactions of the second movement reentering the text, the interpreter engages life, not simply the text, unmasking what is at stake in the situations being faced. In this manner, even problematic events like the Shoah can be incorporated as permanent, although unsettling and disorienting, components of the way the story and its world is configured hereafter. Briefly, then, the diagram represents the differentiated moments in the parabolic dance of midrash with its distinctive rhythms of engagement and critique, even a solidarity-based sense of exile and return, constituted as internal and external critical turns and returns to the unfolding world of *PaRDeS*.[47] Still, we must not forget that this interactive engagement unfolds in a relational field of other interpreters, whether literally present or not. Midrash is not a solitary act—though it may take place in solitude. Midrash is informed by and finally accountable to a community of other interpreters and undertaken on behalf of the community that is called into being by *PaRDeS*; hence, the diagram must be understood as a frozen moment in a more complex communal ecology of knowing.

Indeed, this method is reflected in the story of Jacob at the Jabbok and especially this approach to it. Beginning with our post-Shoah dilemma, we stood poised at the level of *remez*. Next we entered the text and its world and joined Jacob and his wrestling with our own, each shedding light on the other. Then, emerging from that struggle, we withdrew from the text in critical fashion to ponder the midrashic path being followed, entering its world for more wrestling—this time with the texts of critical commentary and midrashic theory. And once again, we pause ready to reenter another text, the Gospel of Matthew, in which Matthew appears to be prophetically oriented, in Neusner's midrashic sense, toward the passion of Jesus while proffering an interpretation of what happened to Jesus in a parabolic reading of Torah. Our subsequent task: to read Matthew from our post-Shoah vantage point at the same time we interpret our post-Shoah situation from the vantage point of Matthew and thereby discern the *PaRDeS* disclosed by Matthew for our time and circumstances.

MEETING JESUS IN GETHSEMANE

After meeting at the Jabbok, Jews and Christians find a different set of issues when they approach the confessional ground of Christians. This is especially clear in approaching such a place as Gethsemane since it brings into focus the centrality of the passion of Jesus in the context of another night of testing and trial. Moreover, it brings into focus, for Jews, the risk and fear involved in trusting their Christian siblings to embrace their Christian identity without at the same time denying Jews theirs in the process—the very issues faced in the post-Shoah encounter at the Jabbok.

The Path to Gethsemane

After the Shoah, the path from the Jabbok to Gethsemane winds through a problematic as well as life-giving confessional history. On the one hand, the path leads to the heart of Christian confession, the passion story. In and through it, Christians know themselves to be included in God's loving and forgiving embrace of creation. Yet in and through this same story, Jews know themselves to be recipients of Christianity's accusation of being a displaced and reprobate people.[48] Moreover, Jews have known in practical terms that during Holy Week, when the Passion Story is dramatically rehearsed by Christians, it is wisest for them to step out of the way of Christian hate and antisemitism. Elie Wiesel's comments illuminate what too many Jews throughout history have experienced.

As a child, I wouldn't even come close to the church. I changed sidewalks. It wasn't because of me: it was because of them. Because twice a year they would beat me up.[49]

Some of that legacy—its supersessionist beginnings especially—was encountered in the post-Shoah wrestling at the Jabbok. However, supersessionism has not been the lone problem. The teaching of contempt and "the myth of deicide" also underlie the long history of hate and antisemitism.[50] Again, because the issues are identity-laden and not simply, and sometimes not at all, behavioral, Christians must face themselves and their shame in a critically integrated adjustment of their narrative identity. This task is nowhere more clearly seen than when Christians who follow such a path make their way to the Passion of Jesus. Hence, the next leg of this post-Shoah, confessional journey moves toward the Mount of Olives and an olive grove called Gethsemane. The setting: another night with echoes of yet another.

The Story

At first glance, the story Christians face in Gethsemane appears straightforward. It begins earlier, in an upper room, in the evening setting of the Seder. The story of deliverance and its celebration in a ritual meal has led to Jesus dismissing his disciples and moving with them to the Mount of Olives. There, after asking all but three of his disciples to wait for him, Jesus withdraws with Peter, James, and John to pray. He briefly tells them that he is troubled and asks them to remain where they are and "watch" with him while he withdraws even farther to pray. After a time, Jesus returns to the three disciples whom he asked to watch with him and finds them sleeping. The story continues with Jesus saying, "[S]o you could not watch with me one hour? [Then] watch and pray that you may not enter into temptation" (Matt. 26:40f.). The scene repeats itself three times, with Jesus' prayer requesting that the cup pass him by while at the same time praying for strength to accept and drink from the cup if it is what God wills. The third time he asks them, "Are you still sleeping and taking your rest? Behold the hour is at hand, and the son of man is betrayed into the hands of sinners. Rise, let us be going; see, my betrayer is at hand" (Matt. 26:45f.).

While the action may be straightforward, the story is far from simple. For Jesus, of course, the story is one of anguish and integration. Like Jacob at the Jabbok, Jesus brings his lifetime to the garden as he struggles with the consequences of his work and message. Somehow, he knows it is not going to turn out well for him. The story itself refers to his sense of what lies ahead, utilizing the ritual symbol of a cup and extending the symbolism of the Seder, which has preceded his going to Gethsemane. Most typically, the cup has been interpreted to refer to Jesus' impending crucifixion and death, drawing particularly from Jesus' own similar identification with his cup and death in the Seder. Jerusalem quite literally overlooks Gethsemane. From there, Jesus ponders the consequences of his life and work as he looks out at the occupied city. He is on a collision course with Roman authorities, and he has frightened Temple leaders who rely on the status quo. In the garden, Jesus dramatically faces the probable outcome of his ministry: rejection and death. He prays that this not be the outcome, yet always in the context of giving himself to the divine will that the text implies may require Jesus' death.

What happened in the garden is also the disciples' story: The disciples are asked to go *with* Jesus to his place of prayer and struggle. There, three (Peter, James, and John) are singled out to go farther and to *watch with him* as Jesus goes still farther into the garden to pray and wrestle with his destiny. The disciples respond by falling asleep, failing Jesus. They are unable to be *with* him, much less *watch with* him.[51] Their struggle is the struggle to be faithful to their companion in his present need. Jesus has asked only that they stay *with* him or *watch with* him. He asks them to do no more. They fail, falling away, as the story remembers it, as Jesus expected.[52]

Interestingly enough, the stories of the disciples, Jesus, and the overarching Passion narrative come together as Jesus confronts his sleeping disciples the third time. Jesus has prayed that the cup pass him by, always with the caveat that God's will be done. After each prayer, he discovers his disciples unable to endure the night and its anguish with him. Then the third time he emerges with a sense of understanding not present earlier. "Arise my betrayer is at hand" (Matt. 26:45). Jesus knows and he is accepting. But what is it that he knows? What is it that he is accepting?

The episode at Gethsemane is surely a threshold or a boundary story for Jesus, Peter, Judas, and any who would follow this one named Jesus. For Jesus, the boundary is often associated with the physical and spiritual sufferings that lie ahead in the trial, rejection, abandonment, and eventual crucifixion awaiting him. However, in this episode, the moment of crisis is tied specifically to the relationships Jesus has with his disciples. What is the limit of the covenantal existence he has offered his followers? Will their inability to stay awake and watch, their inability to share his anguish, their inability to face what he will face, break what they share with him and what he has given them? Will Peter's denial break the bond that ties them together? Jesus has said it would not earlier. Is this the choice immediately facing Jesus in this episode? How fully will Jesus drink from the cup of covenant life? In a sense, Jesus has promised and advocated a covenantal relationship, a marriage, so to speak, that cannot be sundered by the imperfections of those who accept it. In Gethsemane, that promise is tested with sleep, denial, and even betrayal. Will Jesus choose covenant life in these circumstances, with these people? If so, it will cost his life. And in the larger circle of Jesus' covenantal obligations, the issue remains the same. Jesus has chosen covenant life with all of Israel, and he has chosen to focus his embrace with those usually cut off or living at the margins of covenant community. How deeply will he drink from this cup?

The Cup

The central question addressed in the Jabbok story was who or what was the *ish*? In Gethsemane, the parallel question is, What was and is the cup that Jesus anticipated with anguish and prayed might pass him by? But, after the Shoah, one cannot simply ask, What does the cup that Jesus faced signify? One must also, and perhaps first, ask what it can *not*—or *no longer*—signify. Clearly, in the shadowy light cast by the Shoah, the cup cannot signify a divine expectation that Jesus must suffer and die to restore creation. No longer can any human being be used as an instrumental step in some larger scheme of things, even if that grand design is called divine. Nor can suffering itself bear the intrinsic meaning it has carried for Christian belief. Just as surely, the cup cannot be filled with supersessionist interpretations of God's covenantal embrace of creation or Israel.

What, then, is the cup that Jesus faced in Gethsemane? After a post-Shoah journey to the Jabbok, how can and should the cup that Jesus confronted that night in the garden be identified? With whom and what did Jesus wrestle in the night shadows of that place? And how does this vantage point in the late twentieth century affect the way that cup is named? To be sure, the biblical text proclaims that, whatever it was, the cup was a source of anguish. Jesus could feel its presence. In effect, he knew it was coming but not that it was inevitable; otherwise he would not have prayed as he did. Somehow, somewhere, it involved a choice: his, God's, perhaps his disciples', perhaps the local authorities', Jewish and Roman, perhaps all of them.

Also, the Matthean text introduces the symbolism of the cup earlier, at the Seder where Jesus takes one of the cups of blessing (presumably the last one at the close of the meal) and personally identifies with it. The story associates that identification more specifically with his blood and its being poured out for many for the sake of his covenant with them ("Then he took a cup, and after giving thanks gave it to them, saying, 'Drink from this all of you: for this is my blood of the covenant, which is poured out for many for the forgiveness of sins'" [Matt. 26:28]). Traditionally the church has identified the cup in Gethsemane as an extension of this moment, representing Jesus' suffering and crucifixion as a sacrificial death for others. But what of Jesus' own identification?

Jesus does not introduce, de novo, the imagery of a cup to his disciples, nor does Matthew do so to his readers. Rather, Jesus takes the cup in the ritual context of the Seder wherein the cup is richly bound up with the story and images of Israel—more specifically, Israel's deliverance and identity as a covenant people.[53] The cup is a symbol of thanksgiving and recollection of a relationship bestowed and yet still promised. It recalls the Passover gift of freedom and its corresponding relationship of responsible witness. Its meanings are cumulative. Every Passover ritual and experience of this wonderful relationship is poured into this cup. Moreover, every Sabbath meal includes a thanksgiving blessing that is recited with the taking and sharing of a cup of wine. The point: Israel's entire covenantal legacy is bound up, in thanksgiving, with this ritual act. The cup bears multiple meanings, all of which provide gustatory linkage with the covenantal story of Israel. It is this cup with which Jesus identifies his life and passion.

Just as the cup in the Seder signified divine deliverance and God's gracious choice to be in a covenant relationship with the people of Israel, so the cup for Jesus would be identified with his appropriation of that covenantal legacy as well as its and his unyielding commitment to liberation and life. Moreover, Jesus' identification with that cause was an identification that was so complete that he identified his entire life with it. His cause was God's cause, and God's cause was Israel and the covenant life that she represented for the world. After Auschwitz, Christians must see this cup in all its fullness, not simply as it has been reduced by selective liturgical memory.

With this more inclusive and self-critical context in mind, how does one answer the question, What was the cup Jesus faced in the garden? While it might include the suffering he was anticipating and the cost of his life, those components would surely be derivative, no matter how important they were. The cup represented the gift and calling of covenant life, embodied in his own life and that of his people. The question confronting Jesus then would be, Shall Jesus drink from the cup of covenant life so completely that it would bind him irrevocably to those who follow him as well as to those he sought to reach with his message? Like Jacob, Jesus faced a lifetime in one night, symbolized in the cup. What would it mean for Jesus to drink deeply from this overflowing symbol of his life and everything to which he was committed?

If God intends life, God would not intend that which diminishes it. If the cup was given by God, and that is surely the implication of this imagery, the cup does not represent crucifixion but all that Jesus chose and embraced in his life and, derivatively, the consequences of those choices—choices that may very well signify and include crucifixion as well as the quality of life he honored in the choosing. The point: The signification of crucifixion is not primary but secondary as a consequence of embracing covenant life so fully.

Another Night

As our encounter with Jacob at the Jabbok made clear, another more recent historical night casts its shadows on our interaction and interpretation of the texts of faith, no less this one. Realizing the power of Elie Wiesel's well-known point, "[N]ot all victims were Jews, but all Jews were victims,"[54] Jesus' followers must face the unsettling recognition that to follow Jesus after the Shoah is to follow Jesus into the camps and its kingdom of night. With this in mind, the story takes on a frightening dimension. If the night and its garden now include the world of the whirlwind of destruction (or its reverse, the whirlwind now includes this story), then each stage along the path is a stage in the immersion of this world. To be asked to enter the night in Gethsemane with Jesus is frightening enough. To be asked to stay awake and watch, more so. To be asked to go a little farther, and then to watch and pray, increases the challenge even more. But to draw those two nights together and ponder their relationship is something else altogether. After Auschwitz, following Jesus means following Jesus into a Gethsemane renamed Majdanek or Sobibor or some other frightening appellation.

Historically, we know that only a few Christians followed Jesus into the night of the Shoah, and most of them did so problematically. The Confessing Church, for example, followed Jesus there, but without recognizing the pervasive poison of antisemitism in their land and culture. The issue for them was idolatry and Church autonomy.[55] They, like Peter, denied Jesus—that is, the *Jew* from Nazareth, whom they called Christ. Most in that time and place who professed to follow, however, simply fell asleep, unable to stay awake even for the briefest time.

And even now, more than a full generation later, there is a challenge involved in entering Gethsemane, knowing that its night includes this other night of horror. Are we who follow Jesus after the Shoah prepared to step into the night of Gethsemane knowing what it now includes for us? Moreover, are we prepared to hear Gethsemane's story ask us to stay awake, perhaps even to go a little farther and follow our leader even deeper into this little understood olive grove that marks the threshold of his Passion?

Elie Wiesel, in telling his story in *Night*, probes the historic question of his faith—"Why is this night different than any other night?"—with intensely compounded irony, giving the central liturgical question of his people an unexpected twist.[56] The children of the Shoah know another night that mocks the night of deliverance and thanksgiving. In Wiesel's telling of his story, the story of a people is retold in the telling of his own, with characters of each challenging the overarching meanings of the other.

In the shadows of the Shoah, the double edge of the Seder's question can be directed to the account of Jesus' long night of anguish and faithfulness, asking: How is that night different for Christians, especially in the ironic light of the night of the Shoah? Typically, Christians have seen the night at Gethsemane as an intensely focused expression of Jesus' Passion. Jesus' decisions, actions, anguish, and fidelity are all present. In that night, Jesus faced all that he is and has been, all that he is called to be, in the light of what lay ahead for him. Now, after another night, which renders all previous nights fundamentally different, we ask, How is the night of Jesus' wrestling different once again?

What lies ahead is yet another night of wrestling. For Jacob the issues were ones that had accumulated over a lifetime; indeed, they were his lifetime. They included fear, shame, love, hope, healing. For Jesus, the issues were also cumulative. He, too, faced a lifetime in one night. His issues included his vocation, perhaps his self-understanding about any messianic role he might fulfill. Certainly they also included his love and disappointment with regard to the holy city of Jerusalem and its people. As well, they included his relationship with disciples who could not watch with him when he needed them, who even ran away and denied him in his distress.

Now, given their post-Shoah vantage point, modern-day Christians are faced with the awareness that had this story unfolded in the present century, another tragic tale would be laid over this one. Jesus would have been once more asking those who followed him to stay awake and watch with him through the night, this time a twelve-year-long night. Jesus, a Jew, would have been selected, perhaps turned over by those who knew him. His followers and companions who were Jewish would have been taken with him. But the majority of his followers, now Gentiles, would have been spared. Would they have chosen to go with him into this night? If so, would they have managed to avoid falling asleep during that time? Jesus first asked his disciples "to sit here while I go yonder and pray" (Matt. 26:36). From a post-Shoah vantage point, where is "here" and where is "yonder" whither Jesus goes? And why does Jesus next take Peter, James, and John, his closest companions, a little farther along, asking them to "watch" with him while he goes yet a little farther? Does he take them now—invite them—farther into his anguish? And what is it that fills his soul with sorrow and anguish? Then? Now? These are certainly questions that will give critically reflective Christians in this century pause as they ask them self-consciously in the lingering shadows of the Shoah.

Crises in the Garden

In Gethsemane, Jesus faced two major crises: one covenantal, the other political. At the closest, most intimate level, Jesus had asked Peter, James, and John (his closest companions) to go a step farther into the night and to watch and pray with him. To be sure, what he faced, he faced alone—as the story relates. Nonetheless, he asked his three intimate friends to go the extra distance and to stay awake and watch with him—nothing more. They were not asked to change things or to do anything—simply to be present, awake, and to watch. Yet they slept. And the others, whom he asked to go only a part of the way into his night of anguish—they also fell asleep, failing to give even a more limited presence. In contrast, Jesus was fully present—to himself, to his cause, to God, and to his sleeping companions.

The covenantal crisis extended to the people and the city that Gethsemane quite literally faced. What was Jesus' commitment to that place and to those people? Would it be as complete and unreserved as with his disciples? The answer was yes. There was no turning back on his commitment. There was no holding back on embracing covenant life as fully and intensely as he had chosen. He had filled the cup full, to overflowing, and he would drink it. The other crisis, distinct from the covenantal one, was political. Jerusalem was not simply occupied; it was also not infrequently compromised. At the same time, it remained holy and the center of his people's life. It was this crisis that swallowed up the others and then receded into the background in the later stories of Jewish complicity and responsibility for Jesus' death—responsibility that most recent scholarship points out is misapplied to the Jews because of an operative myth of deicide.[57]

In other words, Jesus faced a multifaceted crisis. On the one hand, the crisis was covenantal. It involved those people to whom he was covenantally bound—from the most intimate members of his disciples to the most marginal members of Israel's second commonwealth. On the other hand, his crisis was political. His beloved city and land were occupied by Rome. The leadership of the Temple collaborated with Roman authorities to stay in power and to secure what they thought was needed for their people. Collaboration and oppression were palpable. How committed was he to the message of God's dawning reign and how committed was he to those persons with whom he was convenantally bound, especially those in Jerusalem, the heart of his world? Absolutely so—even if it cost his life!

Yet the story of this crisis has been distorted, confusing some subtle and yet important distinctions. The covenantal crises that Jesus resolves in favor of those who fall away, deny, reject, and even abandon him is confused with the political one, especially as it is focused in the breach between Jesus and Judas. The blame for Jesus' death is shifted from the executioners (i.e., the Romans) to an intimate collaborator whose caricature will eventually emerge to symbolize the central Jewish action in the story—a fact even the stylized account in Matthew does not support. In short, the political crisis with Rome is placed in the background, perhaps originally presumed, while parts of the covenantal crisis are brought to the fore.

Given what can be critically discerned about Jesus' situation then, as well as what must be faced about the distortion and hatred carried by Christianity's legacy of anti-Judaism and its myth of deicide, how should the crisis and its conflict now be understood? To be sure, the issue is covenantal but on a much larger scale. Now it includes not simply individuals and/or parts of the covenantal story of Christianity, but it extends to include the overarching covenantal framework of life to which the Christian story bears witness. The covenantal crisis that confronts critical and thoughtful believers—Jews as well as Christians—is whether or not the world can be embraced covenantally at all. Indeed, this is the heart of Irving Greenberg's point that the Shoah is a reorienting event moving Israel [and Christianity] into an age of voluntary covenant.[58] According to Greenberg, covenant life must hereafter be voluntary, recognizing that in covenant life God has completely embraced human agency. Divine partnership and presence are to be found in the covenantal experience and process, but no longer can the divine partner be expected to act except through the *"called"* human response[59] of faithful people.

Choices in the Garden

The hermeneutical issue facing the post-Shoah Church is how to read such central and important passages in the canon as this one without participating in those traditions that have passed on and contributed to the teaching of contempt. Critical faith calls for a hermeneutical self-consciousness that can situate its interpretive dynamics faithfully within the tradition at the same time it is able to avoid making the mistakes of the past, even if such mistakes were once faithfully motivated. What is required is a double-edged hermeneutic, with distinct but related moments of critique and correction. Clearly that is the critical spirit of this midrashic reading.

Often hope lies in the text itself, once freed from ideologically straitjacketed readings of it. In this case, two crises, one covenantal and the other political, have been confused in the telling, with the political crisis with Rome hidden in the background of the story. Moreover, throughout history, the figure of Judas has emerged as the image in which these collapsed crises have merged. Judas is clearly a collaborator, who makes a political deal in betraying his friend. Instead of excising the role of Judas from the story, one can recover it more fully as that of a collaborator in whom two crises are focused and dangerously confused. The task, hereafter, will be to restore, albeit critically, the fuller political reality that is left in the background—except for its eventual resolution in crucifixion—which, unambiguously, was a Roman act. Toward this end, the text and its story have been critically engaged. According to James F. Moore, the twin hermeneutical tasks of a post-Shoah, midrashic reading of Scripture are

1. To undo the theology of contempt;
2. To provide a foundation for the teaching of respect, not by imposing new meaning on traditional texts but by returning to the text and its narrative with an increased receptivity to its own ambiguity and plurality. [60]

In other words, a truly midrashic reading adds an extratextual dimension that nonetheless remains rooted in the larger story narrated by the text. With historico-critical information about the political context of Matthew's time as well as a more complete view of historical figures like Pontius Pilate during Jesus' time, we can recover a more nuanced understanding of the covenantal and political crises that are not distinguished in the Matthean text itself.

This interpretive strategy is significant. It is at once confessionally critical and critically confessional. It reflects a lively interaction between the received tradition, in this case a text, and how that tradition is experienced, with text and experience each challenging the other to move toward greater authenticity—like wrestling with the text of Jacob at the Jabbok. In essence, midrash is testimony that the story passed on by the text lives in the interaction of the text with an other's significant experience of it. Consequently, there is a deep acknowledgment of the significance of the text on the part of the one engaged with it that simultaneously addresses the critical impact on each with the other. As well, there is a presumption of a critical *relationship* with the text (as well as its interpretive traditions) based on a dynamic and interactive indwelling of the larger story.

Clearly the hermeneutic at work here and throughout this commentary is not unlike that of Paul Tillich's method of correlation. However, in the age of the *Tremendum*,[61] Tillich's Protestant Principle is replaced by something at once more intense and critical—the Shoah, itself.[62] No longer is it enough for the cross to function as prophetic critique. The failure of the Church and its story during the Third Reich requires a stronger and more self-critical principle, which our midrashic approach embraces. The second moment of the dialectic builds on the guidance of covenant life as the divine intention for creation. "Covenant life" avoids the dangers of supersessionism by being more inclusive than Tillich's category of Catholic Substance while retaining its substantive particularity. Moreover, while positive as well as restorative, covenant life is not without its own critical dimension, a quality we might call its covenantal critique.

A Covenantal Orientation

The covenantal orientation guiding this interpretation is dialectically critical and itself rooted in a dynamic, interactive epistemology. At its heart is an understanding that the fundamental intention for creation, which Jesus sought to serve and which Matthew understood Jesus to have fully embodied, was a reality that can be helpfully focused with the phrase *covenant life*. Instead of seeing Jesus in anguish over whether or not God wished him to give his life as a sacrificial offering for others, a covenantal reading, like this one, sees the crisis confronting Jesus to be one of risking probable and imminent death as a consequence of fidelity to a covenantal relationship with God, Jesus' own followers, the people Israel, and even those most marginal in Israel's covenantal community. In Gethsemane, Jesus was, thus, facing the incredible cost of grounding his own life in a radical and inclusive commitment to covenant life at the point of extreme crisis. That crisis included impending death. As well, and perhaps more importantly to this reading, that crisis included the betrayal of one, denial and falling away of the eleven other intimate companions, and rejection by the larger numbers of people whom Jesus sought to embrace. And as the crucifixion scene eventually portrays, the crisis included even the feeling of absolute abandonment in the end. Moreover, a covenantal reading of this story distinguishes this aspect of the crisis from the political crisis, the more direct reason for Jesus' crucifixion. Jesus faced the choice of affirming his covenantal commitments at their point of violation and in the face of a distinct, even if related, political cost. His Passion was a radical and intense commitment to covenant life. Consequently, this interpretation turns away from seeing Jesus' prayers in Gethsemane as moments of resignation and submission to God's will and sees them instead as moments of wrestling with the implications of embracing covenant life so fully that he embraced even the very violations of it (denial, betrayal, abandonment). Essentially, the underlying question confronting Jesus in Gethsemane was, How committed was he to this inclusive and unyielding way of embodying his father's will? The answer, the story reports, is completely so.

How does such a picture fit with Matthew's overall portrait of Jesus? In a gospel that emphasizes with stylistic consistency that Jesus is the one who has fulfilled the Scriptures and is the one hoped for by Israel, the Messiah, continuity is maintained by affirming that Matthew's portrait is one of a Jesus that Matthew sees as fulfilling God's covenantal intentions for creation, which are articulated prophetically in Scripture. Yet the promise-fulfillment motif is directed toward the covenantal intention that lies behind and in front of [63] the prophetic utterances that Matthew cites. The covenantal intention, while singularly God's originating and continuing purpose for life, is not exhausted by claiming that Jesus fully and completely embodied it in an inclusive and radical fashion. Such a claim does not require asking whose covenant, Israel's or the Church's, is truly the covenant intended by God. Rather, God's covenantal intention, singular and uncompromising, lies behind and ahead of each attempt to embrace, serve, and embody it, no matter how successful the attempt. Consequently, supersessionism can be avoided at the same time one can also avoid any divine requirement of propitiation. Likewise, any expectation to view suffering as intrinsically meaningful becomes fundamentally unnecessary. It is the full embrace of covenant life that bestows meaning on the suffering it risks. In this way, the underlying theme of Matthew's portrait, that Jesus is the life that Scripture anticipated and bears witness to, can still be affirmed—however, not in the mutually excluding categories that have hitherto been employed in interpreting Matthew—categories with very specific roots in the conflict between two competing claims for the identity of Israel after the catastrophe of the fall of Jerusalem and the destruction of the second temple.

A Post-Shoah Cup

After the Shoah, the cup with which Jesus' followers have to contend overflows with increased anguish. After the Shoah, Gethsemane's locations shift to places with names like Majdanek, Belzec, Sobibor, and Ravensbrück, and questions of *staying awake* and *staying with* Jesus during the night take on new, unsettling meaning. The notion that suffering might contain inherent meaning requires refocusing on Jesus' choices and concerns in Gethsemane in a more self-consciously Jewish framework. The point: It is essential to clarify that Jesus' choices and anguish are life directed, both individually and on behalf of his people, even if they were made in the face of death. That is, they were not acts of resignation and giving up but moments of resistance to death and its power as it was experienced in denial, rejection, abandonment, and betrayal. Jesus was choosing life, covenant-oriented life, even if the consequence of his fidelity to covenantal existence risked probable death.

The issues of transcendence and power are another matter no less important to the issues raised by the Shoah but not treated here. Nonetheless, they spill out from the cup facing Jesus' followers. The options facing Jesus all emphasize that the covenantal framework of his life was now completely in his hands. Divine intervention did not come from some place else, heaven or otherwise, to confirm or deliver Jesus from his night of anguish. The cup from which he chose to drink did not contain a magical potion capable of removing Jesus from his circumstances. Instead, what lay within his power was whether or not he would choose the covenantal quality of life that characterized life with God and neighbor in an ecology of faith, even if it was confirmed by no one else. In a sense, this is Irving Greenberg's point, embodied in Jesus' choices in Gethsemane. Intervention does not come; nonetheless, covenant life is chosen and extended at its point of crisis. In other words, the transcendence experienced in the garden is one of meaning. A power from outside does not intrude or intervene in the situation. Rather, the power of covenant life is disclosed in Jesus' choice for covenant life in the very moment it is unconfirmed by any visibly significant other, divine or human. At the same time, Jesus is not delivered from the situation by virtue of his action, in contrast to Esther's historic action, which did bring her people liberation and serves as Greenberg's example of a noninterventionist paradigm for voluntary covenantal existence. There remains a real distinction between an authentic Jewish expectation of the Messiah and the Christian assertion that something happened as a consequence of Jesus' actions as he approached and endured the cross. Nevertheless, such a reading, by virtue of its noninterventionist, covenantal perspective,[64] does not require a supersessionist nor contemptuous reading of Jewish action then or now.

SUMMARY

When Jews and Christians meet in Gethsemane after the Shoah, the issues increase. Each brings a difficult history to this confessional garden, compounded by the historic night of the Shoah. For Christians like me, Gethsemane is an essential step in our walk of life, for Gethsemane guards the threshold of the Passion of Jesus, the very heart of our confessional story. However, the post-Shoah journey to the Jabbok is a choice we must make to face ourselves in a new and unsettling way. After the Shoah, Christians who undertake the journey to Gethsemane by way of the Jabbok walk with a limp born of spiritual humility. Moreover, they approach Gethsemane with a responsibility to avoid any victimizing readings of what happened there and after. For Jews, the path to Gethsemane represents a significant and vulnerable choice to accompany their Christian siblings into new and unnerving territory. For them, Gethsemane can be a place that symbolizes fear, as historic memories of persecution are recalled.

To choose to meet there by means of a post-Shoah midrash requires a critical reinterpretation that is able to challenge and correct past antisemitic readings at the same time it is able to establish a legitimate ground in the biblical story of Gethsemane itself. Any post-Shoah midrash, if the encounter at the Jabbok has any lasting merit, will reenter the story itself, not simply the text, to extend Gethsemane's reality into ours and ours into it. Such a meeting will recognize that this story, like Jacob's, is not neatly bound and contained by the specific biblical text. Neither is it solely contained within the larger, scriptural canon, for it is clearly the Church's liturgical story as well. It is a living, breathing, and life-changing narrative, which, like the story in the Seder that it originally extended, is annually rehearsed in liturgical fashion such that it continues to fund the understanding and piety of those whose lives are grounded in the Passion of Jesus. Finally, such a meeting will contend with the ongoing wrestling that the Shoah has provoked for people of critically reflective faith. In the end, approaching Gethsemane by way of the Jabbok may not be sound geographical wisdom; however, it is good critical advice. Critical faith, especially in the age after the Shoah, has no less a mandate than this.

NOTES

1. Alan Segal, in his historical study of the birth of Judaism and Christianity, has developed a more direct metaphorical identification of Judaism and Christianity with Esau and Jacob. Citing Genesis 25:23-24, he contends that rabbinic Judaism and Christianity both grew out of the faith world of Israel's Second Commonwealth as critical transformations of Hebraic life and culture. Consequently, he argues, it is appropriate to equate Judaism and Christianity as "twin religions." See his *Rebecca's Children: Judaism and Christianity in the Roman World* (Cambridge: Harvard University Press, 1986), pp. 1-3, 142-181.

2. See H. Freedman, trans., *Midrash Rabbah: Genesis*, vol. II (London: Soncino Press, 1939), p. 711.

3. Elie Wiesel, *Messengers of God* (New York: Random House, 1976), p. 123.

4. Arthur Waskow, *Godwrestling* (New York: Schocken Books, 1978), pp. 1-12.

5. Paul van Buren, *The Westminster Tanner-McMurrin Lectures on the History and Philosophy of Religion: The Change in the Church's Understanding of the Jewish People* (Salt Lake City: Westminster College of Salt Lake City, 1990), p. 14.

6. Rosemary Radford Reuther, *Faith and Fratricide: The Theological Roots of Anti-Semitism*, with an introduction by Gregory Baum (New York: Seabury Press 1974).

7. Clark M. Williamson and Ronald J. Allen, *Interpreting Difficult Texts: Anti-Judaism and Christian Preaching* (Philadelphia: Trinity Press, 1989), pp. 28-31, 70-72.

8. Van Buren, *Lectures*, p. 15

9. Ibid., p. 16.

10. See Helen Merrell Lynd, *On Shame and the Search for Identity* (New York: Harcourt, Brace & World, 1958), pp. 13-71, for a classic discussion of this distinc-

tion. See Robert Karen, "Shame," *The Atlantic* 269, no. 2 (February 1992): 40–70, for a helpful summary of the current literature on shame.

11. See Richard L. Rubenstein and John K. Roth, *Approaches to Auschwitz: The Holocaust and Its Legacy* (Atlanta, GA: John Knox Press, 1987), p. 59ff., for a helpful discussion of the "problem of the disconfirming other" and its embodiment, "exclusivistic intolerance," as a concomitant dimension of the truth claims of Christianity, as well as those of its Abrahamic siblings.

12. See the discussion of this matter in Daniel L. Migliore, ed., *Princeton Seminary Bulletin: The Church and Israel: Romans 9–11*, Supplementary Issue, no. 1 (1990).

13. Everett Fox's translation in *Genesis and Exodus: A New English Rendition with Commentary and Notes* (New York: Schocken Books, 1990), pp. 103–105.

14. Jacob Neusner, *What Is Midrash?* (Philadelphia: Fortress Press, 1987), p. 13.

15. Geoffrey H. Hartman, "The Struggle for the Text," in *Midrash and Literature*, ed. Geoffrey H. Hartman and Sanford Budick (New Haven, CT: Yale University Press, 1986), p. 8.

16. Ibid., p. 12.

17. Ibid., p. 4.

18. See Neusner, *What Is Midrash?*, pp. 7–8.

19. Ibid., p. 102.

20. Ibid.

21. Ibid.

22. Michael Fishbane, *The Garments of Torah: Essays in Biblical Hermeneutics* (Bloomington: Indiana University Press, 1989), p. 4.

23. The communal role of authority is recounted in a famous talmudic story about R. Eliezer and his disagreement with the Bet Midrash over a matter of ritual purity. Calling upon nature and eventually appealing to and receiving support from heaven, he argued against the combined judgment of his rabbinic colleagues. In the end, R. Eliezer was overruled. Later, the story included a postscript that added that God smiled and laughed because his children had prevailed even against him. See Adin Steinsaltz, *The Essential Talmud*, trans. Chaya Galai (New York: Basic Books, 1976), p. 217f. For a delightful midrash on this story, see Steinsaltz's "The Downfall of Rabbi Eliezer," in *The Strife of the Spirit*, ed. Arthur Kurzweil (Northvale, NJ: Jason Aronson, 1988), pp. 134–149.

24. Sandra Schneiders describes this as the prophetic spirit guiding the work of Rosemary Reuther, whose ideological critique is rooted in the prophetic tradition of Scripture. Structurally and functionally, a midrashic framework can sustain the same spirit, but it must be opened up or adapted for this inclusion. See Sandra Schneiders in Burnham, *Post-Modern Theology* (New York: Harper & Row, 1989), pp. 69–70.

25. Fishbane, *The Garments of Torah*, p. 113.

26. Ibid., p. 118.

27. Ibid.

28. Ibid.

29. Ibid., p. 119.

30. Ibid., p. 120.

31. I am indebted to Zev Garber for recognizing this dimension of midrash. True to the midrashic way, he associates this movement with the differentiated

steps of true dialogue: confrontation, interaction, analysis, and internalization. See his comments in the foreword to this volume.

32. See Paul Ricoeur, "The Sacred Text and the Community," in *Figuring the Sacred: Religion, Narrative and Imagination,* trans. David Pellaver, ed. Mark I. Wallace (Minneapolis: Fortress Press, 1995), p.68. Ricoeur explains that "the critical act is not forbidden by the nature of the text." In fact, it supports the critical reading of it.

33. Distinguishing between a narrated world and a narrative one is essential here. Neither midrash nor *PaRDeS* is restricted to narrative; indeed, a large body of Scripture is law and participates in the very partnership it prescribes. In other words, midrashic interpretation of law can be narrated and thereby located in an overarching metastory, but that overarching story is not exhausted by the category of narrative. It points to behavior and the responsible exercise of covenantal obligations (and the relationships they embody) that stand apart from the story in which that behavior may be embedded.

34. Ricoeur, "Naming God," in *Figuring the Sacred*, p. 235.

35. While the living world of the text is mediated by the text, it is nonetheless greater than the text as well. In this sense, it includes, at least in part, what Lindbeck dismissively identifies as the unmoored reality served by an "experiential-expressive" approach to the text at the same time it renders the always particular reality honored by the cultural-linguistic approach that he prefers. This understanding of midrash thereby resists the dichotomization of Lindbeck's categories and instead seeks to hold them together in creative tension. See George Lindbeck, *The Nature of Doctrine: Religion and Theology in a Postliberal Age* (Philadelphia: Westminster Press, 1984); and Peter Ochs, *The Return to Scripture in Judaism and Christianity: Essays in Postcritical Scriptural Interpretation* (New York: Paulist Press, 1993), pp. 12–23.

36. Ricoeur, *Figuring the Sacred*, p. 242.

37. Ibid., p. 252.

38. Mark I. Wallace, "Introduction," ibid., p. 27.

39. The rhetoric is both intertextual in that the rhetorical action is between distinctive texts within the biblical text and intratextual in that the critical leverage is supplied by the canonical text within its own framework.

40. Fishbane, *The Garments of Torah*, p. 27.

41. Emil Fackenheim, *God's Presence in History: Jewish Affirmations and Philosophical Reflections* (New York: Harper Torchbooks, 1970), p. 21.

42. Ibid.

43. In an interesting aside, this seems to be an integral part of the genius of Elie Wiesel's *Night*, which utilizes the Passover question "Why is this night different than any other night?" to tell the tale of exodus and election turned on its head by the long night of destruction we know as the Shoah.

44. See R. Kendall Soulen for an excellent discussion of the subtleties of structural supersessionism and their lingering possibility, even for post-Shoah theologians. *The God of Israel and Christian Theology* (Minneapolis: Augsburg Fortress, 1996).

45. For Christians, there can and should be an important recovery of law and the abiding reality of covenantal obligation that joins narrative in configuring *PaRDeS*. Even so, Christians and Jews will draw their boundaries of obligation dif-

ferently. As well, they will tell different stories, even when they include shared history and texts. Nevertheless, the midrashic figure of *PaRDeS* and the covenantal reality it represents offer a place where post-Shoah Jews and Christians can stand together in facing each other and the world they share after Auschwitz.

46. Since 1993 I have been working with Zev Garber, Steven Jacobs, and James Moore on doing midrash together as a post-Shoah experiment in Jewish-Christian dialogue. The initial set of essays is collected in James Moore, special edition ed., *Shofar: Jewish-Christian Dialogue after the Shoah* vol. 15, no.1, Fall 1996. This chapter is an extension of that work.

47. In speaking of the narrative world of *PaRDeS*, we must be clear that the story it narrates is also halakhically constituted as well. Large and significant portions are concerned with proper behavior as prescribed and described by legal codes. Consequently, we should refer to *PaRDeS* as also a halakhic as well as narrative world and be more complete in our representation of midrash.

48. See chapter 3 of Rosemary Reuther's *Faith and Fratricide*, pp. 117–182, for a discussion of the patristic roots of Christian antisemitism.

49. Elie Wiesel, *Against Silence: The Voice and Vision of Elie Wiesel*, ed. Irving Abrahamson (New York: Holocaust Library, 1985), 3: 110.

50. See William Nicholls, *Christian Antisemitism: A History of Hate* (Northvale, NJ: Jason Aronson, 1993), for a comprehensive review of this history.

51. Daniel Patte, *The Gospel According to Matthew: A Structural Commentary on Matthew's Faith* (Philadelphia: Fortress Press 1987), pp. 367–369. See also Donald Senior, *The Passion of Jesus in the Gospel of Matthew* (Wilmington, DE: Michael Glazier, 1985), p. 78.

52. It is interesting to note that in this episode the characters are all male. Later, as the Crucifixion draws nearer, the women of Jesus' circle will emerge from the background of the narrative as those few, in contrast to this scene, who did not fall away or fail to watch with their leader and friend.

53. Christians are challenged by Jewish friends to recognize that the Seder is more than a historical *Sitz-im-Leben* for this story. As my colleague Zev Garber has explained, the Seder has an abiding significance for any who would participate in it. That is, the Seder should have an active, living presence in readings that are faithful to the context that Matthew provides. Garber calls it "an unending Seder." See Zev Garber, "Night Encounters: Theologizing Dialogue," *Shofar* 15, no. 1 (Fall 1996): 46.

54. Elie Wiesel, *Memoirs: All Rivers Run to the Sea* (New York: Alfred A. Knopf, 1995), p. 66.

55. See Franklin Littell, *The Crucifixion of the Jews: The Failure of Christians to Understand the Jewish Experience* (New York: Harper & Row, 1975), pp. 44–60, for a classic analysis of this chapter in the history of the Christian Church.

56. See Lawrence S. Cunningham, "Elie Wiesel's Anti-Exodus," *America*, April 27, 1975, pp. 325–327, for an interesting analysis of the paradigmatic structural qualities of *Night*.

57. Nicholls, *Christian Antisemitism*, p. xix.

58. See Irving Greenberg, "Religious Values After the Holocaust: A Jewish View," in *Jews and Christians After the Holocaust*, ed. Abraham J. Peck (Philadelphia: Fortress Press, 1982), pp. 63–86, esp. p. 82 ff., and idem, "History, Holocaust, and Covenant," in *Remembering for the Future: The Impact of the Holocaust and Geno-*

cide on Jews and Christians, proceedings of an International Conference, Oxford and London, July 10–17, 1988 (Oxford: Pergamon Press, 1989), pp. 2920–2926.

59. Greenberg, "Religious Values After the Holocaust," p. 83.

60. James F. Moore, *Christian Theology After the Shoah: A Re-interpretation of the Passion Narratives* (Lanham, MD: University Press of America, 1993), p. 29.

61. Arthur A. Cohen, *The* Tremendum: *A Theological Interpretation of the Holocaust* (New York: Continuum, 1981), p. 25.

62. *Ibid.*, p. 139.

63. The same covenantal intention also grounds a critical *relationship* to the text and the larger canon. Scripture itself can and has grounded antisemitic attitudes. Consequently, a critical relationship as well as a critical reading of the scriptural witness is required.

64. See Henry F. Knight, "Choosing Life Between the Fires: Toward an Intentionalist Voice of Faith," in *Remembering for the Future: The Impact of the Holocaust and Genocide on Jews and Christians*, proceedings of an International Conference, Oxford and London, July 10–17, 1988 (Oxford: Pergamon Press, 1989), p. 641, where I develop a critique of the interventionist perspective and analyze how post-Shoah theology can move beyond simple interventionist and intentional options to a more self-critically dialectical one I identify there with the term *intentionalist*.

2

Looking Back at Sodom with Abraham and Jesus: The Search for Hospitality and Justice in the Face of Destruction

Genesis 18:1–19:29 and Matthew 10:5–15

Having chosen to face the Shoah and its long night of anguish, the wrestling continues. The questions deepen and the struggles increase. Indeed, confronting the Shoah is perilous work, and its call to look back evokes another story where looking back was expressly forbidden: Sodom and Gomorrah, the biblical tale of two cities. In that case, the warning not to look back was offered in the face of immediate danger. Survival depended on action that carried with it a life-threatening consequence if not followed. Survival depended upon action taken in the very presence of destruction. The warning was urgent: Do not delay, or even glance back; the threat is too great. As I hope to demonstrate, the warning was less a moral command, as some might presume, and more an existential imperative—a summons to life in the name of survival.

Our context is different. While looking back may be dangerous, the call to look back is now a moral imperative and even linked to survival.[1] Our looking back is from a distance and therefore removed from the immediate destruction that once was present. Our gaze can linger without the threat of being overtaken by the destruction at hand. We are free to ponder critical moments in what happened, both in the biblical story of the two cities and in the long, historic night of Shoah, learning from each and distinguishing one from the other.

As we begin this chapter, the questions with which we began this study remain: How do we face one another, the Shoah, and our sacred texts with honesty, with integrity, and with hope? However, as we look back from our vantage point and reenter the biblical world and its story of Sodom our questions multiply:

What might we see if we, his modern day visitors, join Abraham in facing the destruction of Sodom, along with the promise and judgment of history focused there, and the demands and responsibilities of covenant life as Abraham saw and passed them on to his ancestors? Furthermore, how do those of us who are Christians take our place there, self-consciously aware of the interpretive moves we choose in the name of Jesus? How do we face history with its judgments and understandings about God's role in history? How do we face our responsibilities for the divine mission of creation and covenant relationship with creation mediated through the descendants of Abraham?

In the shadows of Auschwitz, our work is urgent and its summons to responsibility and solidarity essential. Johann Baptist Metz has put it clearly: We face Auschwitz together with our Jewish siblings. And we face it critically.

We Christians can never again go back behind Auschwitz: to go beyond Auschwitz, if we see clearly, is impossible for us of ourselves. It is possible only together with the victims of Auschwitz.[2]

While not every attempt to do this can be done as an actual dialogue, mutual encounter and accountability provide the context. In other words, Christian interpreters must do their work with Jewish dialogue partners, even when they work in solitude. And where possible, we should make the articulation points of our distinctive views as visible and clear as we can. Consequently, in looking back at Sodom, we will be looking at two texts: the story as it is told in Genesis 18 and 19, particularly the lawsuit of Abraham, and Jesus' reference to Sodom in Matthew 10, as he sent his followers in search of hospitable welcome in the neighboring villages. (In the spirit of dialogue, I shall refer [usually in endnotes] to a project in which I have joined Jewish and Christian colleagues in engaging these same texts. Together, we stand in the shadows of Auschwitz, looking back at its destruction, hoping to learn what we can in the service of so many others we represent. As we pause together at this threshold, we face one another with a sense of mutual responsibility *for* our work and our relationships along with distinctive responsibilities *to* our traditions to represent them, and our interactions with them, wisely and fairly.)

The catastrophe that struck the cities of Sodom and Gomorrah has been interpreted by the covenantal traditions of Judaism and Christianity as an instance of divine judgment in history. We need only mention the name of Sodom, and the entire notion of God as the righteous judge of history is evoked. In modern times, another city has replaced Sodom as the primary reference for how we attend to the problems of God's involvement in history: Auschwitz. However, with Auschwitz, we are oriented differently than we are with Sodom and therefore led in another direction. Instead of presuming the direct involvement of the God of righteousness, we ponder the absence of divine engagement on behalf of righteousness. In other words, Auschwitz appears to evoke the opposite theme usually associated with Sodom. With Auschwitz, the covenantal assumptions of God's involvement in history on the side of righteousness are radically questioned. Yet such questions lie hidden in the reported encounter between Abraham and God that the biblical text places before the destruction it describes in the story. What better way, then, to examine the question "How do covenanted Jews and Christians face the radical destruction focused in the single name of Auschwitz?" than to revisit the biblical story of Sodom and Gomorrah? What follows is one attempt to address this issue by coming to the text of Genesis 18 and 19 and there to meet colleagues who have chosen to face this biblical tale of two cities, viewed from our post-Shoah vantage point, together. And having faced Sodom, we then ask: How shall we incorporate our critical return to that story in a Shoah-tempered encounter with Jesus' presuppositions about Sodom and Gomorrah as recorded in Matthew 10? Are the attendant assumptions recorded there unaffected? Are they altered? And how, then, does that affect us?

LOOKING BACK WITH ABRAHAM

Looking back at Sodom is dangerous. If there is any doubt, we need only inquire of Lot's wife. She turned to ponder Sodom and has remained frozen in her tracks ever since—a pillar of salt, the story proclaims. Do those who ponder Sodom's fate with lingering questions and their own resistance or reluctance to accept the fate of Sodom and her sister city (Gomorrah) risk a similar paralysis or ending to their pilgrimage of faith/life? Since, after all, that is what we are doing, we might be wise to begin with Lot's wife and ask of the story, Why was she punished for looking back, especially when we are told that Lot doubted and resisted the warning from the divine messengers? Lot was reluctant to heed their advice and leave. The story even tells that he had to be led away from Sodom (Gen. 19:15.). Why was Lot's wife the one who faced the greater consequence?

Perhaps our post-Shoah circumstances in asking this question provide our first clue. We know that there are dangers in looking back at Auschwitz. More than once it has broken the spirits and claimed the lives of persons who turn to view its smoke and ashes. Even fifty years after, the danger still lurks in the darkness. As Elie Wiesel has said on more than one occasion, it is dangerous to study the Shoah. Through depression, loss of hope, suicide, through loss of faith, or world, or all of these combined, Auschwitz can transform those who gaze at its pillars of fire into pillars of salt.

Knowing this, perhaps we need only ask, Was Lot's wife a victim of the destruction because she was too close to the destruction? Did she simply get too close to the abyss that was opening behind her when she turned to look and was consumed by what she saw? To be sure, the story said she was warned, but how could she know what was really happening? From this perspective, we should not see her demise as punishment. Neither should we compare her to Lot, or anyone else. Rather, she should be mourned and remembered as one of Sodom's victims. And as one of Sodom's nameless victims, she stands as a warning to any of us who turn back to gaze at Sodom's destruction.

Remembering Lot's Wife

There is another reason we must be careful not to overlook Lot's wife. In addition to the destruction that engulfs her in the story, as a figure she is used by the story in ways that we should question. We never learn her name. We do not hear important details of her life, although she is clearly a victim with whom we identify in hearing her story. In contrast to Sarah, Abraham's spouse and her counterpart in the story, she is a cardboard character. And in many ways, so is Lot, though in his case, he seems to choose his portion in life as a copy of his uncle, mimicking Abraham's hospitality without ever practicing the respect of others, which grounds true hospitality. Indeed, Lot manages to render his hospitality while passing along violence to his own family. In other words, the story passes on the empty shell of Lot's relationships. As a result, meeting Lot's wife as a cardboard figure, a cipher, in Lot's story may reflect the reality of/within Lot's family. If so, her pain is magnified by the absence of her identity in this tale. In addition to not having a place in her own right in the story, she would have none in her life with Lot as well.

Of course, we cannot know her pain or the actual reason for it, but we can see her loss, and ours, as long as she remains missing from the story. Consequently, whatever the reason for her absence, especially now, we dare not leave her frozen in time, unaddressed and overlooked as one who does not matter. Likewise, we cannot do the same with regard to the many women who shared and still share her lot in our world. She must be coaxed to speak—if even in her silent imperative, saying, as it were, "Listen to me! Looking back at Sodom is dangerous, even from a distance."

So why pursue exactly this course of action? Why compound the danger by looking back from the shadows of Auschwitz? After Auschwitz, looking back at Sodom may be even more dangerous; the questions multiply and the covenantal stakes intensify, as this set of reflections will show. Why undertake such a project? Yet, after Auschwitz, is there any other moral choice? Quite simply, after Auschwitz we cannot not look back.[3] The grief and trauma do not allow otherwise; neither do our moral and spiritual obligations to the past and the future, to the covenantal fabric of our world.

While such a task is fraught with danger, it is not without precedent or guidance. Perhaps more important, that guidance is provided by the textual setting in which we encounter our biblical tale of two cities. As we linger here, perhaps we shall be free to notice that Lot's wife may not be the only one who looked back at Sodom. The argument Abraham has with God before the visitation of judgment may very well be a midrashic insertion of questions generated after the historical event in which the message of judgment was perceived—a safe, albeit questioning, way to look back.

Standing with Abraham, Contending with God

Many scholars present a convincing case that the nineteenth chapter of Genesis describing the destruction of Sodom is the older part of the story. They contend that Abraham's argument with God over Sodom's future is from later tradition.[4] Their thesis: A tragic disaster, attributed to an act of God, has befallen the plain cities—perhaps because of an earthquake or a violent explosion of underground natural gas.[5] The argument scene with Abraham is viewed as a later embellishment growing out of the assumption that the two cities had been punished for their sin. Abraham's argument is then read back into the story as a narrative form of theological reflection, in the form of a law court petition[6] in which Abraham questions God about righteousness and justice within the context of receiving and passing on the tradition of judgment about Sodom and Gomorrah. If this thesis is true, then what we have in Genesis 18 is a theological midrash incorporated into the text, wresting meaning out of a disaster by relying on a fundamental belief about God's relationship to history and creation. Namely, God is just, and the ways of the universe follow a just plan. The key line in the text: "Shall not the Judge of all the earth do what is just?" (Gen. 18:25).

With Noah and the Tower of Babel, God acts in sweeping fashion. In the case of the flood, God rescues Noah and his family as ones who walk with God. In the case of Sodom, God acts in sweeping fashion and rescues a family that, while not without its flaws, is part of Abraham's family and modestly practices hospitality, a precondition for righteousness, that is, walking with God. With verse 23, Abraham begins to question the sweeping condemnation of all by asking about the presence of a few who might be righteous. If they are present, would God spare the city? And so the argument develops, fleshing out Abraham's protest on behalf of those who might be innocent of the evil for which Sodom and Gomorrah are punished. The important point to notice is that this portion of the story "wrestles" with the larger narrative by incorporating protest retroactively as an argument prior to judgment, thus justifying the interpretation that Sodom's fate was the result of divine judgment in her history. As midrash read back into the story, Abraham's argument becomes a commentary on why Sodom was not spared. Namely, there were not a sufficient number of righteous persons to save the city.

Why this form? Why approach God in the form of a lawsuit? Why not a straightforward petition for God to save the people of the city? According to Anson Laytner, the law court form of intercession is a distinctive "Jewish response to the problem of theodicy. The law court argument prayer ... calls God to task for His lapses of duty which result in suffering and injustice."[7] When projected back into the story, it becomes a theological as well as legal argument, which in its narrative way clears God of the charges it articulates. It is a midrashic form of protest, that in its grieving restores the relationship troubled by the problem offered up in prayer.[8]

Notice how the argument progresses. In building the substantive case, it moves forward in articulated humility (verses 27 and 32). And not to be overlooked, the entire encounter begins with a divine invitation (Gen. 18:17/ff.). There is no usurping of roles here. This argument proceeds between covenantal partners. In order to understand the significance of this point, we need only remember Jacob's night of wrestling at the Jabbok, treated in the previous chapter, and compare the two encounters. In that episode, Jacob wrestles with God as he faces an unnamed visitor in the night, an *ish*, with whom Jacob wrestles until the break of day. Jacob faces himself, his estranged brother, perhaps his father, and most probably every estranged relationship from his past. He faces a lifetime wrapped in shame in his wrestling, and in his wrestling he found himself contending with God.[9] Jacob emerges a changed figure, Israel. Abraham's contention is unlike Jacob's. Abraham brings a city to God. He brings a people—not even his own, though he includes his nephew's family within his concern. He argues, he wrestles, *on their behalf*. Jacob, on the other hand, brings himself, his shame, and his past. Abraham brings others and their futures—even if encountered in the past after the fact.

In contrast to the outcome of Jacob's encounter, Abraham emerges unwounded. Jacob emerges from his night of wrestling, walking with a limp; Abraham continues walking with God, albeit with more tests, greater tests, ahead. What is different? Why, too, is Abraham spared when Lot's wife was not? Why was he allowed to argue with God and thereby resist what happened to Sodom and its sister city without being consumed by the destruction that overwhelmed its inhabitants and Lot's wife? What distinguishes Abraham?

Here again, the comparison with Jacob's struggle may be helpful. Abraham's boldness was rooted in humility and knowing his place before God. Jacob's was a clutching, demanding struggle—from the very beginning of his life. Jacob's contention was a physical struggle, existentially writ large, deep in the liminal time of night. It occurred in the wilderness prior to a feared encounter with his estranged brother. Rooted in invitation, Abraham's encounter was an expression of partnership. Jacob's was rooted in estrangement, a broken relationship. In facing himself and his significant life relationships, Jacob also faced God. While Jacob's struggle led him to the promise of humility in the wounding of shame, Abraham's began in humility. In his struggle, Abraham faced God and history not for his sake alone or even for his own people's sake. Abraham brought a city to God to press his point. Jacob brought a lifetime—his lifetime—whereas Abraham brought many lifetimes, *other* lifetimes. In other words, in the face of death, Abraham was arguing for others; he was choosing life in the face of destruction, from the beginning.

As we turn to face Sodom and, in turn, reencounter Auschwitz, we might ponder these distinctions. Namely, it matters how one looks back. Abraham pressed for life. He resisted for others. He kept his world open precisely at that point where it was threatened with collapse and ruin. When Abraham looked back, he was looking forward, midrashically. When Lot's wife looked back, she simply turned. We do not know from the text what her motivation was, but its absence from the story makes a telling point. When she looked back the destruction was well under way. It was immediate, and it was starkly overwhelming. So when she turned, she stared directly into the abyss. Perhaps that is all we need to know. She simply turned and gazed into Sodom's stark and naked horror, armed with nothing else. Abraham looked from a distance, though not without personal involvement since he looked back for life and for others. In facing Auschwitz, we confront similar scenarios and options. We risk paralyzing consequences as well. Surely we must conclude that it matters how we turn, how we look back. We should be asking how we face suffering and death: Is it for the sake of life? Dare we face such destruction without any thought for the life-giving energy and strength we need to face the struggle before us?

Revisiting Abraham's Argument

Although we take our stand alongside Abraham, at this point in the story we are not without other problems. We know what the biblical story says, and we know what critical scholarship concludes about Abraham's argument. We can also recognize the warning that accompanies it and any looking back that motivates further questioning. Nonetheless, when we reenter the story from the shadows of Auschwitz to stand beside Abraham, our post-Shoah perspective complicates the situation. More questions are introduced. Let us reexamine the scene.

Throughout his argument with God, Abraham is concerned for the city and all its inhabitants. Why not for the righteous alone? They matter, but only as included ones in the fate of the entire city. Why? Some Christian scholars anticipate the role of vicarious atonement and suggest that Abraham is reversing the typical way of thinking about these matters. Walter Brueggemann explores this option in his commentary on Genesis, although in this case his focus is not on vicarious suffering but on vicarious righteous behavior.[10] Of course, we might also ask if Brueggemann is imposing a veiled theory of *Christus Victor* on this material.

Another option grows out of the material having its origin after the fact. If Abraham's argument arises because of Sodom's complete demise, it would be the city and all its inhabitants that would be at stake. If the argument is understood as midrash read back into the story, it interprets a present and problematic event according to the Abrahamic covenantal tradition. The fulcrum text remains "Shall not the Judge of all the earth do what is just?" (Gen. 18:25), with the direction of its application reversed. As a result, its interpretive field lies behind it, not before it.[11]

Should this surprise us, especially after Auschwitz? When we look at the Shoah, we ask similar questions: For all its victims, we ask, "Why? How could this happen?" The questions are not focused on the ones who could be rescued but on the 6 million lost. However, turning to the 6 million radically challenges Abraham's argument. With regard to Auschwitz, there can be no sense of judgment in what happened there, not without impugning children who died there; not without violating Irving Greenberg's criterion: "No statement, theological or otherwise, should be made that would not be credible in the presence of the burning children."[12] Auschwitz, therefore, changes how we read the biblical tale of two cities and Abraham's argument. It changes how we view Sodom. Now, after Auschwitz, we must ask, though the text did not, What of Sodom's children? Surely there were children there. What of them? How would Abraham frame his lawsuit now?

Dare we recast the complaint and substitute the word *children* for the word *righteous*? Everett Fox in his rendering of this material[13] translates the word *tzadikim* as "innocent" and captures this implication. In that spirit, if we substitute *children* instead of *innocent*, our argument would proceed: "If there were fifty children in the city, would you really sweep it away? Surely not. And what if five of them were really culpable, leaving forty-five, would that be a sufficient number for you to spare the entire city? What if there were only thirty? Dare we press the point further? What if there were only twenty children, or only ten? What about the children?" Greenberg's words echo hauntingly in this recounting.

Is there not a similar logic behind asking why Abraham does not go down to Sodom to accompany God when God declares that to be the next step, to see if the cries from Sodom are true? Where is the bold Abraham in this scene? If Abraham is looking down at an already ruined city, then we understand the answer. There would be no city to visit, only God, in anguish and grief, even in protest. But after Auschwitz we must also ask, If the city is so evil that ten righteous ones could not be found, what about earlier cries from the city's victims? Surely they were uttered. If God could go down at one time, why not an earlier time, before Sodom had essentially consumed itself?

The story relates that God responded to the cries of Sodom, declaring that they were great and weighed heavily on God (Gen. 18:20). Therefore, God decided to see if what God heard was true. Dare we not ask how many cries were sufficient to move God to action? What if there were fifty victims who cried out? Would they be enough to move the Sovereign Giver of Life? What if five of them were responsible for their own victimization? What, then, of the other forty-five? Or what if there were only forty, or thirty? Dare we ask only for twenty? Ten? How many victims are sufficient before God acts? Is this not the other side of how many righteous are required for all the citizens of Sodom to be saved? So we ask, even if the text did not, What about Sodom's victims?

Raising Questions of Judgment in History

Abraham's intercession articulates the presumption that if God is the Sovereign Judge of the universe, then it follows that Sodom is guilty as described. But our probing has raised other questions. If the situation is more ambiguous, then one must reexamine the presupposition either that God is just or that Sodom's destruction is God's doing. After Auschwitz, those presuppositions must be challenged. Otherwise, if God acts in history to judge and/or spare cities and other corporate entities, then if for no other reason than the children, God must be guilty, along with those who are punished. Elie Wiesel has dramatized this problem powerfully in his play *The Trial of God*, also using the form of a lawsuit, echoing Abraham's argument with God.[14] Of course, the companion presupposition could also be examined—and fruitfully, I think. Perhaps Sodom is not God's work—likewise, any tragic event in history. In that case, God would not be directly responsible and therefore not morally culpable. Arthur Cohen explores this option with insightful clarity, challenging the notion that God's role in history must be conceived as intervention or interruption.[15] I follow this option in another essay published elsewhere.[16] The point: One or the other or both assumptions can no longer be presumed after Auschwitz. They cannot be held together without ripping the moral and covenantal fabric of life.

Therefore, we must be cautious in speaking of God's actions in history. The story assumes that Sodom's destruction is God's doing. But as our post-Shoah questions show, that assumption leads to problematic conclusions. Nonetheless, we might say that their destruction is judgment on their unrighteousness. Their being committed to the ways of death led that society to ruin. By not serving life, they opposed God's will and faced a divine "No" in history. But we dare not say that God intervened to bring that judgment to Sodom, and realizing that, we imply something similar regarding the Third Reich, that the Reich's destruction was God's judgment on its evil. If we dare suggest that God finally intervened to destroy the Third Reich, then we must also ask about the 6 million—not to mention the 1.5

million children. Why did God wait to act? Is such a cost just? Thus, Abraham's lawsuit swells to overwhelming proportion.

After Auschwitz, the presumption of God's active intervention in history is seriously questioned. Must God withdraw from history or be conceived to have a different mode of involvement in history? I have discussed the latter option in another work where I develop a more processual view of divine involvement in history while retaining central categories of judgment and redemption.[17] The difference lies in conceiving these categories as being significantly more dependent on human cooperation (or the lack) in doing God's will. And in making that point, another is also made: There are limits beyond which cities, societies, cannot be saved. Beyond these limits, they are marked for destruction, yet with the onus for their destruction being placed on their own actions. Such destruction would not be seen as direct punishment but as the consequence of a morally interconnected ecology of life. In other words, where death rules, life is undone and the results are tragic but not necessarily the result of divine intervention.

Divine judgment is therefore more subtly differentiated in history and shared with God's covenant partners. For all that we do not want to say about God's intervention as the judge of history, we do not want to dismiss God as the One against whom history is judged. Nor do we want to declare that history and judgment in history do not count. That is, we affirm that we are accountable to the standards of justice and righteousness, to the divine intention for life, in history. Yet we seek that affirmation in ways that do not impugn the One who gives life and hopes with us for righteousness and justice. For example, we can say, in covenant fidelity, that judgment counts. And we can say that there are limits to human evil that when surpassed bring destruction. It might even be that Sodom was so evil it was beyond redemption. We can also say that city and her companion city consumed themselves, and do so without violating the integrity of the biblical witness. Similarly, we can turn to the Third Reich and say that its social structure became so evil it consumed itself, and in doing so, it nearly consumed other peoples, as well as its own, in the process. Instead of looking at any corporate entity as the object of divine intervention, we may be better helped by looking at how such entities are accountable in a much more complex social ecology for the character of life (or death) that undergirds their world.

We are not without some support from the text in this regard, although we must resist facile appropriations of its narrative. The entire episode is introduced by the unexpected arrival of three strangers, identified simply as men (*anashim*). As Abraham responds to their presence with extravagant hospitality, the story unfolds. In the telling, the three men become divine messengers, with one eventually speaking on behalf of or representing God. As they depart for Sodom, the number shifts to two, as if the one left behind were God in disguise, lingering to ponder Sodom and the city's fate with Abraham. Critical reflection on this confusion of details suggests distinct strata of tellings in which subsequent experience and later reflection lead to deeper insights as to what was going on in the earlier events. In other words, there is an ambiguity preserved in the text itself that allows us to read it with resistance against a simplistic literalism and in favor of a midrashic literality.[18]

Facing Sodom and Sodom's Sin

If our argument leads to greater human responsibility for what happened in and to Sodom, we must ask, What was Sodom's sin? In what ways was Sodom so evil that Abraham could conclude that an entire city deserved the destruction that befell it? While homosexuality is an implied feature of the scene and figures in the intended action of the crowd, the groups' intention to violate their city's visitors is the more telling focus. The sexual dimension of their violence is more instrumental than essential. The issue, therefore, is the intended violence, the gang rape, regardless of whether it was homosexual or heterosexual. One need only ponder a parallel gathering of robed figures with lighted torches gathering outside the home of a family that has taken in visiting freedom riders during the civil rights movement in the southern United States. Their sin would not be limited to the specific violence intended for such a night—whether a hanging or a shooting. Their sin would be much greater and much deeper. The violence of a single evening is fed by the more pervasive and structural negations of racism that underlie the hatred and bigotry being expressed in one event. In that spirit, Sodom's sin is focused in the violations and disrespect for persons and the absence of hospitality toward others, which, in contrast, is the precondition for any form of moral life. Indeed, the violent inhospitality of Sodom is contrasted with the deep-rooted hospitality of Abraham and the less spontaneous hospitality of his nephew Lot.

Revisiting Hospitality

A close reading of this material invites us to probe the meaning of *hospitality* further. What constitutes real hospitality? Comparing Lot's behavior to Abraham's yields several insights in this regard, notwithstanding Lot's more wooden, imitative qualities in contrast to his uncle's. Each figure encounters strangers at the threshold of his home: the entrance of Abraham's tent, the doorway of Lot's house. There, Abraham and Lot each recognize the presence of the other in an act of respectful encounter—the stranger is greeted with honor. Their greeting is immediately followed by an invitation that Abraham and Lot initiate for the strangers to come into their homes and to take food and rest. At the risk of suggesting a simple formula for hospitality, we may identify and distinguish five important and telling moments in the movement of hospitality portrayed in the narrative:[19]

Recognition The other is recognized as someone worthy of honor and respect even though he or she approaches the threshold of one's life as a stranger.

Invitation The other is invited to share in the rest and safety of one's domain. He may even be implored to do so, but is not forced.

Response The other's response is important. Exchange between others transpires. The guest is guest only when he or she chooses to be so.

Entertainment Life is shared with the other in token abundance. In these cases, special preparations are made with food, and the guest is given a place at the family's table. The boundaries of family are opened to include the stranger as he is feted with food.

Rest Following the inclusive act of eating with their guest, the host and his family provide rest and shelter—sabbath in the midst of life—for the sojourning other. A small sanctuary in time, this gift also includes the gift of safety. In Lot's case, this means protecting his guests, who in response return his gesture as they protect him.

After Auschwitz, hospitality, even as a social ritual, takes on even greater significance. Its absence for Jews was clear. Its occasional presence is perhaps more telling. As Sam and Pearl Oliner have demonstrated in their review of rescue behavior on the part of "righteous Gentiles," the crucial factor in their behavior was not their social sophistication nor the presence or absence of any particular religious identity but the regular practice of making strangers welcome in their homes, what they called an extensive way of living in their social worlds.[20] Often, rescuers, when questioned about their heroic actions, indicated they saw nothing unusual or heroic about what they did. They simply behaved as they always did, embodying conventions of respect for the stranger. In other words, it was simply part of their way of being in the world to practice hospitality.

Facing Sodom Responsibly

The story of Sodom articulates the significance of hospitality in bold and apocalyptic fashion. Its occasional presence in the Shoah renders its significance powerfully. Still, we cannot face Sodom's inhospitality for others without asking about Sodom's victims—those who were victims of Sodom's pervasive violence as well as all the citizens caught in Sodom's tragic ruin. As we revisit the text and its story, we discover that these victims of Sodom are nameless. Sodom, except for Lot and his family, is a faceless city. Its destruction is too easily dismissed without real victims with names and faces. After Auschwitz, no city, no place, should be so.[21] Consider how differently Sodom looks if we try to give it a face. Who were Sodom's victims And what do we mean by *victims*? Were they all like the "men" portrayed in the story? While the implied conclusion is yes, we must remember that the text says only, "[A]ll the men, young and old, all the people were gathered outside" (Gen. 19:4). This is obviously important for concluding why ten righteous men could not be found. But just as we asked about the missing children, we must also ask, What about the women? Where were they? Who were they? Were they filled with violence too? Were they victims? Were they both? In similar fashion, we look for the children. Who were they? Where were they?

After Auschwitz we cannot not look for faces to counter the facelessness of Sodom's situation. (Notice again the use of the awkward double negative.) Without their faces, we cannot distinguish the victimizers from the victims of Sodom. The closest we do come to their humanity is through Lot's wife, and even she is without a name. After Auschwitz, can we turn toward either city, Sodom or Auschwitz, without resisting the namelessness of its victims? Perhaps we should have resisted before, in the name of other critiques. Regardless, we cannot continue without attending to questions about their identity, wondering who they were and what differentiates them still. Of course, we dare not confuse the two cities. Neither do we wish to suggest them as analogues, because they are not. Regardless, their facelessness must be faced.

After Auschwitz we have learned that each story that bears a name and each name that bears a story can be shared as an act of moral and spiritual resistance in the name of human dignity. With every story and every name associated with Auschwitz, we can tell the tale and give them at least that memorial. With Sodom we have no names, yet we can express our disquiet and our protest that they have none. And we can begin with Lot's wife. What was her name? Was her name unique or shared by any of her ancestors or descendants? Was it Ruth or Naomi? Was it Miriam or Hannah? Similarly, we ask about Sodom's children: Where were they? Who were they? What were their names? In facing their absence, we must also remember an earlier point: We ask our questions for the sake of life, lest we who look back be consumed by the death that smolders in their ashes. Therefore, for the sake of life, the life of current children, our children, the children of Sarajevo or Kosovo, the children of Chechnya, the children of Jerusalem, the children of any city, we ask about Sodom's children.

In a subtle but important way, this insistence extends the test of hospitality that was originally put to Sodom. How does Sodom treat people? What is the fate of the "other" in their everyday encounters? What is the fate of the "other" in our historic reflections? The test of hospitality is thereby *our* test as it was *their* test. Without question, hospitality mattered then, just as it matters now. In Abraham's reception of his visitors and in Lot's partial imitation of his uncle, hospitality mattered. And in negative fashion, hospitality counted in Sodom, in its violent absence and abuse. In short, Sodom's fate was determined by the absence of hospitality. How they treated others, the matter of hospitality, was the key to how they fared.[22] At least, that is how the biblical text tells the tale.

In making this point, we dare not forget that in Nazi-occupied Germany, hospitality mattered significantly as well. Most acts of rescue indicate that the primary value of the households that sheltered Jews was that strangers were welcome in their homes. The critical factor was not directly tied to religion or any form of heroic action. Rather, it was tied to the virtue of hospitality to the stranger.[23] By contrast, the absence of hospitality was a fatal flaw in much of Nazi Germany and occupied Europe. Its absence allowed for the near annihilation of a people and other discounted groups of persons.

LOOKING BACK AT SODOM WITH JESUS

As a Christian, I come to Abraham and his vision of Sodom by way of Jesus—even when I seek to recover the midrashic dimension of Abraham's relationship with historic tragedy that is too often overlooked by Christian interpreters. And for that reason, I place my articulated journey in collegial review, before Jewish colleagues as well as fellow Christians. But that, as critical as it is to responsible post-Shoah Christian witness, is not enough. I must also ask, How does what I have recovered in my looking back at Sodom in the light of Auschwitz affect what I see in approaching the Jesus I follow in my walk of faith? What better way to get at this than to look at Jesus as he looks back at Sodom, while self-consciously including what I have learned from looking back at Abraham from the shadows of Auschwitz? Consequently, this reflection turns toward Matthew's account of Jesus as he glances back at Sodom in a brief and allusive reference to that city's destruction while sending his disciples off to extend his ministry to neighboring villages in Galilee.

Looking back at Sodom over Jesus' shoulder, as it were, requires more than a restoration of its midrashic dimension, however. It also asks responsible Christian interpreters to revisit their history, often passing through tragic terrain: sanctuaries in conflict, battlefields of the Crusades, pyres of the Inquisition, pogroms in Eastern Europe, the *lager* of the Third Reich. The path evokes shame and consequent penitence and change.[24] It invites a rethinking of fundamental purpose as Christians examine their confessional identity vis-à-vis Jews. As a result, the journey is complex and convoluted and can be dangerous for Christians, leading to the kind of paralysis that facing Sodom can evoke. Nonetheless, this legacy must be faced. In this case, Christian return passes through the confessional domain of the New Testament, where assumptions about providence and mission are refracted in an episode in which Jesus obliquely alludes to the fate of Sodom and Gomorrah.

In Matthew 10, as Jesus' disciples were sent out to proclaim that God's kingdom has drawn near, they were instructed to look for hospitality. When hospitality was found, the house that offered it was deemed worthy. Consequently, the disciples were to bless it with their peace and to share their message of the nearness of God's reign among them. And where needed, they were to bring healing. On the other hand, if they were not welcomed, they were to move on, shaking the dust from their feet. In this context, Jesus alluded to Sodom and Gomorrah, accepting the traditional reading that they were utterly destroyed because of their sin and lack of hospitality. To that Jesus added a warning to be careful because there was animosity in the land, particularly among the synagogues. Critical scholarship tells us that Matthew's wording of this comment reflects a situation some time after Jesus, one in which there was competitive hostility between synagogue leaders and the sect constituted by Jesus' followers. Embedded in this story is a record of the relationship between Jews and Christians sometime near the end of the first century of the common era, as well as the message Jesus' followers were to proclaim to their Jewish siblings. In our post-Shoah context, we know the tragic outcome of the supersessionist reading of this material and the displacement logic undergirding it. Aware of this tragic story, we see the conflict between Church and Synagogue in the very telling of Matthew's testimony. As a result, we may be forced to ask, Is there even room to reread this story for post-Shoah guidance?

Consider Jesus' introductory charge to his disciples in this story. What does it mean for him to say, "[G]o to the lost sheep of Israel"? One way of reading this story is to view it as a commissioning action whereby Jesus judges his own for straying from the ways of God, and, more pointedly, if they do not heed his call, they remain lost. We know, especially after Auschwitz, the tragic consequences of reading his statement in such judgmental terms. But does the story require that? Can the story support an alternative reading and retain integrity in the process?

First of all, let us not overlook that Jesus differentiates those who are the focus of his concern, "the lost sheep," as being "of Israel." Being "lost" and being "Israel" are not equivalent. "Israel" is the larger, more inclusive term. Second, being "of Israel" identifies these persons as Jesus' own people. His concern is for them because they are his own. Third, being "lost sheep" can mean that these persons have strayed on their own. It can also mean they have been led astray by others or even that they are trapped in dangerous or oppressive situations. That is, they may be victims in need of rescue from victimization and violence. Many of us have read "lost sheep" pejoratively, but we might be more authentic in reading it as an indication of Jesus' fundamental concern for his own people in situations he views as oppressive and/or violent, therein needing his message with its good news. Thus his charge can be one that expresses solidarity, not judgment, though judgment may follow as a consequence of not receiving those he sends with hospitality and respect. In the latter case, the judgment falls as a consequence of lacking hospitality.

To illustrate, let us pretend we heard Jesus commissioning his followers as if he were Martin Luther King, Jr. telling a team of civil rights leaders:

Go to the folk in Selma, not the White clergy or those who say they support us but our folk, the sons and daughters of former slaves, and proclaim to them the good news, telling them the Kingdom of God has drawn near. They are free. If they welcome you and take time to listen to what you have to say, they are worthy of your goodwill—even if they do not choose to join us in our work. Bless them and their families. Bring peace to their homes and, where they are in need, bring healing. If you are turned away, do not linger or grieve but move on. Shake the dust from your feet. Their judgment will come in its own way and time. Our time, however, is urgent, and the message you bear is critical. Go now, for the Kingdom of God is at hand.

The point is not whether such a conversation happened (or could happen) but whether viewing Jesus' charge to his disciples within the context of solidarity and concern can be supported by the text. If so, would it alter how we understand the story and the issues it focuses? The illustration concretely demonstrates that such a shift in perspective does matter and can be borne by the story. Notice how such solidarity can be expressed urgently and in the spirit of renewal and change without communicating an "over against" attitude. The issue of judgment turns on whether those sent are met with hospitality and respect (the embodied promise of the very message they bring), not whether those who welcome them agree with them or join them thereafter. In other words, when we view Matthew 10 from this perspective, we see that Jesus sends his apostles out instructed to bear witness to the very message their hosts embody in welcoming them—hospitality.

What, then, are Jesus' followers sent out to do? Clearly, they are to announce that the Kingdom of God has drawn near. Moreover, they are to articulate their news in those places where the promise of God's Kingdom has been manifest in hospitality. In other words, they are sent to declare how they view the ultimate significance of hospitality and in that manner be true to themselves and the one whom they serve and follow. Mission is thereby linked to hospitality with a dual emphasis: an articulated witness encountering an embodied promise.

And what is asked of those whom they meet? Are those who welcome the apostles required to agree? Interestingly, nothing about agreement is mentioned in the text, however much it may have been presumed in its long history of interpretation. After Auschwitz and the tragic history of antisemitism, Christians know too well the Jewish "no" that greets their historic witness. Is there room within the rearticulated commissioning explored here to accept that "no"? If what the disciples are to seek is hospitality, knowing that those who receive them may perceive the significance of their hospitality relative to God's reign in history differently than those who proffer it, then the answer can be yes. Is there likewise room for witness, even conflict, relative to the difference in how one sees God's actions in the world? Again, the answer is yes, so long as the conflict is rooted in hospitality and respect for one other. Thus we, as Christians, can bear witness to the nearness of God's reign that we know "in and through Christ." But we dare not feel compelled to replace our covenantal siblings in the larger story of divine embrace we each proclaim. Instead, we can look for and ask for hospitality and respect as together we serve the ideals of God's ways of covenant life.

What, then, of the notion of judgment in the allusion to Sodom and Gomorrah? If we recall the urgency of apocalyptic sensibilities, we may read Jesus' warning as rooted in the urgency of his sense of the end time. For him, the very outcome of history is at stake in whether or not one finds hospitality. Can such a claim remain true now? If rooted in an interventionist understanding of God, that warning has a cluster of meanings that need to be challenged or rethought. If rooted in a more processual view of history, there is room for understanding creation to be a place where covenant life can take root and grow. Covenant life, therefore, in this perspective, is always at stake in how persons are welcomed and whether or not there is hospitality extended to strangers. In this fashion, the focus shifts, and Jesus' warning can be read as an expression of what is at stake in the visit of his disciples—how they are received—not on whether or not those who receive them view their situation with the same understanding.

What implications does our discussion have for the problematic topic of mission? We know the tragic legacy of Christian mission toward the Jewish people. We know, too, the way it has been fed by displacement theology, anti-Judaism and antisemitism, as well as by fears of being rejected. All these issues are focused in this text. Yet after Auschwitz, we must still ask, Is there nothing distinctive we have to offer our Jewish siblings except shame and repentance?[25] To be sure, we bear responsibility for what has happened, along with many others. But is there nothing positive from our identity as Jesus' followers with which we can face them? With a proper understanding of this episode and our post-Shoah hermeneutics of hospitality that guide it, we are freed to look at ways in which we may offer distinctive understandings to what it means to walk in God's ways and to share in the partnership of covenant life that is the legacy of Abraham's descendants. That dialogue needs to happen and in the context of hospitality and respect.

Even so, we can make the rather strong claim that the linkage of mission to hospitality is not coincidental but essential, especially after Auschwitz. The proclamation that the Kingdom of God is near can make sense for Jews and Christians only in the presence of hospitality, since the presence of hospitality experientially configures the grace and relationship that Jesus commissions his disciples to identify as the good news of their proclamation, thereby bringing into explicit clarity the very promise and intention of creation that hospitality embodies. In the shadows of the Shoah, Christians may be helpfully guided by this recognition as they announce the good news they are called to serve in the world. That is: Where hospitality is present, they are to identify its significance for new life and hope in the midst of oppression and misery. Where it is absent, they should move on, but toward those in need of the hospitality being sought, with the clear understanding that the closer one moves to the victims of inhospitality and violence, one must embody the same good news one seeks to proclaim.

Our post-Shoah situation forces us to return to the biblical mandates, especially this one, regarding Christian mission to the Jewish people. We return to the story and ask, Does it truly mandate what has happened in the name of the apostolic mission, or may we read the story anew and correct our abuse of it? Such is the case with this text. As we make our way back *from* Sodom, we discover many consequences of our post-Shoah return *to* Sodom. For one thing, the relationship with any tragedy is transformed. Likewise, our views of God's embrace of history. Moreover, the importance of hospitality to and for the other is intensified, especially if it is the precondition of righteousness and a test of its promise. Without hospitality, life is diminished, and there is little hope in tragic or critical times. Research into the behavior of rescuers during the Shoah makes this point abundantly clear. As the Oliners discovered through their interviews with those who risked their lives to rescue Jews in Nazi-occupied Europe, the distinguishing factor linking them to one another was not religion, education, or the like, but whether or not they grew up in families that practiced what they call "extensiveness"—hospitality to the other regardless of who that other was.[26] Our return to the story places us face-to-face with the dynamics and ultimate significance of hospitality, not just for these texts but for our own time as well.

Another Side to Hospitality

There is another side to hospitality that we must not overlook and ignore, especially in the aftermath of the Shoah. In responding to life hospitably, life does not always reciprocate the gesture. More specifically, there are others who do not welcome otherness in their lives and in whose presence anyone other to them is fundamentally threatened. Hospitality to them is not simply dangerous; it can be perilous in the extreme. Clearly after Auschwitz we cannot simply advocate a naive approach to the other with an equally naive understanding of the virtue of hospitality. With this critical recognition then, how does one proceed, remaining committed to the movement of hospitality in life yet alert to its violation and the perils of its practice?

Of course, one option is to restrict the circle of others to whom we give ourselves in hospitality. In this case, we look for criteria that allow us to encounter others who are relatively safe for us to encounter and approach with our invitations to hospitality. However, the danger in such an approach is that we never really embrace the full significance of otherness. Too easily, our worlds can become circumscribed to include only those sufficiently enough like us that we reach out to them. Others we either shun or avoid.

Another approach could be argued from the perspective of a Christian theology of the cross. Namely, we are called to mirror God's ways, as did Jesus. His embrace of the other included the other who could, and would, betray, deny, and crucify him. He withheld his hospitality from no one as he looked for hospitality from others. However, as Matthew reports the commissioning in Matthew 10, he describes a more nuanced scenario. Here, Jesus instructs his disciples to look for others who are hospitable to them. When met with hospitality, they are to articulate its significance and to extend and deepen it by declaring how it fulfills the very intentions of God for creation. Still, Matthew reports Jesus' awareness of the danger of this task, warning his disciples to be "wise as serpents and gentle as doves."[27] This caution immediately follows the commissioning and is accompanied by a depiction of conflict and persecution that includes the resistance of synagogues and their leaders. With our understanding of the conflictual circumstances of Matthew's time near the end of the first century, we can assume that we are most probably encountering aspects of that conflict in this report. Nonetheless, Jesus advises his disciples to exercise caution and good judgment as they undertake this mission. As we read the material post-Shoah, we can likewise practice similar caution, attempting to be wise as serpents and gentle as doves for the sake of hospitality. Retaining the spirit of caution and openness that Jesus advocates, we can resist the negative portrayal of Jewish leaders while retaining the wisdom that comes from knowing hospitality's violations. Such an approach indeed suggests that it may at times be appropriate to withhold the invitation to hospitality or its invitation; at other times (pun intended) circumstances might require qualifying it. Nonetheless, the practice of such wisdom would always occur within the larger movement toward hospitality, with the moment of recognition taking on increased significance in the light cast by the pyres of Auschwitz.

In other words, the traditional logic of a theology of the cross can be placed within the larger framework of a theology of creation, oriented by the divine movement of hospitality toward life. In creation, God embraces otherness fully. In so doing, we cannot forget that this act embraces the very negation of itself as one of the dynamics that is risked and borne in such a choice for life. This is God's hospitality to life in its otherness. Are we expected to take a similarly all-embracing risk? If so, we are asked to risk the same possibility of death from the hands of the other; however, if each human partner in such an enterprise were always to follow in similar fashion, we would move no closer to the fullness of life originally pursued by the choice for life in the beginning. Instead, if we were to reject the otherness that rejects its own ground in the other, then we move forward toward the realization of the divine project of a fully cooperating ecology of life. The task is to approach otherness and the other, with a form of hospitality that has fully grasped the significance of its practice, with regard to both its promise and peril; and one that has embraced hospitality on the other side of innocence, as it were, and chosen to still live hospitably with otherness, now knowing what is at stake in its absence and risked in its practice. How we understand and practice this post-Shoah hospitality may take more time to develop and understand. But it will be a critical form of hospitality that adds to the fivefold characterization an important dimension to the moment of recognition as we approach otherness and the other.

DRAWING CONCLUSIONS, RAISING UNFINISHED QUESTIONS

Looking back at the Shoah is a dangerous yet necessary task—likewise, the return via Matthew's story. They require confronting overwhelming death and consequently rethinking a great deal of our received tradition. Such work occasions unsettling and sometimes paralyzing responses that are further complicated by their thoroughgoing existential and theological dimensions. Through reentering the story of Abraham's encounter with the fate of Sodom and Gomorrah, we find warning and guidance in how we might look back at such tragic and traumatic history. The critical task of looking back surely remains unfinished; nonetheless, we may draw some conclusions, however tentative, for our ongoing work.

Facing Sodom, we know what Abraham has said and done. He argued boldly with God, though always knowing his place in such an audacious act. He spoke out on behalf of the righteous. He spoke out on behalf of the few for the many. He set the scene for a test for righteousness and justice. Hospitality was the key. While Abraham did not define either righteousness or justice, his argument with God signaled its importance. At the same time, however, we recognize that Abraham's argument is no longer sufficient. We must bring other issues, other questions, in our walk with God to the very One Abraham confronted. We do so, with a similar boldness, trusting as well that we may stand with him in extended, though critical, covenantal partnership.

Facing Auschwitz, we ask, What would Abraham do and say? Our clues lie in returning to Sodom midrashically,[28] asking, Is there something about Abraham's way that invites us to read and interpret our post-Shoah experience according to the Scriptures (in this case, Gen. 18 and 19 and Matt. 10) that can be uttered in the presence of the burning children of the Shoah?[29]

In this way, that text invites us to return to the scene overlooking Sodom and there, with Abraham and his descendants and companions in faith, gaze upon what happened. There, upon the mountain overlooking the plain cities of Sodom and Gomorrah, we may ponder with Abraham their unfolding tale of judgment. From there, we can take our midrashic vantage point and look in both textual directions—back at Abraham's argument with God as well as ahead to Sodom's visitation and destruction. And from our twentieth-century starting point in the shadows of Auschwitz, we bring questions that lead us to see the scene anew, yet in critical continuity with what Abraham and his descendants have subsequently seen all along. Likewise, we reenter another scene in which Sodom is referenced by Jesus, to retrieve older, embedded meanings uncovered in Shoah-tempered dialogue with Jesus and his story.

Looking back at these episodes, we are able to draw out several implications. With regard to hospitality, we are invited to linger with our biblical hosts and feast on its stories and learn more about the character of hospitality and its linkage with the promise of new life in the midst of old, its role in divine providence, its place in justice, and its commensurability with the rule and realm of God as a sign of its adorning presence. More specifically, we are enabled to distinguish some interrelated and telling moments in the movement of hospitality: recognition, invitation, response, entertainment, and rest that together provide sabbath time for others whom we encounter at the boundaries of our safely circumscribed worlds. In addition, we are challenged to see that any elaboration of mission and the work of Christian proclamation must be intimately tied to the presence and practice of hospitality if it is to be true to the witness we meet in these episodes. Finally, as we conclude our looking back at Sodom, with Abraham and with Jesus, we should not fail to recognize that looking back midrashically can be a way of looking and moving forward for the sake of others and for the sake of the hospitality and respect not present in the past. And perhaps in this fashion we *can* heed the angels' warning about looking at destruction at the same time that we search for a way of looking back at it responsibly.

NOTES

1. Literally, living over; in this sense, implying a movement from mere survival as a victim to surviving as a witness.

2. J. B. Metz, *The Emergent Church: The Future of Christianity in a Postbourgeois World* (New York: Crossroad, 1987), pp. 19, 32.

3. The double negative, though awkward, is intentional.

4. See, for example, Walter Brueggemann, *Genesis: Interpretation—A Bible Commentary for Teaching and Preaching* (Atlanta, GA: John Knox Press, 1982), pp. 163, 167.

5. See Charles Pellegrino's provocative study *Return to Sodom and Gomorrah: Bible Stories from Archeologists* (New York: Random House, 1994), pp. 139–182, for an intriguing reflection on the archeological possibilities lying behind the story.

6. Anson Laytner, *Arguing with God: A Jewish Tradition* (Northvale, NJ: Jason Aronson, 1990), pp. 3–8, 45–48.

7. Ibid., p. xv.

8. Ibid., p. 47; Brueggemann, *Genesis*, p. 167.

9. See my earlier article "Wrestling with Two Texts: A Post-Shoah Encounter" as well as the longer record of our panel's dialogue over this text in the special edition of *Shofar: Jewish-Christian Dialogue After the Shoah*, Vol. 15, no.1 (Fall 1996), pp. 3–118. ed. James F. Moore.

10. Brueggemann, *Genesis*, p. 172.

11. See Peter Ochs's overview of postcritical biblical studies, *The Return to Scripture in Judaism and Christianity: Essays in Postcritical Scriptural Interpretation* (New York: Paulist Press, 1993), pp. 3–51, and his essay "Returning to Scripture: Trends in Postcritical Scriptural Interpretation," *Cross Currents* 44, no. 4 (Winter 1994/95): 437–451.

12. Irving Greenberg, "Cloud of Smoke, Pillar of Fire: Judaism, Christianity, and Modernity After the Holocaust," in *Auschwitz?: Beginning of a New Era?*, ed. Eva Fleischner (New York: KTAV Publishing House, 1977), p. 23.

13. Everett Fox, *Genesis and Exodus: A New English Rendition with Commentary and Notes* (New York: Schocken Books, 1990), p. 74.

14. Elie Wiesel, *The Trial of God*, trans. Marion Wiesel (New York: Random House, 1979).

15. Arthur Cohen, "In Our Terrible Age: The *Tremendum* of the Jews," in *The Holocaust as Interruption*, ed. Elisabeth Shussler Fiorenza and David Tracy (Edinburgh: T. & T. Clark, 1984), pp. 15–16.

16. Henry F. Knight, "Choosing Life Between the Fires: Toward an Intentionalist Voice of Faith" in *Remembering for the Future: The Impact of the Holocaust and Genocide on Jews and Christians*, proceedings of an International Conference, Oxford and London, July, 17–18, 1988 (Oxford: Pergamon Press, 1989), p. 641.

17. Ibid.

18. Here I want to distinguish between a literal correspondence with history and the literal configuration of the story, which allows the reader to dwell in the literally rendered telling of the narrative in order for it to unfold with full figurative power.

19. I am indebted to Claus Westermann for his thorough analysis of this material and his organizational categories for suggesting this way of identifying the ritualized movement of hospitality. See Westermann, *Genesis 12–36: A Commentary*, trans. John J. Scullion (London: SPCK, 1985), p. 276.

20. Samuel P. Oliner and Pearl M. Oliner, *The Altruistic Personality: Rescuers of Jews in Nazi Europe* (New York: Free Press, 1988), pp. 171–186.

21. See Zygmunt Bauman, *Modernity and the Holocaust* (Ithaca, NY: Cornell University Press, 1989), for a provocative study of the significance of social distantiation as a prerequisite for the bureaucratic dimension of the Shoah.

22. See Thomas W. Ogeltree's *Hospitality to the Stranger: Dimensions of Moral Understanding* (Philadelphia: Fortress Press, 1985), for an introductory analysis of hospitality as the precondition for the moral life. He builds on the work of Em-

manuel Levinas, whose philosophical work is grounded on the very presence of the other in anyone's life.

23. Oliner and Oliner, *The Altruistic Personality*, pp. 171–186.

24. See Henry F. Knight, "From Shame to Responsibility and Christian Identity: The Dynamics of Shame and Christian Confession Regarding the Shoah," *Journal of Ecumenical Studies* 23, no.1 (Winter 1998): 41–62.

25. I explore this issue in ibid.

26. Oliner and Oliner, *The Altruistic Personality*, p. 258.

27. Matt. 10: 16.

28. See Michael Fishbane, *The Garments of Torah: Essays in Biblical Hermeneutics* (Bloomington: University Press, 1989), pp. 19–32.

29. Greenberg, "Cloud of Smoke," p. 23.

3

The Transfigured Face of Post-Shoah Faith: Critical Encounters with Root Experiences

Exodus 24:12–18 and Matthew 17:1–9

Facing one another in the shadows of Auschwitz brings Christians and Jews face-to-face with the root experiences of our traditions: for Jews, the gift of Torah at Sinai with its covenantal realities and imperatives; for Christians, our Christological confessions that God has been fully encountered in Jesus of Nazareth. Consequently, our attention turns toward two key biblical texts: Exodus 24:1–18 (especially 12–18) and Matthew 17: 1–9, which incidentally are paired for many liturgically oriented Christians to be read in worship on the last Sunday before Lent begins—Transfiguration Sunday.[1] The Exodus passage takes us to the foot of Sinai, looking on from a distance at Moses's mediating work with the Giver of Torah. The Matthean passage presents how the Gospel of Matthew views Jesus through the lens of Sinai and Torah, seeing him as "Emmanuel: God with us."

FACING ROOT EXPERIENCES AFTER THE SHOAH

How do Christians and Jews approach and embrace their root experiences after Auschwitz? Do we proceed as if nothing fundamental has changed, or do we find ourselves having to reorient ourselves to the confessional foundations that ground who we are? This study has proceeded with the latter assumption, drawing on the work of a number of thoughtful colleagues—Jews and Christians alike.[2] There is no need here to rehearse their plea, but there is a caveat. Facing root experiences after Auschwitz and reorienting ourselves in the light of the Shoah constitute convoluted work. Our conversation moves in and out of present and traditional understandings of the world driven by the searing images and questions from the Shoah. Our paths twist and turn, intersect and diverge. For example, as a Christian, my path to Sinai passes through Jesus, but in often problematic ways, which must be acknowledged and amended. Corrected, that path finds a metaphorical anchor at Sinai and returns to face a transfigured Jesus now reconfigured in the post-Shoah light of the late twentieth century. Consequently, when I stand with this figure, I am challenged to reintegrate the covenantal orientation of Sinai in a specifically Christian way of embracing life that is capable of affirming Sinai and the Jewish identity of Jesus at the same time it is able to incorporate a Jewish rejection of the Christian embrace of this transfigured Jesus as the Christ—as the incarnate face of God. This is no easy affair or one that can be adequately accomplished in a single work. Nonetheless, these issues punctuate the terrain that must be explored in working with these stories and the root experiences they mediate.

According to Emil Fackenheim, Jewish tradition modifies and qualifies its relationship to its root experiences within a midrashic framework characterized by a dialectical form of narrative resistance.[3] From within the story, those faithful to the narrated root experience raise the probing questions generated in their own unfolding history and pose them to the root events themselves, pushing and resisting the story they trust. On the other hand, the story and its narrated event resist the present experience as it is probed with questions. What results is a narrative "stubbornness" that meets equally "unyielding realism"[4] from which emerge new learnings about the story and hitherto unperceived dimensions present in history.

While the root experiences remain fixed in our confessional traditions, how we relate to them is influenced by key events in our histories. Moreover, our reading of the root experiences often changes as a result of the experiences we bring to them. This is especially true with regard to the Shoah. In contrast to Fackenheim, Richard Rubenstein views the traditional tapestry of midrashic interpretation as having been radically severed and no longer capable of sustaining the tension generated by the Shoah.[5] While I join others who have not drawn this conclusion, I am, however, persuaded by Greenberg[6] that the covenantal fabric of creation is threatened significantly enough that the reorientation occasioned by the Shoah has revelatory import even if the event itself is not revelation. Simply put, the Shoah shapes and colors how we see the world and the traditions that give us place and meaning in our world. The following commentary examines how the Shoah refracts the light given by Sinai and the Transfiguration, in a sense reconfiguring their essential elements in such fashion that we are called upon to address the issues and realities introduced by the Shoah while seeking to remain true to the covenantal witness to which they are ultimately accountable.

The Path to Sinai

As a Christian, I come to Sinai by way of Jesus. This is, of course, an oversimplified way of putting the matter, but it is nonetheless true. I cannot approach this confessional terrain any other way. More precisely, I come to Sinai by way of a transfigured Jesus, whom I identify as Christ, and in whom I meet and know the Eternal One of the universe. Moreover, I approach the sacred ground of covenant existence for Israel, and thereby for Jesus, through the filtering layers of Christian tradition—additional configuring that further transfigures the Jesus I meet and follow. After Auschwitz, all this is brought into question. As a twentieth-century Christian, my journey to Sinai is interrupted by the Shoah and my shameful encounter with its legacy. Facing the searing criteria of history, I must now ask in its transfiguring of this Jewish figure, To what degree have those of us who follow him distorted his image and the image of all those who, like him, stood with Moses at Sinai? More troubling, I ask this question knowing the presence of the 6 million victims and the 1.5 million children who, because they stood at Sinai, also stood in Hitler's shadows.

J. B. Metz, in a frequently quoted essay, has asserted that any responsible Christian theology produced in the post-Shoah context of modern life must occur in solidarity with Jews.[7] Approaching Sinai, especially through a text and story that celebrate the presence of all Israel—past, present, and future—standing at its foot, intensifies Metz's admonition considerably. Consequently, any Christian approach to Sinai occurs in humility as well as solidarity. Likewise, it includes self-critical clarity regarding the path to a more responsible encounter with Sinai and what it represents. Having learned about Sinai and its key figure Moses by following Jesus, the known in my confessional tradition, the Gospel portraits of Jesus, have been the ground from which I have extended my knowing with regard to Sinai and its traditions. However, the epistemological dynamics of my knowing, typical of many if not most Christians, may not actually reflect the analogical knowing depicted in the Gospel of Matthew and in the Transfiguration scene specifically.

Clearly, Jesus and Moses are analogically linked by way of explicit and implicit comparisons. However, in Matthew's case, the knowing is *from* the Sinai and Moses material *to* the figure of Jesus. Matthew knows from Sinai to Jesus and in turn reflects back upon the Sinai material. Typically, most Christians know from the Gospel portraits to the Sinai traditions, often reversing the epistemological directionality of their foundational witness.[8] Post-Shoah, this epistemological loss is significant.

The stylistic rendering of the Jesus story we meet in Matthew utilizes the larger story of the Jewish people to tell his story of Jesus. It requires a thorough knowledge of the Exodus tradition, the story of Moses and the midrashic style of relating to it. What is known and cherished by Matthew and his audience is used to illumine and clarify the identity of Jesus. Allusions to existing Scripture, whether explicit or implicit, are at best unclear or arbitrary unless the larger narrative context of the Torah is used by the hearer/reader in orienting and understanding Matthew's task. When we try to learn this contexting story by way of the narrative embedded in the larger one, we reverse the hermeneutic employed by Matthew. To be sure, Matthew reads the Torah from his experience of following Jesus. But he begins knowing Torah first. His knowing is interactive, moving from Torah to Jesus and then back. Typically, Christians have read the Matthean tradition in the reverse manner and, more often than not, failing to retain the interactive quality of midrashic knowing. After the Shoah, this hermeneutic is not simply problematic; it is unacceptable. It participates in the very logic of supersessionism, a logic of replacement, which will haunt our confessional identities and our relationships to our own faith traditions unless otherwise confronted and corrected.

Approaching Sinai

What happened at Sinai? To be sure, we cannot reexamine the entire tradition. Still, we can examine this representative portion of that material as we pair it with the delimited portion of Matthew that uses the same material to tell his story of Jesus. In this way, we can take our place at Sinai and learn how better to accompany Matthew in his portrait of Jesus' relationship to Sinai and Torah. Even more significant, Matthew has provided a case that recalls the giving of Torah at Sinai and expresses his view of Jesus' relationship to it and to those who follow Jesus as his disciples. The scene: a mountaintop, reminiscent of another, wherein Jesus is transfigured before his disciples and is seen by them as standing with Moses and Elijah, addressed and confirmed by God as his beloved. However, in order to comprehend fully the story that Matthew tells, we must return to Sinai and allow the story he is retelling to be present and assertive in its own right.

At the beginning of Exodus 24, we find Moses and his people encamped before Sinai. Earlier (Exod. 19), they had arrived and set camp, where they were to remain for quite some time (until Num. 10:10). Here they would continue to receive instruction and clarification of the covenant relationship given and sealed at Sinai. The scene opens with Moses having made more than one trip up the mountain to meet with God, with each meeting described as one wherein God has descended to meet the ascending Moses. The tradition has already reported (chapter 20) the reception of the Ten Commandments (more accurately words, *devarim*), but without limiting the divine instructions to only those commands. Indeed, Jewish tradition asserts that during these times Moses was fully instructed in the divine intention for life that is passed on as Torah, both written and oral. Moreover, the language of Moses's ascent and God's descent is punctuated with dramatic descriptions of extraordinary natural phenomena as well as stylistic references to the ritual settings in which these events are later remembered.

This part of the story begins with a divine summons for Moses to ascend the mountain to meet with God, with accompanying directions for the seventy elders to remain below in reverent attendance to what transpires above. Moses shares this instruction, and the people respond in the enigmatically recurring response "all these things we will do." Moses then records the words of God. The scene shifts to the foot of the mountain during the early morning where Moses, before ascending, sets up an altar and twelve pillars representing the twelve tribes of Israel. Selecting representative young men (not elders), Moses guides them through a ritual, presenting burnt offerings and sacrificed bulls to God during which Moses dashes blood against the altar and reads the written record to the people. They respond as before: "[A]ll that God has spoken we will faithfully do." Then Moses dashes the remaining blood on the people, declaring it the blood of the covenant that God has made with his people.

Following this, Moses, with Aaron, Nadab, and Abihu, along with the seventy elders, ascends the mountain and there beholds the God of Israel in majestic fashion (verse 10). Importantly, the story reports that they beheld God unharmed; then they ate and drank before their divine host.[9] Once more Moses is summoned by God. Verse 12 reports that God called to Moses to come up the mountain and there to wait to receive stone tablets on which God would inscribe the commands and instructions for the people. (Here God writes them in stone; later, after the confrontation over the golden calf, Moses will record them in a significant act of encounter and distantiation [Exod. 34].) At this stage, Moses is described as being attended by Joshua, with the elders being told to wait with Aaron and Hur.

The story continues with Moses ascending the mountain that the text describes as enveloped in a cloud. The text specifies that God's presence resided there on the mountain, hidden for six days. Then on the seventh day, God spoke from the midst of the cloud, calling Moses. To the Israelites the presence or glory (*kevod*) of God appeared as a consuming fire on the top of the mountain, and Moses entered the cloud, once more continuing his ascent. There he remained for forty days and forty nights.

Sinai Revisited

In returning to Sinai, we should note several key vantage points. First, we should linger a bit with Israel camped at the foot of Sinai. The text is clear to say that all Israel gathers here at Sinai's foot. Jewish tradition has been explicit in interpreting "all Israel" to mean that every generation stands there along with all those present in any generation. Post-Shoah Christians who follow Jesus will be led to Jesus taking his place among his generation. He, too, stands at Sinai's foot, as does Matthew. Following Jesus post-Shoah inevitably leads faithful Christians back to this sacred place and to join in solidarity with those they meet there. After Auschwitz, this is a most significant place.

But what does it mean to stand there? What does one see? Or do? In the story, the people are presented with the relationship that Sinai signals and asked to commit to it before knowing all that the relationship entails. Jewish tradition is clear about this; the people are to do before they understand. The commitment to the doing of the relationship comes first. Post-Shoah Christians are invited to see this as a fundamental commitment to the covenantal relationship that precedes any understanding or elaboration of the relationship that will follow. The relationship comes first, and it always involves an active support, doing. Too easily, Christians can speak of the primacy of relationship and forget the doing without which the relationship is not whole.

Indeed, the journey to Sinai brings one face-to-face with a ritual of covenant making, a marriage between God and God's people that Moses celebrates. The return to Sinai cannot overlook this either. Christians who accompany Jesus to this place cannot overlook that the sealing of this pact comingles the blood of the ceremony with the destiny of all Jews, whether they are present in the wilderness or not.

Standing with the people of Israel, we observe the ascent and descent of Moses on the mountain. There is not simply one journey up the mountain, but several. At the heart of the encounter is the memory of the final ascent, but the work of communion is not a onetime affair. Furthermore, even those looking on from a distance are invited to see an ascending Moses toward whom God turns and moves. Their divine-human encounter is a meeting. Even though Moses must climb the mountain, God moves toward him in descent; and the text reports this movement for those gathered at the foot of Sinai to know.

The movement of ascent is shared, to a point, by a smaller circle of leaders, lastly including Joshua. The leaders accompany Moses, in stages, up the mountain. And in rehearsing the stages the story indicates first a recognition on the part of those ascending the mountain that their ascent is possible because God has made it so. Their ascent is a response to God's hospitality. Indeed, the very movement of the ascent echoes the movement of hospitality as Moses moves closer to the last threshold, where alone he eventually crosses over after six days to rest and delight in God's presence on the seventh. And there he remained, enveloped in God's care and instruction for forty days.

Standing at the foot of Sinai, we are invited to see all this and more to come. In following Jesus to Sinai, we journey by way of another mountain and from there move to Sinai, just as Jews are led to Sinai from other parts of their scriptures and the living witness of their tradition. Nonetheless, we must pause here to take in what we can, knowing that we approach the other mountaintop from this one.

Covenantal Configurations after Auschwitz

Of course, this story does not stand alone and uninterpreted by the larger tradition. Still, it invites further interpretation. Indeed, the narrative calls forth this ongoing interpretation by inviting every generation of Israel to stand with the seventy elders at its foundation and to participate in its covenantal ratification, in effect, further inviting those who stand there to join all Israel in declaring "all this we will do." Those of us who approach this story from the shadows of the Shoah have very specific questions we bring, with the hope that the story is able to resist and provide helpful theological clarification in our attempts to reorient ourselves post-Shoah. And since our questions are generated by the tearing in the covenantal fabric of creation, it is with regard to the covenantal dimensions of the story that we turn.

Where shall we begin? Jewish tradition celebrates the presence of all Israel (past, present, and future) at the foot of Sinai when God gave Torah—represented by the seventy elders and ritually by the twelve pillars. In the light of the Shoah, 6 million now stand at Sinai's base and bring with them a set of questions and concerns that critically challenge the way Sinai has been approached through the ages. Their blood is now mingled with the blood in which the covenant at Sinai was ritually sealed or purified. How can the sealing of covenant life in blood, especially blood associated with a burnt offering, not call to mind the blood of Israel's children during the Shoah? The cutting of the covenant invariably and irrevocably initiates a solidarity that has borne an unforeseen cost. Fackenheim has penetrated the tragic dimensions of the covenantal embrace of every generation:

Like Abraham of old, European Jews some time in the mid-nineteenth century offered a human sacrifice, by the mere minimal commitment to the Jewish faith of bringing up Jewish children. But unlike Abraham, they did not know what they were doing, and there was no reprieve.[10]

Not a single one of the six million died because they had failed to keep the divine-Jewish covenant. They all died because their great grandparents *had* kept it, if only to the minimum extent of raising Jewish children.[11]

The crisis of the Shoah, because it is covenantal, is foundational. Consequently, we must ask, Can the story sustain the unyielding countertestimony of 6 million victims, 1.5 million children? Fackenheim concluded that the midrashic framework could be salvaged, but only if a midrashic reading of the Sinai story could still be identified. That reading he found in the notion of a commanding voice, which he linked directly with Auschwitz as a command not to allow Hitler a posthumous victory—what he called the 614th commandment. Namely, Jews must survive as Jews; otherwise, the covenant linkage across generations is irrevocably broken.[12] In this fashion, fidelity across generations is honored; the slaughtered are not subjected to insensitive explanations of punishment; nor are illusory affirmations of salvation maintained that collapse in the face of what actually happened. In short, the presence and power of covenant life are maintained in the face of a God hidden in exile.[13]

From this vantage point, we might ask more directly of the story, Where is God in this revelatory event? The text points to a cloud, an important and richly ambiguous image. Although God is claimed to have been seen directly and beheld by Israel in verse 10, the theophany at Sinai concentrates on the presence of God as mediated by a cloud. In the story the cloud is the means by which God descends to meet Moses. It is the cloud that envelops Moses. It is from the cloud that God speaks. Still, the cloud does not yield a clearer, less ambiguous figure. To be sure, the story says the people perceived God's presence as a consuming fire. But on the mountain, the cloud remained throughout Moses's encounter. In other words, the presence of God, even in this theophany, is a hidden presence, which only Moses is invited to enter.

The story conveys more. This hidden presence establishes relationship with Moses as he ascends to meet it. There is a dual movement: God to Moses, Moses to God. After the Shoah, can there be any secure place for the notion of God acting without human cooperation? Greenberg makes the same point.[14] No longer can the covenant at Sinai be conceived as involuntary. With the deaths of the burning children and God's nonintervention to deliver them, the notion of God acting in history without human cooperation would be blasphemous. So if we ask, Why does the story again and again emphasize that Moses goes up the mountain, while God descends upon it? we must answer, Because God's presence requires human cooperation, human partnership. Moreover, even that cooperative meeting is hidden in plain sight, in a cloud, which in continuity with Sinai we can identify as a cloud of covenantal presence and partnership. Such is the form of covenantal presence that is able to resist the fires of Auschwitz, but only if other human partners act in the partnership of covenantal obligation and responsibility articulated at Sinai.

Greenberg identifies a further imperative that he links specifically to Sinai: He argues that for those who know themselves to be created in the image of God along with every other human being, the most significant command emanating from Sinai is to honor that image in the face of any person, Jew or Gentile. Greenberg puts it succinctly:

We also face the urgent call to eliminate every stereotype discrimination that reduces—and denies—[the] image of [God] in the other. It was the ability to distinguish some people as human and others as not that enabled the Nazis to segregate and then destroy the "subhumans" (Jews, Gypsies, Slavs).... The indivisibility of human dignity and equality becomes an essential bulwark against repetition of another Holocaust. It is the command rising out of Auschwitz.[15]

To put the matter simply, the covenantal presence mediated by Moses at Sinai and now refracted through the flame-tempered prism of the Shoah is able to resist its searing questions insofar as the Divine Presence is thoroughly covenantal, engaging human partnership and responsibility and commanding a covenantal regard of the other in whatever guise or identity the other is met.[16] In this sense, Israel is both an involuntary and voluntary witness—involuntary in the sense that Israel's descendants have not chosen the role in which history has now placed them vis-à-vis the Shoah, yet voluntary vis-à-vis their choosing to dwell in this covenantal framework knowing what they now know is at stake for them, their children, and their children's children.

REVISITING THE TRANSFIGURATION

How does this post-Shoah return to Sinai prepare us to read Matthew's account of the transfiguration of Jesus? How does it prepare post-Shoah Christians to approach the root confession that Jesus is the Christ? In order to grapple with these questions, we must remember that the Gospel of Matthew is a stylized account of the life and ministry of Jesus. Matthew alerts his readers early on to the stylized nature of his work. He tells us Jesus is to be called "Emmanuel, God with us" (Matt. 1:23). However, no one *in* Matthew's story thereafter ever calls Jesus "Emmanuel" except in the overall telling of his story. How does Matthew accomplish this? How does he tell us who Jesus is?

When we step back from the narrative to look at it in its entirety, we see that Matthew uses images from the Exodus and Sinai traditions to tell the story of Jesus. Michael Goldberg in his book *Jews and Christians: Getting Our Stories Straight* and Dale Allison in his book *The New Moses* both contend that Matthew is relying on his audience's familiarity and understanding of the Moses, Exodus, and Sinai traditions to comprehend his stylized portrait of Jesus.[17] Indeed, they point out that Matthew tells Jesus' story in such a way as to assert that Jesus' life is a fulfilling of, by way of refilling, these sacred stories. Not to be confused with the fulfillment of predictions, they mean that Jesus' story is a filling out of the root stories of Israel so fully that they overflow with meanings conveyed in and through them. That is, the cups of blessing, which these stories represent, overflow with life—Jesus' life.

As Brandon Scott points out, Matthew was drawing on the background of his Jewish readers and was using the trusted, cherished, liberating, and orienting story of Moses to make sense of the events of Jesus' life, death, and resurrection. That is, Matthew comes to his understanding of Jesus by way of his understanding of Moses, not the other way around. What Matthew and the Jewish community he sought to convince knew best was this set of Mosaic traditions, and Matthew utilized them to paint his stylized portrait of Jesus in order to show his Jewish audience who he believed Jesus to be: God with us.[18]

How, then, does Matthew's transfiguration scene unfold? Six days after a pivotal scene at Caesarea Philippi in which Peter confesses Jesus to be the Christ, Matthew takes his readers to an undesignated mountaintop, where Jesus has taken three of his disciples to be by themselves. There the text recounts that Jesus was transfigured in their presence, with his face and clothing brilliantly transformed. The story continues, describing the appearance of Moses and Elijah as Jesus' companions and conversation partners. One of the three disciples, Peter, proposes to build three booths or dwellings, one each for Jesus, Moses, and Elijah. Then, while Peter is still speaking, a bright cloud overshadows them all, and from it Matthew reports hearing a voice that proclaims: "This is my Son, the beloved; with him I am well pleased; listen to him" (Matt. 17: 5). At this the disciples fall to the ground, overwhelmed by fear. Jesus responds by coming to them, touching them, and telling them to get up and not to be afraid. Upon looking up, they see only Jesus, for Moses, Elijah, and the cloud have disappeared. Matthew then reports that as they come down the mountain, Jesus commands his disciples to tell no one about their vision until after the Son of Man has been raised from the dead.

Before looking at the refracted configurations of this event and the questions that grow out of our interaction with them, a contexting comment about this scene may be helpful. The Transfiguration occurs six days after the confession at Caesarea Philippi and narratively near the middle of Matthew's full text; it also prepares the reader for the concluding journey to Jerusalem and the events that unfold there. This unspecified mountain, cast in the images of Sinai, provides a vantage point for viewing the greater landscape of Matthew's gospel, literally and figuratively. It is a promontory, as it were, for viewing Jesus' work in and around Galilee as well as a vantage point for understanding the more encompassing message of Matthew's Gospel. Moreover, the time reference, after six days, suggests the temporal and liturgical vantage point of the Sabbath's place in the rhythm of the week and recalling the portrayal of Moses on Sinai recounted in Exodus 24.

Reconfiguring the Transfiguration

To be sure, the central question driving the Transfiguration scene as well as that of the entire Gospel is, "Who is Jesus? What is so important about him?" As Scott maintains, the point of the Gospel is to unpack the name "Emmanuel" even though it is not used within the text by anyone in the story to address Jesus directly. Instead, the Gospel proceeds midrashically.[19] Still, the post-Shoah Christian cannot avoid its central claim—God with us—since it is fundamental to Christianity's root experience. Nonetheless, it matters significantly how that claim is made in the narrative, and after Auschwitz, it is important to discover if the narrative is capable of fully addressing the questions put to it by the Shoah.

With this in mind, let us return to the mountaintop with Jesus, Peter, James, and John and examine the scene utilizing the light cast from Sinai. The six-day reference provides an interesting context: the time span of a week and the place of the Sabbath in the rhythm of Jewish life. Was Matthew alluding to Sabbath time with Jesus as a time to go with him to a mountain high and apart? Was Matthew recalling a similar allusion his audience would know of another mountain, liturgically climbed every Sabbath, namely, Sinai? To begin with such questions is to place ourselves in the story liturgically as well as midrashically, hearing the echoes of the larger, enveloping tradition (a cloud in its own way) without receiving definitive answers that Matthew meant *this* and not *that*. That is, we bring our Shoah-tempered questions into dialectical tension with the stubbornness of the story while dwelling in the narrative framework of the overarching Sinai tradition.

So in this context, what happens next? Moses and Elijah appear, "talking with Jesus." If echoes of the Sabbath continue to reverberate, we have a dramatic image of a faithful student of the Torah and the Prophets. To be sure, such an image comports with the larger Matthean portrait. In this scene, the accompanying disciples are overwhelmed as they recognize his mountaintop companions. According to Matthew, all three figures are conversant with each other. Jesus knows them well, and they seem to know him. Peter, James, and John are overwhelmed by all this as they see Jesus transfigured in its light. (Notice what is known and trusted, thereby casting light on that which needs to be better understood. Moses, the covenant at Sinai, and Elijah come to illumine Jesus.)

Peter speaks up and offers to build three booths: one for Jesus, one for Moses, and one for Elijah. Ready to act, Peter reaches into his tradition to honor the moment and those present in it.[20] He proposes ritual housing for what was happening—booths. But he and his proposal are interrupted. Matthew says, "Peter was still speaking when a bright cloud overshadowed them, and a voice from the cloud said, 'This is my beloved Son with whom I am well pleased; listen to him."

The echoes from Sinai resound but with some additions. As at Sinai, a cloud descends to envelop the encounter. And God speaks from the cloud, as God did with Moses. The covenantal presence and partnership identified at Sinai are represented here. However, the reported voice from heaven reflects another setting: the Jordan and Jesus' baptism, adding the phrase "to this one you shall listen" to the language of even earlier texts.[21] With this development, the disciples are thoroughly overwhelmed. They fall down, and Jesus comforts them, telling them to rise and not to be afraid. As they get up, they discover they are alone with Jesus. Moses and Elijah are gone. Likewise the cloud. Why? What do we make of the disappearance of Moses *and* Elijah and the cloud?

Before dealing with that question, however, let us consider the significance of the overshadowing cloud, for that and its accompanying revelation drive the disciples to the ground, not the presence of Moses and Elijah. What, then, does the cloud signify? Jesus and the disciples were enveloped in a bright cloud, what the Sinai tradition has linked to the presence of God, the *Shekhinah*. Indeed, the Exodus tradition remembers that only on this single occasion was God ever *directly* observed. Only then was God ever beheld by Israel—by Moses within the cloud, by others from a distance. There God spoke directly to Moses, in the cloud that descended to meet him in his ascent.[22]

A cloud is a wonderfully ambiguous and self-critical image, which we associate with the covenantal presence of God at Sinai. In itself, the image of a cloud is at once richly revealing and concealing. With a cloud a presence that is invisible can be seen. We can make out where one can begin to encounter its presence and where that encounter ends. And yet what we see remains hidden from view by the very presence we perceive. Indeed, a cloud can be the image of knowing and unknowing at the same time. And that is the case here.

Peter, James, and John had encountered *in Jesus* one who knew intimately the Law and the Prophets. Moses and Elijah were Jesus' intimate companions in the walk of covenant life. Everything about the way of Torah was intensified in this teacher of theirs. And with this in mind, it is not inappropriate to say that on this occasion his intimacy with Torah and the prophets overflowed and overpowered them. Moreover, the very presence of God, the *Shekhinah*, enveloped them as they pondered Jesus' intimacy with the heart and soul of Torah and the prophetic spirit. And what they beheld, they could not contain. Indeed, it contained them! In a cloud of simultaneous knowing and unknowing.

However, let us not forget Moses and Elijah. They did not remain in this scene. What is the significance of their disappearance? One possible response follows a trajectory that in the light of Auschwitz is tragically problematic. That is, Jesus not only embodies and intensifies the spirit of Moses and Elijah; he surpasses it. Morally, after the Shoah, we must resist such an interpretation, in the name of those who have suffered as a consequence of the supersessionism it expresses. However, there is an additional reason rooted in Matthew's text. If Sinai is the interpretive anchor of this scene, then Sinai and its traditions are the light source illuminating what happened, and they participate in the transfiguration of Jesus. Reversing the analogy breaks the analogy, but that is nonetheless what has happened for centuries. Indeed, for more than one interpreter, Moses and Elijah disappear because they are no longer needed. They are surpassed. But we can no longer go along with this tradition knowing that both history *and* the story support our resistance to this supersessionism.

The presence and then accompanying absence of the enveloping cloud supports such a reading as well. Not only do Moses and Elijah disappear, but the cloud does, too! Even those adhering to a supersessionist interpretation would not wish to argue that the cloud that mediates God's presence would be also left behind. But that would be implied if we interpret the disappearance of Moses and Elijah to mean that they were left behind. All three disappear from the scene together. Quite simply, any accounting for the disappearance of Moses and Elijah must be commensurate with the disappearance of the cloud.

What, then, do we make of their disappearance? Knowing what we know about supersessionism and its complicity in the conditions that made the Shoah possible, we cannot say Jesus surpassed them. Likewise, what we know about the rhetoric of Matthew requires a similar response. Neither can we separate Jesus from Moses and Elijah because they disappeared, for we would separate Jesus from the presence of God as well. Still, we must come to terms with their disappearance. Perhaps our midrashic reading of the scene provides a clue.

With the recovery of the midrashic dynamic present in Matthew's text, we have learned to approach this portrait as Matthew has, by way of Sinai. He, like the disciples he portrays, has come to Jesus knowing the Torah and the Prophets in familiar ways. They constitute the way they know the holy and the realities of covenant life. Bringing this knowledge to Jesus, they see him standing atop another mountain, representatively, with Moses and Elijah and enveloped in a radiant cloud. They know Jesus from their knowledge of Sinai and in turn are challenged by Jesus to look back at Sinai and the Prophets with new insight. Read in this way, the scene is dialogical and reflects the interactive character of midrash, interpreting experience from tradition and tradition from experience—as Fackenheim describes, with the stubborn resistance of Moses and Elijah meeting the unyielding experience of Jesus, the focus of Matthew's contemporary experience. The dynamic begins with Sinai and moves to Jesus and is confirmed by the very presence of God. But the experience does not end there. Rather, it moves on, focusing now more particularly in and through Jesus, who has more to show his followers as he sets his face to Jerusalem. Furthermore, the same interactive dynamic draws us into the interpretive mix as we come to Jesus and Sinai haunted as we are by the aftermath of the Shoah. Here we are reminded that even though as Christians we come to Sinai by way of Jesus, his followers came to him the other way round, and we must get the tension in the relationship right. Moses and Elijah are his companions whom we restore to the story even when we approach him standing alone and transfigured with his followers.

Yet even reading the scene midrashically, Christians cannot overlook that the emerging rabbinic community rejected Matthew's portrait. The support of Moses and Elijah was withdrawn by the rabbinic community of Matthew's time. Jews said no to the transfigured Jesus we Christians know as the Christ—then and now. While Christians affirm continuity with Moses and the Prophets, Jews see discontinuity. Whatever else this scene preserves for Matthew, it also preserves a historic tension that has been the source of confusion and conflict ever since. Given this, we must find a way to affirm Jesus' Jewishness at the same time we face the reality that he was not accepted as the one we Christians believe him to be.

A great deal is at stake: Christianity's relationship with Judaism, as well as its distinctiveness. Christians like me must find a way of reclaiming Jesus as a Jew but recognizing his distinctiveness then as well as now. Furthermore, we must not forget that, for Christians, Jesus must bring something new to our condition for his presence to be salvific. The Christological test of continuity and discontinuity[23] must be honored, but in a way that avoids the supersessionism and displacement theology that has distorted most attempts to deal with this tension. In terms of the story, the presence of Moses and Elijah is essential. Jesus is a child of the covenant and aligned with those who honored the role of the Prophets. He was a Jewish reformer, speaking like Elijah from within the tradition. And yet these figures do not remain with him, just as Judaism did not remain with or continue to embrace his followers. After Auschwitz, this need not, and must not, mean supersessionism. Nonetheless, reclaiming Jesus' Jewishness and reconfiguring this tension do not justify failing to recognize that the tension remains and separation evolved. Rather, it calls Christians and Jews, but Christians especially, to get the story straight.[24] Christians must account for the Jewish "no" to Jesus, but not in such fashion that Moses and Elijah are denied their place, for a time, on this mountain with Jesus as his companions.

As we begin our descent along with that of the disciples, we recall that Jesus told them they were not to tell anyone about what they had seen. Why? Was Jesus promoting secrecy? Perhaps. I am more inclined, however, to think his concern was for encouraging the three disciples to wait, to let their experience mature. To allow the whole picture to emerge with the completed story, especially in the light of Peter's tendencies. In the light of what we know now, it seems especially wise to take this perspective. So where we read "tell no one," I would read that to mean (*kivyakhol*): "Do not tell anybody about this now, not yet. Wait. Wait until you understand. You are not ready. And you won't be for a while. You need to live with this until . . ."

Before leaving the mountaintop there is another question that our post-Shoah perspective draws from this encounter: Why did the disciples fall on their faces before the transfigured Jesus? Whatever else it meant then—awe, respect, a sense of unworthiness—the reason now includes for post-Shoah Christians like me a recognition that in his Jewish face I also see the faces of 6 million victims of the Holocaust—1.5 million of whom were children. With that knowledge and the additional knowledge I have of Christian complicity in the legacy of antisemitism, I can only add that the shame of any supersessionistic transfiguration would drive true disciples to the ground. Moreover, from this posture, and perhaps only from this posture,[25] I, and others like me, can experience this transfigured Jesus touching me and telling me to get up and not to fear. The shame leads to spiritual maturity rooted in a humility born of true confession. The subsequent question, then—why be told, "[T]ell no one?"—leads directly to a posture of caution and modesty (a positive and healthy dimension of shame) that in effect declares, "Know the whole story, the story stretching from the first three decades of the first century B.C.E to the last decades of the twentieth century, before speaking. Know what has been done and said in the very name of this transfigured Jesus. Know the shadow side that accompanies the positive affirmations. Even so, arise and do not be afraid of what you see and know." There are transfigurations upon transfigurations!

In the light of the Shoah, the commanding and covenanting voice of God is midrashically reconfigured. Likewise, the transfigured Jesus and the light shed on him by Sinai. How, then, shall we return to the enveloping cloud that still hovers over this scene and interpret the divine declaration Matthew reports coming from it?: "This is my beloved son, with whom I am pleased. Listen to him." Greenberg asserts that there is an abiding and commanding covenantal voice that speaks from Sinai saying: "The overriding command and the essential criterion of religious existence after the Shoah is to honor the absolute and equal dignity of any other, for every human being is created in the image of God."[26] Is this not the covenantal imperative of Sinai and the abiding work of creation that we are obliged to see in the transfigured face of Jesus? He is one who wholly and steadfastly fulfills that obligation. Surely, that is what it means, especially after Auschwitz, for us to know Jesus as an intimate companion of Moses and Elijah. If we are to see Jesus as one who represents, as a beloved son, the covenantal image of God, can we see any less?

Rethinking Christology

For most New Testament scholars, and Christians generally, the Transfiguration story is a Christophany. It raises and answers in narrative fashion the question "Who is this Jesus whom we follow?" If Sinai is the illuminating tradition in Matthew's Christophany and not a foreshadowing or allegorical typology, then the presence of God revealed in Jesus in this event and its consequent covenantal imperatives take the form of what

Schubert Ogden calls a representative event,[27] bringing into human articulation (even incarnation) that which was present at Sinai and articulated by Moses. Christians may claim that Jesus intensified or extended that reality beyond traditional boundaries; nonetheless, the logic of Matthew's portrait is representative.

For Matthew, Jesus is disclosed and illumined by the event at Sinai. Matthew approaches Jesus by way of Sinai. He sees Jesus embodying the very reality revealed at Sinai to Moses. Consequently, he uses the Sinai tradition to construct his Gospel portrait of Jesus. That is, Sinai is the base for the metaphors he employs. Jesus represented for him what Matthew trusted to be revealed at Sinai. After the Shoah, how do we understand the question of Jesus' identity and Matthew's answer? Our answer? When we Christians turn to this story and ask, "Who is this one we follow?" we answer with many who have gone before us, like Matthew, "He is the Christ," meaning, as Matthew did, "God with us."

According to Schubert Ogden, Christians can distinguish between two different kinds of Christologies as a way of moving beyond Christocentric or theocentric options in relating to people of other faith traditions. In distinguishing between constitutive and representative events, he describes two very different ways of understanding the experience of salvation mediated by Jesus. A constitutive understanding of the saving character of Jesus' life believes that salvation is not simply represented by Jesus; it is constituted by his life and work. Jesus' life and work bring salvation about. Without his life and action, its reality is missing. Therefore, a constitutive Christology would be one that dictates that Jesus has constituted a new reality that does not, and cannot, happen in any other way. On the other hand, a representative understanding of the saving character of Jesus' life recognizes that the promise and possibility of salvation have existed prior to the event that may make it manifest, much like a marriage ceremony articulates and represents a reality begun before the ceremony and continuing long after it. The celebrant represents or brings into focus that which the couple serves in their shared promise making and their willingness to articulate it in the presence of God and others with whom they share their lives. Ogden's categories provide helpful clarification in understanding the implications behind these styles of Christological thinking. A constitutive Christology must necessarily partake of supersessionism. A representative Christology provides a way of confessing Jesus as the Christ without partaking of supersessionism. Furthermore, we can claim with Matthew that Jesus was the representative image of God without having to discount or displace the covenantal tradition that provides the foundation for making such a claim.[28]

To be sure, a representative Christology may still be *confessionally* constitutive for Christians, but if it is to be true to Matthew's midrashic rhetoric, its Christology is not *ontologically* constitutive. That is, Jesus' life and work represent the promise given at creation and sealed in covenant at Sinai. In similar fashion, Sinai articulates and thereby represents the covenantal intentionality of creation. Hence, Sinai is confessionally constitutive of Israel's life, making possible the understanding of a covenantal project of life we identify as creation, in turn representing what is given from the beginning at creation. Similarly, Easter and this Christophany are confessionally constitutive of Christianity but not of creation and its covenantal intentionality.[29] Ernest Nicholson has hinted at this point by saying a relationship is not a covenant until it is so articulated as one. It may partake of its qualities, but until it takes on the articulated self-consciousness of promise in the presence of witnesses, it is not yet fully what it is, though it may very well participate in its promise to be so.[30] For example, creation is relational from the beginning, but that relationship is not yet a covenant until a covenant is articulated. Nevertheless, one can look back from the articulation of that covenant to understand that the nature of the intended relation has been covenantal from the beginning.

This kind of thinking is an important post-Shoah step since it grounds a representative Christology not in the process categories of philosophy, which are analytically helpful, but in the narrative imperatives of Matthew's portrait of Jesus. Confessing Jesus as Christ need not lead without compromise to displacement traditions and consequent theologies of contempt. Indeed, the covenantal narrative of Sinai, as mediated by Matthew, is able to resist supersessionism at the same time it can support the foundational claim of Christianity that Jesus is the representative one whom we are to follow and who faithful Christians can recognize as "God with us" while remaining faithful to the burning children who perished at Auschwitz.[31]

Significantly, a representative Christology rooted in the traditions of Sinai leads to understandings that emphasize the covenantal traditions of Israel. The confession "God with us" re-presents these covenantal dimensions emphasizing the relational quality of that confession—its "withness." Jesus as the image of the invisible God becomes the incarnate face of a covenanting God turned toward those who follow him. Jesus as the image of a shared humanity becomes a representative face of a covenanting humanity, choosing covenant life even in the face of inevitable death. The transfigured Jesus seen by the light of Sinai represents the covenantal realities mediated there, too. In the light of Sinai's hidden face of God, which is radiantly reflected in the face of Moses, Jesus is seen by Christians as the one who represents this covenantal reality abundantly, mediating the covenantal and covenanting presence of God and the subsequent responsibilities of covenant life with others: what Greenberg identified as the criterion of any religious claim after Auschwitz and what earlier I identified as the post-Shoah covenantal imperative of Sinai. Of course, the discontinuity represented by the disappearance of Moses and Elijah remains as well. Likewise the Jewish "no." But the contention is now directed to the character of covenant life and how best to honor and represent it. For Christians, Jesus extends the embrace of covenantal partnership to include the marginal Jews and eventually the Gentiles. Even at these boundaries, he shows the face of God at the unveiling of divine-human encounter. Where for Jews the veil remains, for Christians the transfigured face of Jesus becomes the face of God (2 Cor. 4:6), their *Peniel*—"the place" where Christians meet God and know the divine embrace of covenantal relationship. Yet the veil in another sense remains for Christians as God is still hidden in and through him—a finite life and figure.

In the post-Shoah light of Sinai those of us who follow Matthew's guidance can make out the contours of a distinctly representative and covenantal Christology. In the face of Matthew's transfigured Jesus, we meet an intimate companion of Moses and Elijah, as one who walks intensely and extensively the way of Torah with the reforming spirit of the Prophets and who stands with all Israel at the foot of Sinai addressed by its covenantal and historic realities. The Jesus we meet in Matthew represents the manifold relationships revealed at Sinai. He stands illumined by its covenantal light and enveloped in its covenantal witness. At the same time, he represents Matthew's distinctive confessional assertion that in this figure his disciples meet the one they call "Emmanuel—God with us." Continuity and discontinuity are retained with the covenantally articulated common ground of its confession recognized as the place where it is my hope the distinctive claims of Jews and Christians can be faced and honored.

CONCLUDING THOUGHTS ON THE TRANSFIGURED FACE OF POST-SHOAH FAITHFULNESS

In the reconfigurations of Sinai's light, we glimpse our unfinished portrait of post-Shoah faithfulness with increasing clarity. Just as Matthew stood with his people at Sinai to portray the transfigured Jesus, we have taken our place there as well. Hopefully this commentary has exposed the serious problems that accompany how Christians typically make their way to Sinai—starting with Jesus and presuming they may do so without regard to how prior witnesses came to him. In Matthew's case, his way to Jesus and his way of presenting Jesus to his followers proceeds from Sinai. By restoring that rhetorically essential move to Matthew's hermeneutic, we enable the Mount of Transfiguration to continue being for Christians, even post-Shoah Christians like me, a vantage point for recognizing who we are, with whom we dwell, who we follow, and why. Furthermore, Matthew's portrait allows for, indeed it invites, a representative Christology pointing faithful followers of Jesus back to Sinai, not to appropriate it in supersessionistic fashion but to reclaim it as a confessional anchor for living a covenantally informed and dedicated life, able to recognize in the covenant of

Sinai the very intentionality of creation; and at Sinai, to stand in solidarity with all who faced the Shoah and the imperative to honor the other, in whatever fashion one meets the other, as created in the image of a relational deity seeking covenanted life with all of creation. Yet even here, continuity as well as discontinuity remain but hopefully on a more respectful and inclusive covenantal base.

To be sure, these reflections have focused on the orienting terrain of the mountaintop. However, both scenarios are richly textured by what lies on the other side of the mountain in its shadows. For Moses and his people, it is a covenantal crisis in which the divine-human partners confront the catastrophe of the Golden Calf. The covenant survives, but at a cost and with a loss of innocence that the story remembers and preserves. For Jesus and his disciples, their descent leads to Jerusalem on a path that will pass through Crucifixion before it ends in Resurrection. Indeed, the narrative location as well as the liturgical placement of this story at the threshold of Lent (according to the *Common Lectionary*) combines with Matthew's anticipation of the Passion to orient the reader: There is a cost, an attendant risk, that accompanies covenant life. From our post-Shoah vantage point, this sobering perspective intensifies our descent from the mountain. For Matthew, Jesus, as the representative one of covenant life and a covenanting God, embraces life in the most vulnerable posture possible, choosing covenant life in the face of its rejection and abandonment with a covenantal "nevertheless."[32] He chooses covenantal solidarity with his disciples, with Jerusalem, with the Judean people, and with the traditions of Moses and Elijah even in spite of their response to them. From the Mount of Transfiguration, Jesus moves on to Jerusalem to complete his mission and to fulfill his vocation. From this mountain peak somewhere in the Galilee, he moves down into its hills and valleys and makes his way to another mount and its holy city. After Auschwitz, that embrace includes the children of the Shoah gathered at the foot of Sinai even as Sinai's light illumines him. After Auschwitz, our journey to the Mount of Transfiguration takes us back to Sinai where we take our place with the transfigured face of post-Shoah faithfulness.

A MIDRASHIC POSTSCRIPT

Fackenheim, in describing the midrashic framework guiding post-Shoah reflection like that of this project, points out that midrash explores its own contradictions by exercising a dialectical tension between a stubbornly resistant story and its limits exposed by an unyielding sense of realism. This rhetorical strategy insists on remaining faithful to the root experience narrated by the story while at the same time experiencing great freedom and trust in pressing the very same story to address the limits exposed by the painful realities of everyday life as well as life *in extremis*. Fackenheim makes it clear: History is not transfigured by the narrative. The saving presence mediated by the narrative occurs in history—fully experienced for what it (history) is. In the case of Sinai, history is not changed when social circumstances challenge the assertions of Sinai. The story is re-entered to discover how in midrashic configuration (or reconfiguration) the story can remain true to itself and also address the new circumstances confronting it. In other words, in clashes between root experiences and historical realities, midrash remains open to and expressive of these contrarieties at the same time it seeks ways to honor the fundamental assertions of the root experience.[33]

This rhetorical strategy is similar to what happens in jazz. Where the stories are the basic melodies, midrash is the elaboration and stretching of the melody that transforms a rather simple structure into a complex and rich exploration of that melody's commentary on the world. The original composition is stretched, played in different rhythms, modalities, configurations, and the like; yet throughout the musical interpretation the original tune resists the player or players interpreting the piece, providing an encounterable structure—an "other"—that serves as the interpretive anchor to which the player is finally accountable in the presence of other interpreters of the same piece. In the end, the song is bigger than its musical interpretation, but it often takes a master interpretation to make that clear. In similar fashion, the story is bigger than the text that mediates it, and it often takes a meticulously probing and thoughtful interpretation to demonstrate that as well.

NOTES

1. Roman Catholic liturgy celebrates the Transfiguration in the Ordinary time midway between Pentecost and Advent. Nonetheless, the same biblical passages are paired for the day.

2. Numerous figures can be cited as influencing my work. Emil Fackenheim, Irving Greenberg, Arthur Cohen, Franklin Littell, J. B. Metz, Roy and Alice Eckardt, Clark Williamson, and Paul van Buren are only a few.

3. Emil Fackenheim, *God's Presence in History: Jewish Affirmations and Philosophical Reflections* (New York: Harper Torchbooks, 1970), pp. 20–31.

4. Ibid., p. 26.

5. Cited in ibid., p. 71.

6. Irving Greenberg, "Cloud of Smoke, Pillar of Fire: Judaism, Christianity, and Modernity After the Holocaust," in *After Auschwitz: Beginning of a New Era?*, ed. Eva Fleischner (New York: KTAV Publishing House, 1977), pp. 9–13.

7. J. B. Metz, *The Emergent Church: The Future of Christianity in a Postbourgeois World* (New York: Crossroad, 1987), pp. 19, 32.

8. Michael Polanyi's work on epistemology is helpful here. He explains that "all knowing" has a from-to character. We know from something to something else. The *from* dimension is known tacitly as background, whereas the *toward* or *to* dimension is known focally and attended to in the foreground. See Michael

Polanyi and Harry Prosch, *Meaning* (Chicago: University of Chicago Press, 1975), pp. 34–42, for a concise explanation of Polanyi's distinctions.

9. While Matthew does not develop the story in this direction, we should not overlook the movement of hospitality reflected in the telling of the episode. The ascent is made in stages of hospitality, with the nearness and presence of God carefully approached.

10. Fackenheim, *God's Presence in History*, p. 70. Italics in the author's text.

11. Ibid., p. 73.

12. Ibid., p. 84.

13. Ibid., p. 60.

14. Irving Greenberg, "Voluntary Covenant," in *Contemporary Jewish Religious Responses to the Shoah*, ed. Steven L. Jacobs (Lanham, MD: University Press of America, 1993), pp. 77–105, esp. p. 85 ff.

15. Ibid., p. 44. Judith Plaskow, in the light of feminist critique, offers a model for returning to Sinai in which she reconfigures this task in the face of power and its abuse. I have chosen to address this issue in the context of covenant partnership. She emphasizes the issue of distance and control in the pervasive notion of God as One who is unapproachable and wholly other. These are important cautions, and her insights about healing (*tikkun*) as the restoration of relation in what she calls an embracing wholeness in which the returning child of the covenant may abide are instructive. However, she identifies the problematic nature of distance with otherness in such a way that the problem occasioned again and again by otherness and radically posed by the Shoah is not fully addressed. After Auschwitz, we are obligated, commanded as Greenberg asserts, to face otherness as a primary human and creational datum in need of being reconfigured in relational terms. In this regard, I offer a friendly amendment, suggesting her critique of otherness focus on what she calls "dominating otherness" while developing a relational category of "embracing otherness," which her work can easily and conceptually support. See her book *Standing Again at Sinai: Judaism from a Feminist Perspective* (San Francisco: Harper & Row, 1990), chaps. 4 and 6.

16. Emmanuel Levinas's work makes the same point. The imperative of the other is rooted in the face of that other. And faithful people of the covenant are to see the other as created in the image of the One who calls us to life, into life.

17. Michael Goldberg, *Jews and Christians: Getting Our Stories Straight* (Nashville, TN: Abingdon Press, 1985), pp. 135–148; Dale C. Allison, *The New Moses: A Matthean Typology* (Edinburg, Scotland: T & T Clark, 1993), pp. 131–165.

18. Brandon Scott, personal conversation, February 7, 1996.

19. We do not need to determine whether or not the gospel is actually midrash or derived from a midrashic framework to make this point. Matthew relies on a rhetorical style that draws from a way of living in and out of the narrative framework of Jewish tradition that is reflected in midrash.

20. Note the continuity with action preceding full understanding that is rehearsed in the Sinai tradition. In the very spirit of Sinai he was ready to act or do and then to hear (Exod. 19:7; see also Exod. 24:4,7).

21. The "beloved son" language has an even longer tradition behind it than the baptism tradition associated with Jesus: It stretches back to the "beloved son" traditions of Genesis and their associations with sacrifice, death, and resurrection.

Jon Levenson, *The Death and Resurrection of the Beloved Son* (New Haven, CT: Yale University Press, 1993), esp. pp. 220–232.

22. The implications for divine-human partnership identified in the covenantal meeting between God and Moses at Sinai hold just as strongly in this scene as well.

23. Jesus must be like us in all respects; otherwise, he does not participate fully in our humanity. He must be unlike us in such fashion that he can offer us what we cannot offer ourselves.

24. This is the critical point of Michael Goldberg's excellent book *Jews and Christians: Getting Our Stories Straight*.

25. I treat this issue in several essays, most thoroughly in one presented at the 1995 annual meeting of the American Sociological Association in Washington, D.C. See Henry F. Knight, "From Shame to Responsibility and Christian Identity: The Dynamics of Shame and Christian Confession Regarding the Shoah," *Journal of Ecumenical Studies* 35, no.1 (Winter 1998): 41–62.

26. Greenberg, "Cloud of Smoke, Pillar of Fire," pp. 42, 44.

27. Schubert Ogden, *Is There Only One True Religion or Are There Many?* (Dallas: Southern Methodist University Press, 1992), pp. 83–104, esp. p. 97.

28. Douglas John Hall's book *Professing the Faith: Christian Theology in a North American Context* (Minneapolis: Fortress Press, 1993) utilizes Ogden's distinctions in a very helpful development of a representative Christology. See especially pages 506–548, where he explores the hermeneutics of representation for contemporary Christology. Clark Williamson relies on Ogden's distinctions as well and utilizes them for his reading of Christian Scripture and the development of his Christology. Clark M. Williamson, *A Guest in the House of Israel: Post-Holocaust Church Theology* (Louisville, KY: Westminster/John Knox Press, 1993), pp. 160–201.

29. Symbolically, of course, Christianity refers to the constituting intentionality of creation as the *logos* of God, whereas Judaism extends its understanding of Torah in similar fashion.

30. Ernest Nicholson, *God and His People: Covenant and Theology in the Old Testament* (Oxford: Clarendon Press, 1986).

31. This, of course, is Irving Greenberg's criterion for doing theology after the Shoah, that it be held accountable to the children who perished in it. "No statement, theological or otherwise, should be made that would not be credible in the presence of the burning children." "Cloud of Smoke, Pillar of Fire," p. 23.

32. See my reflections on this theme in our first set of reflections: Henry F. Knight, "Wrestling with Two Texts: A Post-Shoah Encounter—A Midrash on Genesis 32:22–33 and Matthew 26:36–46," *Shofar: Jewish-Christian Dialogue After the Shoah* 15, no. 1 (Fall 1996): 54–79.

33. Fackenheim, *God's Presence in History*, pp. 20–31, esp. p. 25.

4

From the Bush to the Vineyard (and Back): A Post-Shoah Return to Holy Ground

Exodus 3:1–15 and Matthew 20:1–16

More than one theologian has asked, "How do we live *with* God after Auschwitz; and how *without*?"[1] At the heart of any theological wrestling with the Shoah is the multilayered and multivoiced question of God. For many, it is asked by Elie Wiesel in *Night*: "Where is God now?"[2] For some the question is posed directly to God in lament and/or protest, crying out, "Where were you?" For some, it is raised in anger and rage and posed to those who have not dealt with the theological implications of Auschwitz, demanding of those who still speak faithfully of God, "Come to terms with what happened. How dare you speak of God in the same way now, after what happened there!" However the question is raised, it haunts faithful Jews and Christians, especially those who wrestle with their faith in the shadowy light of Auschwitz.

No one has argued more persuasively than Irving Greenberg that the Holocaust is an orienting event of revelatory significance. His 1974 essay "Cloud of Smoke, Pillar of Fire: Judaism, Christianity, and Modernity After the Holocaust" was a landmark exploration of this theme. Thereafter, his criterion of the burning children [3] of Auschwitz has haunted theologians, like me, who seek to find reorientation and balance in the fiery shadows of the Shoah. The "way to wholeness," he wrote, "[passes] through the demonic, consuming flames of a crematorium.... Neither Exodus nor Easter wins out or is totally blotted out by Buchenwald, but we encounter both polar experiences; the life of faith is lived between them. And this dialectic opens new models of response to God."[4]

Perhaps there is no better scriptural passage to focus this dialectic than that of Exodus 3:1–15, recording as it does the call of Moses to lead his people to deliverance and the self-disclosure of the God of Israel in the burning bush at Horeb/Sinai. For Jews, God is the Holy Other, the great I AM, who hears the cries of Israel and delivers them as a covenant partner eternally committed to their welfare. After Auschwitz, how do any of us approach this burning bush? For Christians, God is the One whom Jesus describes as reaching out to include the left out, lost, and least in the divine movement of deliverance and covenantal fidelity.[5] After Buchenwald and Treblinka, how do any of us approach the holy ground of covenant life described by Jesus? To focus our wrestling with these issues, the burning bush story is paired with Jesus' parable of the workers in the vineyard wherein Jesus focuses on the including grace of God's continuing invitation to enter the dawning reign of God, in effect echoing the later disclosure to Moses "I will be gracious to whom I will be gracious" (Exod. 33:19), which Matthew reports Jesus using to conclude his parable.[6] These passages preserve the covenantal structure of God's commitment to creation as they place the Eternal One Who Is at the center of the stories of deliverance and salvation that give life and meaning to Judaism and Christianity. After Auschwitz, how might these passages speak of these touchstone realities and the life of God?

APPROACHING THE BURNING BUSH

The episode of Moses at the burning bush is familiar. Moses, while tending his father-in-law's sheep, comes to Mount Horeb, the mountain of God. There Moses encounters a burning bush, which he turns aside to see because it is not consumed in the burning. As he does, he hears a voice calling his name from the midst of the burning bush. Moses responds forthrightly, "[H]ere I am [*hineni*]," presenting himself in readiness to be further addressed by the as yet unidentified voice.

In just fifteen verses the text mediates the story of Moses's call to deliver his people; it narrates the giving of the divine name to Moses; it reveals God's attentiveness to the Israelite people and their plight in Egypt; it establishes the significance of Sinai in the history of Israel; and it identifies the Eternal God of the Universe as one with the God of Abraham, the God of Isaac, and the God of Jacob (as the God of Israel's ancestors) and a God who desires freedom for a people chosen for relationship (i.e., covenantal partnership). The story of the burning bush is rich and inexhaustible, revealing how the Israelite people come to know themselves embraced by a covenanting God of deliverance and life.

Attending to the Burning Bush

What calls and speaks with such force that Moses, or anyone else, would turn aside to see what is taking place? The story describes a bush (*s'neh*) that is on fire but not consumed. Magical images in the tradition of Cecil B. DeMille conjure up a bush made of fire or a bush that burns yet is untouched by the flames that engulf it. Of course, the text tells us neither; we supply such images in the absence of a textual explanation. The text relates only that the bush was not consumed.

The traditional compilation of midrashim on this episode inquires about the significance of the bush that Moses turned aside to see. What kind of bush was it? According to the text, it (*s'neh*) was a common thorn bush. But why should a common bush be chosen as an instrument of divine disclosure? Here midrashic interpretation draws the following connections between the bush and Israel:

> just as the thorn bush is the lowliest of all trees in the world, so Israel was lowly and humble in Egypt;
>
> just as the thorn bush is the prickliest of all trees and any bird that goes into it does not come out unscathed, so was the servitude of Egypt more grievous before God than all other servitudes in the world;
>
> just as one makes of thorns a fence for a garden, so Israel is a fence to the world.[7]

The connections are built on the ordinariness of Israel. God speaks through an ordinary people, a prickly people with very specific claims about their relationship to God and their role in history as a priestly people. Elizabeth Barrett Browning conveys this kind of association in her allusion to the burning bush in her poem *Aurora Leigh*:

> Earth's crammed with heaven,
> And every common bush afire with God;
> And, only he who sees takes off his shoes—
> The rest sit round it and pluck blackberries.[8]

But there is more at work here than Browning portrays. The common thorn bush is also identified with Israel's prickliness (like a hedge around a garden or vineyard). Israel's specific, historic identity as a priestly people elected for that purpose is an essential part of the revelatory disclosure; and that identity can be prickly. Even so, it is not the bush per se or its boundary marking or witness qualities that draw Moses's attention in this episode;[9] rather, the bush/Israel is burning (oppressed and threatened), and Moses turns to look because the bush/Israel is not consumed. Indeed, *The Midrash* on Exodus makes a similar point even though the midrashist sees the bush more literally than I will be suggesting:

Why did God show Moses such a symbol? Because he (Moses) had thought to himself that the Egyptians might consume Israel; hence did God show him a fire which burnt but did not consume, saying to him: "Just as the thorn bush is burning and is not consumed, so the Egyptians will not be able to destroy Israel."[10]

Could the revelatory power in the episode be that the bush did burn but nevertheless survived? Such a recognition would lead to considering a different, and much less magical, possibility than the one offered by filmmaker C. B. DeMille and his ilk: a living entity that is being burned but that upon inspection we discover is not being wholly consumed. In this case, the intensity of the story would be directly related to recognizing how the power of the living, growing entity is not overwhelmed by the image or force of its own destruction. Only in surviving the fire could the bush not be consumed. That is, we can look at a bush that has burned and not been consumed only if the bush still lives. Consequently, the image would be one of endurance and resistance (if the fire is still raging) or of an aftermath (if the fire has gone out) that includes survival. Either way, the image is powerful without having to be magical.

This phenomenon is not unfamiliar. Consider Martin Luther King, Jr. and the burning images of a bombed-out church or synagogue; or the flaming torches of the Ku Klux Klan and its burning cross; or Mohandas Ghandi and the searing shame of untouchability unmasked for the oppression it truly is. Or consider Nelson Mandela and the burning hatred of apartheid. From the strength of a people surviving oppression (or who in the midst of oppression are nonetheless struggling to live with hope and pride and who can then rise from the flames of that destruction into something more), we might talk about a fire that does not consume the people it threatens to consume.

In other words, the disclosure is not focused simply on the fire or on the bush alone but on the gestalt of a bush, burning *and* surviving to bear witness to something more. This point is crucial; the revelatory power is in life and its witness to itself, even in the face of destruction. After Auschwitz, this point grows in significance.

The hope and future of covenant life beckon forth, in this case especially in its violation. Yet Moses must turn aside to see, before he is in a position to hear any call coming from its midst. He attends, alert, fully present, covenantally ready. The Hebrew term is *hineni*: Here I am. The orienting begins in attentiveness and the offering of his presence, also implied by the term *hineni*.

As the scene progresses, the drama intensifies. God commands, "Come no closer! Remove your sandals, for the place where you are standing is holy ground." Then God declares God's own identity, in effect responding with a divine *hineni*. Presence invites presence and responds to presence. Moses's presence to the reality of the burning bush evokes a corresponding divine presence with the accompanying recognition that the "place" of this encounter is holy ground. Moreover, Moses has attended *with* God to God's people who are also Moses' people. This, too, is part of the gestalt of the burning bush. Solidarity and mutual presence together constitute covenantal presence; and that is holy.

Consider what is at work here. The encounter and its covenantal dynamics are holy. The place of covenantal meeting is holy. Furthermore, we need not specify which aspect of the event is the source of holiness. It is the overall gestalt that comes together to reveal what is of ultimate significance for Moses and the Holy One who embraces him. It is the configuring and reconfiguring gestalt (*HaMakom*?) that reveals what is holy for those who follow Moses. And this is the ground of divine-human encounter that is sacred.

The story continues to deepen. God explains that the suffering of Israel has been the focus of divine compassion and concern. Furthermore, the divine intention is to deliver them from their oppression, leading them from the constricted land of oppression (*Mitzrayim*/Egypt, literally means narrow land) to a broad land overflowing with plenty—an abundant land. Yet God cannot act alone, or so it is implied. God needs Moses' help, and the sacred summons emerges as the divine intention unfolds. The presence of mutual attention leads to the revelation of Israel's oppression and Moses' divinely appointed task. Throughout, the scene is interactive and mutually disclosive. As Moses reveals more of himself, likewise God reveals more of God's self to Moses, but never without retaining the ultimate mystery and divine freedom that are God's. The scene and its mutual disclosure press on toward increased responsibility for Moses and unfolding clarification of the covenantal pact between God and Israel.[11]

The Summoning Call

Who and what call Moses? The story is ambiguous, saying first that an angel of the LORD called from the bush. Thereafter, the text tells of God speaking to Moses. Why? What does the text preserve, or gain, in retaining an ambiguous designation of the one speaking to Moses? Perhaps we, the listener/hearers of this language, are invited into the ambiguity that surrounds any true encounter with that which is holy and sacred. Perhaps the text preserves the mystery of the encounter and the burden of interpretation of that mystery with a designation that signals a threshold of identification. Maybe the text, with its ambiguity, tells us something about the dynamics of vocation as well. From whence does a sense of calling come? With what does the call speak? How does it speak? In this case, the story speaks, even as the bush and the flames (aspects of the story?) speak. The text speaks as the story speaks; however, the story and the text are not equivalent, for the story transcends the text, even though it is mediated by it.[12] Just as Moses turns aside to attend to the burning bush and hears God speak from its midst/configuring gestalt, faithful readers of this text/hearers of this story are invited to assert that *in all that*, the narrative's configuring gestalt, the text and more, God speaks.

The story, in its simplicity, does not specify how or why the bush is burning, or what the bush might represent, or say what or who set the bush on fire. Because it does not offer such specificity, it leaves room to examine important distinctions that we are compelled to make in the aftermath of orienting experiences. If the bush is the people Israel, would it not be appropriate to say that Pharaoh has set it aflame? Perhaps. But what is gained by refraining from this kind of specificity? The bush calls Moses to attend to it after the fire is under way. Is that not a more accurate reflection of how oppression is recognized, after it is well under way and taking victims? Was that not the case for Moses regarding his people? He had seen their suffering firsthand. He even acted in passion regarding what he had witnessed earlier in his life. But the suffering and oppression did not go away. Instead, Moses did; he fled. Can we read Moses' response to the burning bush to mean that he could not let his people's suffering remain unattended to, no matter how much he might wish, despite his prior history and despite where his attention would soon take him?

We might also ask, To what is Moses drawn? Is he drawn to the flames? the bush? or the survival of a bush that is burning? The bush is not consumed in the burning; according to the text, that is what draws his attention. The attention Moses gives is a confirming gaze directed to a still or yet living bush, threatened by fire, but reaching out to him with its witness to life. Moses is drawn to the bush's survival, not its burning. Therefore, we must specify that the witness of that truth is not the work of whom or what set the fire. Instead, it is the power of life to live through and transcend its own destruction that we must respect. Again, the orienting character of such an event resides not simply in its parts but in its overall gestalt, aspects of which may still remain unknown or unarticulated. If we turn aside to face the searing reality of the Shoah, we can say Hitler and his henchmen set the bush we identify with Israel on fire, but not simply Hitler. The fuel of antisemitism was an essential part of its kindling, as well as the atmosphere that fanned its flames. The overall gestalt must be confronted here, too. And we are called by the story and by history to turn aside with Moses to face the burning bush again. We are drawn by the witness to life, in its extreme violation and in the resistance to annihilation, not simply to the pain and suffering embodied in the flames. The Shoah, however, is not the bush, though it may be the flames that engulfed the bush. The overall gestalt of the burning bush that is not consumed causes us to turn aside and see.

Facing the Bush (and Its Ashes)

As we turn aside to face the bush and its searing imagery, we must insist that after the Shoah we ask further questions about the branches of the bush we have identified with Israel that *were* consumed. Wiesel has made a similar point with regard to the *akedah* (the binding of Isaac). The binding of Isaac is a revelatory tale for survivors; however, with regard to the victims, it fails to disclose the embracing, covenantal purposes of God except in their violation.[13] In the case of the Shoah, there were 6 million "Isaacs" who were not spared. Likewise, in reading the burning bush as a threatened Israel that resists its destruction, there were many children of Israel who knew utter victimization. In respect to them, we cannot build our affirmations and commitments to life at their expense. Nonetheless, Israel has survived, and the story remains instructive; but it must be sensitively and respectfully qualified. We must walk carefully on the ground before these images.

In the scarlet shadows of Auschwitz, the burning bush takes on terrifying dimensions and intensity. If the bush is truly Israel in burning need, then the post-Shoah image of that bush assumes the visage of 1.5 million children, the human tender of a victimized people. Their agony-filled cries silenced by hatred and indifference reach out to those with courage enough to hear a summoning call to responsibility and witness. The mystical and revelatory dynamic of I AM-you are also includes the cries of the burning children in the crackling sounds of leaping flames. Ka-Tzetnik 135633 (Yehiel De Nur) writes:

Auschwitz is a flaming pyre. I know. I have been summoned to witness the fire belching sight.[14]

The I AM-you are summoning dynamic takes on a profoundly unsettling summons for those who survived their encounter. The summons to witness as survivor calls for the survivor to reenter a nightmare that will not die—by choice. And the burning children of Auschwitz, forever embraced in the burning bush, summon forth our covenantal readiness. How shall we respond? In the post-Shoah shadows of the late twentieth century, the burning bush can be a terrifying figure. To return to the imagery of the narrative, we must remove our shoes and face this burning bush with great care, for here we stand with vulnerable others on holy as well as terrifying ground. Still, we must attend to its summoning visage, however unsettling it might be. And we must hear the urgency of its summons to act, knowing now the cost of not doing either before it was nearly too late.

The story as preserved in the text (Exod. 3:1–15) is silent about any branches that have been lost in the burning. Instead, the focus is on the bush that is not consumed. Nevertheless, there were branches lost in the burning; after Auschwitz, we cannot ignore this. Consequently, we must ask about branches that were lost under Pharaoh as well as those lost under Hitler. Indeed, as we ask about Israelites who perished under their oppression in Egypt, we find ourselves giving Moses a lamenting voice in much the same spirit that subsequent readings and interpretations of Torah saw themselves giving the teachings of Moses long after Moses had passed on. In this fashion, we remain true not only to Moses as the mediator/giver of Torah but also to the 6 million—especially the burning children of Auschwitz.[15] So we ask about branches the text overlooks, believing that the larger story that the text mediates must do so as well. This insistence is an essential part of our post-Shoah *hineni*.

In unsettling fashion, our post-Shoah return to the burning bush links us to Moses, turning aside to see what is yet burning but not [yet?] consumed. And in turning aside to attend to this event, we discover ourselves summoned into covenantal presence. In other words, even now, the response is *hineni*, a confessional presence that brings full acknowledgment and responsibility to the narrative as well as to history as they meet in the event we identify as the Shoah. Equally unsettling is the recognition that if the burning bush is aflame with a life-destroying fire that does not consume itself, then it still burns. Consequently, any responsible *hineni* requires our asking "Where?" In the shadows of the Shoah, this question is hauntingly acute. Where are God's people oppressed and suffering? Furthermore, who are they? In the age of Shoah, Israel's representative witness cannot be forgotten even as we deal with Israel's particularity. Together they are a critical warning as well. What can happen once can happen again. Hence, the pledge "never again" must attend to other situations as well as other people at the same time it speaks for Israel and her people near and far.

This imperative is not foreign to the biblical witness. Indeed, it permeates the heart of Torah. Over and over again, Israel is reminded to treat the strangers in their midst honorably, for once they were strangers in a foreign land.[16] Greenberg makes the post-Shoah context of this ethical claim urgently clear:

We also face the challenge to create the conditions under which human beings will grow as an image of God.... It was the ability to distinguish some people as human and others as not that enabled the Nazis to segregate and then destroy the "subhumans" (Jews, Gypsies, Slavs).... The indivisibility of human dignity and equality becomes an essential bulwark against repetition of another Holocaust. It is the command rising out of Auschwitz.[17]

After Auschwitz, Israel, as the people of God, represents the claim of every person to be viewed as created in the image of God. In that reflected light, we are summoned by the burning bush in her story to attend to the burning bushes of others. To be sure, it is no easy task to incorporate this admonition. Yet this is the tension of living within the beckoning reach of the burning bush.

Of course, antisemitism still burns in human hearts across the world. So it cannot be dismissed or left behind as attention is directed toward others set apart for victimization. Rather, the task grows more complex. And with the political realities and difficulties of modern Israel, the dilemma grows even more convoluted and acute. Nonetheless, Israel and the Jewish people remain set apart, often tragically, summoned to a representative role (however more difficult it has become) as "priests" for a covenantal way intended for all peoples to follow.

Coming to Terms with God

Our *hineni* includes a deep insistence that the Shoah has radically affected how we can think and talk about God. We even insist on criteria like Irving Greenberg's haunting imagery of "the burning children."[18] We ask about the innocent victims, the 1.5 million children who perished in the flames. Any talk of survival must be tempered by coming to terms[19] with their loss. So, how does the story about a burning bush help us face such deep and searing questions? To draw help from the narrative, we must first ask how Moses comes to terms with his experience. What happens to Moses? What does Moses learn about God? How is divinity present for him?

Moses discovers an embracing, covenanting God who remains always other even though steadfastly committed to a continuing relationship with the people of Israel. Likewise, this covenanting One is a summoning Other, who in some fashion calls Moses to act on behalf of his people. More specifically, Moses discovers God to be present in the summoning gestalt of relation and responsibility configured in and through the burning bush. Still, God remains the One who is whatsoever and whomsoever God chooses.

After the Shoah, talk of God is difficult. Particularly trying are the classical ways of thinking of God's relationship to history and the interventionist assumptions that characterize how the biblical traditions face these issues. Throughout, God talk is punctuated with images and metaphors of monarchic (imperial) notions of power that express interventionist assumptions. Even the covenantal imagery participates in many of these assumptions about divine power. With the Shoah, such assumptions about power, divinity, and covenant come under fire, literally and figuratively. How, then, does one conceive of God, given the radical way in which the covenantal fabric of life (among peoples and between God and God's covenant people) has been torn?

Arthur Cohen, Richard Rubenstein, and Irving Greenberg have addressed the fundamental assumptions about God's relationship to history within a covenantal framework and the ways in which those assumptions about history and God's relationship to it are shattered by the Shoah. For Cohen, the interruptive character of a divine pledge to act in history on behalf of a covenant people is sharply challenged. God did not intervene. Consequently, Cohen is led to rethink the use of covenantal categories without the assumption of an interruptive or interventionist relationship between God and history.[20] For Rubenstein, the notion of a covenant with a

God who can intervene and who does not breaks the divine-human covenant.[21] To be sure, Rubenstein wants to retain the significance of covenantal categories, but after Auschwitz, they are focused among the persons who constitute the people Israel, between the generations, and voluntarily chosen within history by human partners. Singular divine action expected as a consequence of those covenants can no longer be expected. Irving Greenberg raises similar concerns and argues for a thoroughly voluntary covenant for which Jews must take responsibility as they accept their role as the covenant people Israel.[22] In each case, the problematic nature of a God who is outside history and intervenes as a consequence of a covenant with a people in history is brought into focus. In the light of the Shoah, that kind of covenantal configuration breaks down. Either God is portrayed as capable of acting and does not—a sadistic figure; or God cannot act at all—unless the covenant is inadequately configured.

A close reading of this episode reveals, even when the monarchic and interventionist patterns of the Exodus tradition are present, a strong processive and partnership model evocative of critical appropriation. The episode at the burning bush begins with encounter and moves through mutual disclosure (Moses: "Here I am"; God: "I am the God of your father, the God of Abraham, the God of Isaac, the God of Jacob") to call, and from call to the interventive action of a representative agent empowered and accompanied by God who chooses to be known as the One who calls forth being and life from the beginning and forever. That is, from beginning to end, the enterprise is a partnership, unfolding in greater and richer differentiation along the way and increasing responsibility for human agency in that partnership. From beginning to end, the realities indwelled by both partners are mutually constructed. From beginning to end, the reality constituted by the participating partners takes the shape of a covenantal gestalt. Where in the past the assumptions of interventionist power as the appropriate form for conceptualizing divine power were not questioned, after Auschwitz such assumptions fall short. A thoroughly covenantal reading, however, can address the hard and unyielding questions generated by the Shoah without dissolving the covenantal gestalt that enlivens the passage and sustains its participants and followers. As a consequence, we are invited to revisit the terms we employ for addressing and talking about God, focusing on the processive and relational nature of what is revealed at this bush/in this story.

In other words, we cannot avoid asking, What kind of covenantal agent/partner is silent in the face of 6 million victims, 1.5 million of them under twelve? What kind of agent (divine and/or human) watches without acting when over a million young "branches" and 6 million total are allowed to burn? Is this God just a shibboleth? A cipher for the language of covenant that breaks down in the face of massive, innocent suffering? Perhaps the best we may respond, without attempting to remove such questions, may be:

An absent presence/a present absence.
A silent presence that says, "I am what I am, as you are what you are."
A presence that is absent, giving room for covenantal responsibility even if not accepted.
A covenantal gestalt in which attentive human response and intervention take on greater significance, reflecting the very intention of creation and the life of God. A place that is no place; a name that is ultimately empty of speculative content yet a promise-bound place of inclusion and care.

The I AM of divine self-disclosure is an identifying and summoning *you are* to Moses. Confronting the self-defining and absolute otherness of God, Moses finds himself affirmed and confirmed in his identity. The encounter is deeply relational and prefigures its unfolding covenantal character. As Peter Hodgson remarks in *Winds of the Spirit*, this encounter is the configuration of a covenantal gestalt in which God, the One Who Has the Power of Being Absolutely, calls Moses forth to be who he is.[23]

In addition to this mutually covenanting, relational power of I AM–you are, the divine name conveys a delimiting quality that I have tried to replicate in using the different cases to convey the overall gestalt. Lawrence Kushner captures this in his rendering of the divine name as "I am God—you are not!" where he alludes to the first two utterances of the Decalogue.[24] Kushner also captures the open-ended quality of the imperfect action of Hebrew verbs in another rendering that he makes: "I am not yet who I am not yet."[25] We might adapt that as "I am who I am not yet, or I am not yet who I am yet to be."[26] Importantly, all of these associations are carried by the three-word Hebrew phrase *ehyeh asher ehyeh*, which interprets (but does not articulate) the divine name in the text.

Summoning Covenantal Partnership

After Auschwitz, how do we view such a project of covenantal partnership? In the Exodus tradition, Moses and the people must act for God to act as well. But the tradition remembers plagues, magical staffs, and other aspects of divine intervention into human affairs/history. After Auschwitz, we are forced to see the burdens of covenantal partnership increasingly as a human responsibility to uphold.[27] And God's presence is hidden in the dimensions of our humanly configured covenantal acts. Still we must ask, At what point do the realities of history exceed the reach of covenantal metaphors? What is the burden of this kind of partnership?

In this regard, we must rethink how we speak of intervention. By itself, especially in the shadows of the Shoah, intervention is an insufficient covenantal category. This is most apparent now, but perhaps it has always been so; only now we are forced by what happened in our century to ask tougher questions of our theology. At the burning bush, if we have the eyes to see it, intervention is not necessarily direct but summoned. Moses is called to act in partnership with the divine will for deliverance to occur. Yet Moses is free to choose; indeed, he resists. In an age in which the absence of divine intervention signals a covenantal crisis of ultimate significance, this point is critical. To be sure, intervention is a part of the story, but the divine intervention that is perceived by the eyes of faith is intimately and thoroughgoing in its dependence upon the intervention of Moses. Furthermore, the intervention is not simply Moses' alone. His intervention is inadequate and even dangerous by itself. Recall that earlier in the story, Moses intervened out of his own passion—and he brought death (Exod. 2:12). He intervened again in Midian at the well and presumably struggled with his own violence yet again, but keeping it under control (Exod. 2:17). In this episode, he hesitates, hopefully, in a matured sense of his own capacities for harm in acting again. But this time, he is called to act *in partnership* with the divine will and the divine presence.[28]

After Auschwitz, intervention is problematic. Divine intervention as well as human intervention is subject to critical scrutiny. From what we now know about power and its abuse in the intrusive acts of intervention, we know the limits of power and its abuse. The Nazi actions, bureaucratic or SS (*Schutzstaffel*) directed, were intrusive interventions in the life of European Jewry. Intervention alone is problematic. On the other hand, no intervention is likewise a problem; we know the dangers of its abdication as well. Consequently, power must be rethought and transfigured as well. How that power is exercised and for what purposes must likewise be reviewed.

Clearly the only way the covenantal language can hold is for its human partners to accept more and more of the responsibility for creation and its relational qualities. God as an intervening figure in history must be rethought as a covenantal presence known in the transcending gestalt of covenantal actions that reveals a quality of mystery and significance not fully accounted for by the cumulative historical arithmetic of meaning. That is, there is a surplus of meaning given by the covenantal embrace, even with greater and greater human agency. There is something sacred and holy in the mix, in the process, happening more as a verb than as a noun and requiring the action of human agency.

A Deepening Summons

At the burning bush Moses is summoned to life beyond himself: I AM–you are *for others* in partnership with the Summoning One's fidelity to covenant life as embodied in the promise and deliverance of the people Israel. Indeed, Moses had previously heard and responded to situational needs to help others beyond himself—at the well in Midian and before that in Egypt when he went out to his people and saw an Egyptian beating an Israelite slave. In the first case, Moses intervened but without bringing deliverance. Instead, his actions brought death to one oppressor and fear to those that he tried to help. Later, at the well, he intervened on behalf of Jethro's daughters who had been driven away by a group of undesignated shepherds. In this situation, Moses defended the daughters and watered their animals. Whether Moses struck out at the intruders at the well we do not know. The text is silent about the nature of his defense, focusing only on the subsequent relationship that grew out of his respect for the women and his concern for their vulnerability. These earlier episodes are important for how we see Moses and his summons at the bush.

Indeed, there is an ongoing and deepening dynamic in this story. In recognizing it, we discover that the summons at the bush is not an isolated call but a focused and richly textured continuation of an ongoing summons that begins with our initial glimpse of the adult Moses. It comes just after the birth and adoption narrative. The transition is abrupt and immediate as the story of the adult Moses begins; likewise, his summons:

One day, after he had grown up, he went out to his people and saw their forced labor. He saw an Egyptian beating a Hebrew, one of his kinfolk. He looked this way and that, and seeing no one he killed the Egyptian and hid him in the sand. When he went out the next day, he saw two Hebrews fighting; and he said to the one who was in the wrong, "Why do you strike your fellow Hebrew?" He answered, "Who made you a ruler and judge over us? Do you mean to kill me as you killed the Egyptian?" Then Moses was afraid and thought, "Surely this thing is known." When Pharaoh heard of it, he sought to kill Moses.[29]

Perhaps Moses is simply unable to watch the oppression of his people? Notice how the text points out the importance of Hebraic kinship in the telling of this episode. First, the Hebrew people are identified as Moses's kinfolk. Then Moses expresses distress at the violence between two "fellow Hebrew[s]" who were fighting. In each case, Moses cannot remain a spectator. He is called by what is happening to intervene. Later, at the well in Midian, the situation calls him into action. Once more he intervenes—this time for strangers.

In all three instances, Moses seeks to act on behalf of others. But simply acting on behalf of others is not enough. First, Moses is summoned by the predicament of his kinfolk, where he acts, violently, to stop the violence. Yet the violence continues: The oppression does not end, and alienation even marks his relationship with his kinfolk as they respond to him in fear and accusation. Still, Moses appears to be summoned by what he has failed to recognize in the vulnerabilities before him. Furthermore, acting as he has, he has now cut himself off from Pharaoh and his adopted culture. Moses is thoroughly alienated and accused. So he flees in exile from Egypt and the people of Israel. Yet in the wilderness he is moved again. At the oasis in Midian when several women are driven from the well by some shepherds, Moses comes to their defense. Once more, he is called out of himself by the vulnerability of others, although this time they are strangers, not kinfolk. And he acts decisively for their welfare. How, we do not know; on this matter the text is silent. And then, in the context of a persisting summons, Moses confronts his burning bush. But in the face of its call, he balks. Why?

In his journey from Egypt to Midian he has lost privilege and place, only to regain it again. As a person of privilege and power, Moses acted in the presence of violence with violence and failed to bring liberation from the violence that prompted his intervention. As a consequence, he lost both his privilege and his power and became the object of intended and sanctioned violence in the culture that had provided his authority and place. Then without either, he acted on his own authority in the face of need at the well in Midian, a place in which he himself was a stranger. As a result, status and privilege were returned, but in limited scope as a member of Jethro's family, as Jethro gave him the hand of his daughter Zipporah in marriage. Once more he is taken in by a family not his own. His place is granted by others, in hospitality to a stranger.

In other words, in facing the bush, Moses has faced himself, first with privilege and power, then without. He has faced himself as a man of violence trying to stop violence but failing. He has faced himself as a man who acts in the face of need on behalf of others, relying on himself as one with and then without recognized authority. What does it mean for this figure to ask, "Who am I to go to Pharaoh . . . ? Who am I to act on behalf of my people whom I have earlier failed?" In the light of his actions before and after the encounter at the bush, and particularly his deep reluctance to respond to the call to return to Egypt on behalf of his people whom he had earlier failed, we notice an important change.

The text does not tell us of Moses's inner disposition. We do not know whether he experienced guilt or shame. To be sure, we can guess, but the text is silent in this regard. Its concern is with the summoning response. Moses is assured that he will not be alone but accompanied by the divine, covenantal partner of his people. In other words, Moses is summoned out of his limited intentionality (whatever that is) and self-sufficiency into partnership with the One Who Is Absolutely; he is called upon to return to the people that are his people (i.e., he is called to move from alienation to reconciliation), and in the process, he is set apart for their deliverance. Moses' freedom is connected to his reconciliation with his people and their subsequent emancipation. In brief compass, the story describes Moses' personal deliverance from his past, reconciliation with his people, and his action on behalf of their liberation.[30] And in doing so, the story relates a deepening summons that is focused at the burning bush but that begins earlier and continues beyond the encounter at the bush. Furthermore, that deepening summons is dependent upon the maturing ability of Moses to face himself and thereby become more and more available to the summons unfolding in his life.

A Perilous Enterprise

Coming to covenantal terms with this One we call God can be perilous. Moses was compelled to step into dangerous territory—physically, politically, and ethnically, as well as confessionally. Returning to Egypt would be physically dangerous, with his life at risk, given the circumstances under which he fled. Returning to Egypt would bring him face-to-face with the political power of Pharaoh as an adopted insider to power who had alienated himself from that very base of support. Returning to Egypt would bring him face-to-face with his birth people, from whom he was also estranged and who certainly saw him as an outsider to their plight. And returning to Egypt would bring him face-to-face with himself and, presumably, his own sense of shame and inadequacy. Nonetheless, that was what he was called to do and accept if he was to act in partnership with this Summoning Other of the Covenant. In a very real sense, any who would accept the covenantal terms of this kind of divine-human relation after Auschwitz must recognize the risk as well as the urgency of such an enterprise. The interventionist character of divine agency now adheres more to the power of the narrative to speak to receptive human beings who, themselves, must accept responsibility for any embodied intervention in human affairs. Furthermore, such intervention must occur without any divine guarantee of the outcome, since responsibility is given over to human agency. The risk and stakes thereby increase. Still, the character of this enterprise, a covenantal gestalt of choosing agents seeking relation of perduring value, reflects the image of the covenanting other who has entered into this enterprise we call creation.

Classical notions of omnipotence and omniscience yield to truly covenantal configurations of power and knowing. Presence, too, must be reconsidered. The power configured in covenant is the power of partnership. It is dependent upon the response of the covenanting other. It is not intrusive, although it can lead to intervention, as any parent can identify with regard to his or her children. Likewise, as the same parent can attest, covenantal power cannot control outcomes. In similar fashion, covenantal knowing is interactive and interdependent. Covenantal knowing recognizes what is fundamentally at stake in situations; and the covenantal knowing of God can be conceived as that knowing that recognizes with complete and absolute understanding what is at stake in this and any situation, but because it is covenantal, it cannot know the response of the covenanted other who acts and responds in his or her freedom. Furthermore, covenantal presence, because it is a partnership gestalt as well, requires a responding other for its expression. In this kind of covenantal context, we may declare with the psalmist that there is no place where such presence cannot occur (even in Auschwitz, the darkest valley of the shadow of death), but covenantal presence requires the responding partner for configuration and confirmation. Moreover, because life is plural, others in their freedom can prevent still others from having the freedom to participate in this mutually constituted covenantal gestalt.[31] This dimension of sin, an insidious consequence of evil, must always be reckoned with in a world in which something like the Shoah can happen. Sin, like covenant life, is bigger and more extensive than we may have thought.

Coming to covenantal terms with God after Auschwitz is indeed a perilous undertaking. The partnership is not equal, but the disproportionate distribution of responsibilities may not be as previously conceived. Instead of God as the all powerful sovereign who establishes a covenant with a vassal of inferior power, God now must be thought of as the Eternal Giver of Life who in the covenantal project we call creation ventured into the risk of relation with that which is other than God—the supreme and divine act of hospitality. Furthermore, in this venture, God seeks relation with an other (creation) and others (creatures), who while other than God can choose or reject relation in return. Thus, God has in effect chosen to be limited by the ever-differentiating expressions of otherness that we know as life. Consequently, with regard to responsibility and power in this domain, God is dependent upon the covenant partnership of humanity, by the very divine choice that initiates and undergirds creation.[32]

The summons to covenantal partnership calls for more than deliverance. The text preserves the memory that God's people were to return to the land given to Abraham, the land of the Canaanites, Hittites, Amorites, Perizzites, Hivites, and Jebusites. According to the text:

[A]nd I have come down to deliver them from the Egyptians, and to bring them up out of that land to a good and broad land, a land flowing with milk and honey, to the country of the Canaanites, the Hittites, the Amorites, the Perizzites, the Hivites, and the Jebusites.[33]

The story unfolds with further elaboration of how God will accomplish this action with Moses. The text clearly gives expression to interventionist assumptions in rendering God's role and actions in the partnership, but we have reentered the story critically. A noninterventionist reading invites a figurative appropriation of these claims: God can still be perceived as an active participant in very confrontational acts, but that participation depends upon the kind of action that unfolds. Still, even such a figurative reading must confront the literal qualities of the figure and important realities associated with the promise conveyed in the divine summons. Why would God "resolve" to "bring" Moses and his people into the land of others (Canaan-

From the Bush to the Vineyard (and Back)

ites, Hittites, Amorites, Perizzites, Hivites, and Jebusites) as the land of Israel's promise?

Of course, we could argue that what God promised to Israel was given at the exclusion of those others. That is, the land was theirs alone and to be taken, if necessary by force. Indeed, there are texts and traditions that grow from them to support this.[34] But if we are going to read the summons at the bush as a call to covenantal partnership, surely we must look for that to be carried out as the fruit and fulfillment of its promise even in a land of others. The plain meaning of the text is clear: Israel is called to build its life of covenantal partnership in a land already populated by others.

If this dimension is an essential part of the summons at the bush, would we not expect Moses to have seen the vulnerabilities and problems of such a venture? After deliverance, more struggle and risk would follow. After fire, perhaps more fire. Surely, we can imagine Moses crying out long before Micah (and long after, too):

What does the Eternal One require of us? To do justice? To love and pursue kindness unflinchingly? To walk humbly in our way with this summoning, covenantal Other?[35]

Knowing what we know of the struggles the people faced with the others in this land, a covenantal partnership read in this manner would be no easy affair. Indeed, the enterprise would be perilous at best. Yet this seems to be the higher calling to which Moses' successors responded as Israel's Prophets reminded her people not a few times: "You are to be a light to the nations."[36] Torah, as well, makes the case strongly, admonishing the people of Israel to receive the stranger in her midst with hospitality, remembering that they were once strangers in Egypt.[37]

While this reading can be supported from the summons at the bush, and would not be altogether new, it is perilous—as if the other path of conquest were not. However, after the Shoah, the risk is intensified. Furthermore, as the path to security and peace for modern Israel demonstrates, the risk remains fraught with obstacles. Survival is at stake in every step. And so we ask in even more haunting terms: What does the Eternal One require now?

Why would God resolve to bring his people into the land of others as the land of their covenantal promise? Indeed, the question intensifies. And yet in the light of what is at stake, there is perhaps no more profound way to fulfill the promise of covenant life than to embody it in such circumstances where it will be tested in the extreme. If this is the logic of the covenantal way, then to what is modern Israel summoned now? After Auschwitz, idealistic romanticism cannot obscure the risk of such a path. After Auschwitz, we live, as Greenberg remarked, in a dialectic between Exodus and Auschwitz, Easter and Auschwitz.[38]

The Returning *Hineni*

Our approach to the burning bush reflects a continuing summons to responsibility that is summed up in the Hebrew word phrase *hineni* (here I am). Indeed, each movement of the story builds, like a fugue, on this theme: Moses quite literally responds to the summons of the burning bush: "Here I am." God responds similarly, declaring a commensurate divine presence: "[Here] I am, the God of your father, the God of Abraham, the God of Isaac, and the God of Jacob." Moses continues the thematic development, deepening his presence by revealing his resistance and perhaps his shame with a further disclosure of who it is that has declared readiness before the summoning Other. God again responds, not to Moses' question but to Moses' deepening self-revelation, "I will be with you." Finally, Moses speaks from his need to identify the One who has called him to responsible action for his people, asking for that One's name. God discloses the divine name, declaring *"ehyeh asher ehyeh"* ("I am . . ." in all its implications). Now we declare, reading this story in the shadows of the Shoah and in the presence of another burning bush: "Here we are." Opening ourselves to its interrogating power, we stand accountable and covenantally bound to the witness of this searing story. We are called out of familiar territory to go back and to bring out those who dwell in this oppressive place. We are called into responsible action, to intervene—an intervention that absolutely requires our action if there is to be any intervention whatsoever.[39] We hear ourselves called to act by the God of Moses, the God of Moses' father, the God of Abraham, the God of Isaac, the God of Jacob—the God of Israel. When we ask in fear and/or shame, Who are we to undertake such steps? we are promised nothing more nor less than "this One who is, who and what that One is," will be *with* us. Nothing more, nothing less. Presence: Mutual, deeply vulnerable and covenantal presence. And when we inquire what terms we can use, what name and understanding we can give to this summoning, eternal, covenanting Other, we are given a confounding answer: *ehyeh asher ehyeh*. The summons to responsible action and the responding *hineni* are the recurring legacy of this biblical story and the post-Shoah framework we bring to it. Together they configure a covenantal gestalt of meaning and action that points us toward a more responsible way of talking about God and founding (not to mention confounding) the covenantal partnership we identify as the ultimate goal of creation.[40] God is the eternal and covenanting Other, Holy Other, who remains other even in the covenantal embrace of life we know as creation. The otherness of the Other remains other, declaring, in effect, its own *I AM* as it simultaneously confers a corresponding *you are*, summoning its encountering other to a reciprocating presence in an unfolding, relational gestalt. We encounter a fundamental mystery we cannot penetrate but that still gives definition to our mutual relationship, leaving our inquiry unfinished but nonetheless with an orientation to life and its sacred significance before the Eternal One Who Is.

Such an understanding of covenant life (reflected in the use of the noun as an adjective modifying *life*) moves traditional emphases on discrete covenants to the prior and more inclusive embrace of life as the divine choice made at/in creation. Covenant, then, becomes a shaping figure for organizing and guiding how we as creatures take up our responsibility for caring for the gift of life. As well, covenant helps us conceptualize the promise of this gift and God's steadfast commitment to it. In the biblical narrative, the actual term appears first in the story of Noah and the flood, then more particularly as Abraham's legacy and in fuller articulation at Sinai with Moses. This reading places covenant in the service of life as an expression of creation and its fundamental choice for life given in and through relation self-consciously expressed and nurtured covenantally.

FROM THE BUSH TO A VINEYARD

Typically, the issues focused by the burning bush and its story are addressed under the rubric of revelation: "How does Israel come to know its God?" Through the story of the burning bush the question is posed, not as an abstract dilemma requiring detached reflection but as a problem of relationship and relational knowing. For Jews, how do they know themselves addressed by a covenanting God? For Christians, how do they know themselves to be included in this Eternal Covenanting One's embrace of life? More still, what do they learn about this one who addresses and embraces them in this story? And what are the consequences of this relationship? All these questions are focused by this story. And after Auschwitz, they cry out with a burning intensity not unlike that which caused Moses to attend to the burning bush in the first place. For Christians, any return to the burning bush and the divine self-disclosure mediated by this story will pass through the filtering lens of Jesus and his parables of God's rule and realm.

A parable is a narrative riddle much like the figure of a burning bush, revealing and concealing the presence of God and the holy ground of the divine realm. Parables, short narrative figures, work like a metaphor to push beyond the boundaries of our present knowing to reach new understandings. They work by way of comparison, knowing from the familiar to the unfamiliar, yet they extend our reach beyond the familiar by casting their comparison in the reorienting ways of a riddle. Attending to the world at hand, a parable is a brief narrative about familiar experience that is configured in such fashion as to invite its hearer to reconfigure his or her perception of and action in that world.

Meant to bring reorientation, parables were used by Jesus to focus the issues of divine sovereignty and the fulfillment of God's intention for life in the coming reign and realm of God. Beginning, "The reign/realm of God is like..." Jesus drew stories from common, everyday experience yet rich in reference to the identity of Israel and its heritage in which he lived (e.g., vineyards, tending sheep, sowing seeds, and tilling soil), but he took these familiar figures and configured them in ways that reoriented his hearers to see and be challenged by the holy or sacred in their midst.

Our path in these reflections moves through a specific parable that portrays this holy ground for Christians. The reality portrayed by Jesus in his parable of the workers in the vineyard is sacred for Christians. It represents what is called the rule and realm of God,[41] abundant life, what I have chosen to call a gestalt of covenant life. How we understand and dwell in that gestalt reveals what we believe about ourselves, this holy realm, and God, the Giver of this sacred domain/dimension of existence. So it is doubly appropriate both in form and in content.

In coming to terms with this parable the story is primary even though the context in Matthew is important. Matthew, the only Gospel to report this parable, has Jesus tell it in the context of his debate with the Scribes and the Pharisees as he challenged their notions of who is included in the domain of God's sovereign care that Jesus called the realm and rule of Heaven. Following the sequence of Mark, Matthew situates the parable in the midst of Jesus confronting the religious leaders with the challenge that their expectations about these matters must be rethought. The recurring theme "The first will be last and the last will be first" ties Jesus' parabolic commentary together. However, if the parable is one that Jesus told more than once (and there is every reason to believe this possibility),[42] then the story remains primary and demands our closer attention.

The story is compressed and easily held in memory due to its simply structured story line. But its impact is far from simple. A landowner goes out early one morning (dawn) and, after reaching an agreement with them, hires some laborers for a denarius a day[43] to work in his vineyard. In recurring intervals of three hours, the landowner goes to the marketplace and hires more laborers, declaring, "[W]hatever is right, I will give you." Then with only an hour left to work, the landowner makes a final trip to the marketplace and finds one last group of laborers that he sends to work with no reference to wage or even to what is right, just the summons: Go and work. At the end of the day, the landowner returns to pay the laborers and tells the steward to pay all the workers beginning with the last first. He directs the steward to pay this last group the one denarius that he promised to pay the first-hired for the entire day. The steward then pays the middle hires the same, one denarius. And last of all, the steward pays the first-hired the very same, according to their contract/agreement. These first-hired grumble, unhappy that the last-hired have been treated the same as the first-hired, as their equals. The landowner hears their complaint and responds to one of them, "I have done you no wrong, for I have treated you according to our agreement. Take what is yours and go. I choose to give to this last group the same as I give to you. May I not do what I wish with what is mine? Are you envious because I am generous?" Matthew, presumably adds, "The last will be first and the first will be last."[44]

By Way of Parable

How does the story actually work? First, we must identify the characters and other figures that, together, configure the overall gestalt of the parable. To begin, there are three primary characters[45] and at least two secondary ones: the landowner, the first-hired workers, the last-hired who are complemented by the other workers hired at three-hour intervals throughout the day, and the steward. In addition to the characters, there are key figures that exercise a critical presence of their own: the vineyard, the marketplace, and the wages paid to the workers.

As critical as the characters are, they are unspecified in the parable except for the role that they play in the unfolding narrative. That is, their specific identity appears to be less important than the unfolding action they generate. First, an unnamed landowner goes out to find workers for his vineyard. The landowner first reaches an agreement with the laborers that he finds to work from the beginning of the day. The landowner then proceeds to go to the marketplace seeking more workers. Finding potential workers idle in the marketplace, he recruits their help, promising to pay them "what is right." Then at the close of the day, the landowner makes one final gesture, recruiting those who were idle even at the last hour. They are simply told, "Go and work," receiving a simple and unencumbered invitation. By not specifying anything more than being the owner, the landowner's action must establish his character and identity. He is unswervingly committed to his vineyard, over and over again seeking laborers to work in it. The workers are similarly unidentified except for how their inclusion has been secured. The first group had a formal agreement to which the landowner and each worker were accountable. The workers secured from the third hour through the ninth were secured only with a promise. And the last-hired were given no promise, only a place in the vineyard to work, however brief their work might be. Emphasizing their action in the story and their role in its enactment, the hearers of this story are free to identify with more than one character. The action and the roles in the drama together configure a powerful gestalt that invites multiple identification.

The landowner is never identified. He need not be a divine cipher but a symbol capable of representing any who might stand in the ownership relationship in which he is portrayed, God certainly included, but not in an exclusive nor restrictive sense. Similarly the workers hired with a formal agreement can refer to any members of the covenant people who view their role in the work of their people's mission as work in the vineyard of Israel's life. However, by not specifying that, hearers can focus on the dynamics and relationships that the parable expresses and apply them again and again to more than one situation in their life. To repeat, the focus is the gestalt of the overall story, not any single character in it.

This configuration includes not only the characters in the story but other figures as well, most specifically a vineyard. If Jesus can compare the realm and rule of heaven to a story about a vineyard, surely it is worthwhile pausing with this figure to inquire what images and associations it would have evoked for Jesus' hearers, as well as Matthew's readers. Brandon Scott makes this connection succinctly:

[T]his is not simply any farm work but labor in a vineyard. The vineyard implies a metaphor, for vines and vineyard have a rich symbolic heritage in Israel's language stock. One need only recall Isaiah's Song of the Vineyard (5:1–7) or God's mournful complaint in Jer. 12: 10 that "many shepherds have destroyed my vineyard," the vineyard being Israel.[46]

For Jesus' hearers and for Matthew's early readers, any comparison of the rule and realm of heaven to a vineyard would have evoked images of Israel like those cited by Scott. In addition, the literal qualities of the figure[47] would have evoked the notion of a tended ecology not unlike that of a garden, but in a vineyard's case, set aside for a specific purpose. Moreover, such imagery of a tended ecology would underscore the double identification of a vineyard with a land of promise—the promise of bearing fruit of the land that could be made into wine and the land of promise known as Israel. Even more, such a land would evoke the promise of this covenanted land in such fashion that its promise transcended the very place it was to occur. Nonetheless, that land, like its people, would be set aside and protected by very clear boundaries.

In corresponding fashion, the figure of a vineyard operates in tension with that of a marketplace, the public square of first-century Judaism. The image is secular and economic, and neither domain provides the work or the value that is the focus of the parable. Yet the marketplace is where the landowner does his work of inviting. Time and time again, that is where he goes to find workers for his vineyard.

With these characters and narrative figures in mind, let us sharpen our understanding of how the parable works. Consider how the parable begins and how the comparison (with the reign and realm of heaven) is made:

The rule and realm (*basileia*) of heaven is like a landowner who went out early in the morning to hire laborers for his vineyard. (Matthew 20:1)

The comparison is not simply to a landowner nor a vineyard nor the laborers hired to work in it. Rather, the comparison is made to the overall gestalt that the parable relates. Leaving any part of that gestalt out of the comparison not only diminishes the parable but it changes the picture that Jesus has painted with his story. Each figure contributes essentially to the configuration of the narrative as a whole, weaving the spell of the parable's power to reconfigure the hearer's world.

The parable generates conflict regarding conventional understandings of the rule and realm of God. It does this by resisting simplistic interpretations and piecemeal allegorizations. It also generates dislocation by generating conflict within its narrative as well. Within the story, the conflict is focused on the expectations that the first-hired have regarding how they and their work are perceived vis-à-vis the later and more particularly the last-hired. Indeed, the first-hired are asked to reexamine their response when the other workers, even the least productive, are treated the same as they. Conversely, the later and last-hired are challenged to comprehend that they have been treated according to the agreement entered into by the first-hired. While the workers in the parable are challenged to deal with the generosity manifest in their encounter with the landowner, the hearers of the parable are challenged to deal with the generosity as well as the multiple identifications they might have with the various characters and figures portrayed in the story. Furthermore, the movement of invitation and inclusion to work in the vineyard, not the distribution of wages, which in a first-century context would be minimal, challenges the expectations typical listeners bring to the parable. Moreover, the overall gestalt challenges the hearers to rethink what it means to have a place in the vineyard and to make room for others to take their place in the same vineyard. In each of these ways, the parable generates some measure of hermeneutical dislocation.

The parable also does its work by not addressing typical expectations and thus raising questions that lead the hearer into new perceptions and actions. For example, in attending to the way in which time is specified and at the same time not addressed, one might ask, Why does the story identify the hours when the landowner goes to the marketplace and not identify the season in which the vineyard's work takes place? Of course, a simple answer might be that the hours of the landowner's goings and comings are specified to make the story easier to tell and to remember. Even if this is the intention behind the telling, the openness about the seasons allows the hearer to apply the story to times of harvest as well as those of pruning, sowing, and general maintenance. One might also note that the landowner's hiring, especially at the last hour, leads the hearer to ask, "What is so urgent?" The story does not tell, except to suggest that the work of the vineyard is urgent no matter when it happens. And this observation leads the hearer to ask, Just what is the real nature of this work? Is it what it seems?

Further still, the story ends with the expectations of the workers being challenged by the equal payment of wages to every worker, from the last-hired to the first. If the challenge to this expectation were neither desired nor anticipated, the simple solution would have been to pay the first-hired according to their agreement and then pay everyone else in the order of their coming to work. But the order of payment allows the first-hired to observe and listen. Is that an intended outcome of the landowner's actions throughout the day? If so, the first-hired are being challenged to move into a new relationship with the landowner, in their attitude toward the vineyard, its work, and the place each one has in the tending of the vineyard. Likewise, those who hear the story are asked to reconfigure their notions of what the realm and rule of heaven might be like.

The questions continue. Why choose a vineyard to be the focus of the landowner's care and the work of so many? What is so special about its tended ecology and its fruit? Scott has pointed out that there is a treasure trove of images that Jesus' hearers would have associated with this figure. In Isaiah and Jeremiah the vineyard is Israel, in her historicity and in her promise. As well, the vineyard, as Jesus extends the figure, embodies the divine intention that Israel represents as the intention for all creation. That is, a vineyard carves out identifiable ground where the garden intentions for creation can be experienced, in part, as the promise for all who would accept the invitation to work for it. The vineyard is nothing less than land with promise that has been cultivated, holy ground for those with eyes to recognize what it is. And the divine intention for life unfolds in the recognizing, cultivating, and sharing of that truth in an interactive gestalt of meaning and an ethos of care and responsibility.

Elsewhere I have identified this divine intention for creation as the desire of God for relation that has been embodied in Israel's covenantal history with God. Covenant life, like the work in the vineyard, was entrusted, by covenant, with Israel. But the quality of this life, righteousness, is not restrictively served by Israel. Her task is to bear witness to its light and truth and to invite others to respect and serve its promise. Like the landowner, she is to call others to the work of righteousness. And like the vineyard, she is set apart in order to bear this fruit of the tree of life for the sake of others. The parable works to mediate all these associations, not just an allegorical identification with the vineyard. And in doing so, the parable invites any who would make it their own to make similar multivalent connections. Furthermore, the parable compares this encounterable gestalt with the rule and realm of heaven. In effect, Jesus is saying, "The rule and realm of heaven are like this.... It is an encounterable gestalt, which we may meet in our midst. It is the very promise of covenant life, breaking into our broken and oppressive realities like a landowner who ..."

Coming to Terms with a Post-Shoah Vineyard

Perhaps the first and most obvious point a post-Shoah Christian encounter with this parable must assert is that any displacement reading of the Matthean postscript must be actively resisted in the name of the burning children as well as in pursuit of a more authentic rendering of Jesus' story.

Furthermore, careful attention to its constitutive figures as well as to its internal logic support a nonsupersessionistic approach. In addition, the covenantal gestalt that the story evokes challenges the ways in which many have typically read the covenantal intentions of life. Instead of discrete covenants (agreements or contracts) that can be disputed, the reality they embody and serve is larger than any single agreement. That is, the rule and realm of God is[48] greater than any single attempt to embody or serve it. Covenant life is larger than any singular covenant. This should come as no surprise.

After the Shoah, this insight is magnified in importance, for many have been taught otherwise. Christians have been taught that they have replaced Jews in their marriage with heaven: Christians are the New Israel, indwelling the *new covenant* as if the old covenant were over. Yet our common sense tells us, especially if we apply what we know about covenant life from married life,[49] that it is not necessary for our marriage with heaven to supersede a previous one in order to honor the inclusive power of covenant love that grasps and caresses us in the life of Jesus. An honest encounter with Jesus' parable about "the landowner who . . ." challenges such supersessionist thinking. And our post-Shoah vantage point reveals what is at stake. Consequently, no matter how much grumbling might be occasioned by "the first will be last and the last first," we can never overlook that the first-hired remain included even as the last become the immediate concern of the landowner who includes. No one is displaced even though any worker who grumbles might be challenged to rethink why he withholds equal place in the work of the vineyard.

Of course, this last comment invites more reflection on the vineyard and its work. What is this promised ground that bears the fruit of life when responsibly tended? As a tended, promise-bearing ecology, a vineyard is a plot of land with its own boundaries, set aside for the specific purpose of growing grapes for wine. Its fruit is to feed and refresh others. In a larger story about the covenantal purposes of creation, symbolized first by a garden of delight, it is not out of line to ponder how a vineyard might be linked to the cultivation of life as intended for that garden. Those first-hired know, by way of their agreement, not only what they will be paid but also the purpose that their work in the vineyard is to serve. This work can be nothing less than the right relations of covenant life to which they are elsewhere called to bear witness.

By identifying the vineyard as a configuration of the covenantal project of creation, we are led to place the redemptive work of God, which Jesus served, in the larger, more inclusive framework of creation. The covenantal history of Israel and its God need not be relegated to a prefigurative relationship to the work of Christ (nor as a prehistory of the Church). Rather, the work of Christ can be seen as the restorative work of one fully committed to this covenantal project he identifies as the rule and realm of God, with his work grounded in the covenantal intentionality of God for creation that is given expression and embodied in the life of Israel. Seeing that intentionality fulfilled in his singular life, those who do may confess him as Christ. Importantly, such historical embodiment is particular and essential in its particularity, since covenantal relation can only be known and expressed in specific relationships. Furthermore, to say, as Christians do, that Jesus fully embodied this covenantal intentionality does not require (and should not be allowed to require without contradicting itself) the displacement/replacement of the covenantal partners from whom one has learned about and been nurtured in this covenantal project of life.[50]

The boundaries of this vineyard serve the holy ground of its work, its mystery, and its grace—and the identity of its owner and those who have found a place therein. The boundaries serve all this, not the other way round. Too often we get it the other way, with mystery evoked to serve our boundaries, no matter how important those boundaries might be. It is interesting to note that vineyard boundaries, in the context of this story, might be marked by stone fences or living fences—hedges constructed from the common thorn bush, a *s'neh*, the common bush that Scripture reports burning without being consumed. When Jesus tells of a landowner intentionally bringing in anyone from the marketplace who would accept the landowner's invitation to work, Jesus was pushing the traditional boundaries of any vineyard identified with Israel. But he was not challenging the reality such boundaries were meant to honor and protect. The landowner, the grace of inclusion, and the responsibility to work in the vineyard remain shrouded in ambiguity and mystery. In short, through this parable we are given an image to configure Jesus' parabolic offerings: vignettes of and from the vineyard of God's dawning covenantal project variously identified as creation, the rule and realm of God, the beloved community, covenant life, abundant life.[51]

Jesus, the Burning Bush, and Holy Ground

Matthew places the parable in the conflict between Jesus and the religious leaders of Judea in his day and echoes the rendering of the divine name that occurs in Exodus. 33:19: God will include whomsoever he includes. With this in mind and recalling how a parable works, let us revisit its figures, attentive to the conflict Matthew emphasizes and the expectations that Jesus seeks to subvert in telling his story. In doing so, let us also be alert to how this conflict might be reconfigured in the light of our concerns about Jewish-Christian relations after the Shoah.

First, we should note how Jesus refers to his focusing concern: *basileia ton ouranon*, or the rule and realm of heaven. The Greek term *basileia* calls to mind both the notion of who is sovereign and the quality of life lived within a domain that is properly oriented to God and neighbor. The designation "heaven," instead of God, is a circumlocution indicating a sensitivity to the divine name and identity that hearken back to the story of the burning bush. For those who respect this holy ground, God's name is not spoken; other references are made when the name is encountered that express an interactive relationship of respect and devotion to the One whose name it is. The phrase "the rule and realm of heaven" expresses such an understanding and relationship. Figuratively, Jesus has removed his shoes in making his approach to this holy ground.

The gestalt configured in this parable is holy ground for Jesus and for those who follow him. That gestalt is what I have been referring to as covenant life, recognizing that it is an interactive ecology of responsibilities and actions, attitudes and connectedness, which together are the life intended by God. Jesus' story, while not reducing it to a vineyard, identifies it as such—a tended ecology with boundaries and caretakers, witnesses and upholders. His story gives prior but not privileged nor exclusive place to the first-hired who know their duties and rewards by virtue of their articulated agreement. He also gives significant place to other workers, some who have received only a general promise they will receive what is right and some who have only an invitation to join in the work of the vineyard. The later ones are rewarded in such fashion that they learn they have an equally valued place, which causes consternation for the first-hired. Not only did the first-hired bear the longer burden, but surely they have had to show the late arrivals what to do and how the vineyard works. They retain their valued place; yet they are given increased responsibilities for tending the vineyard as well as the latecomers, bearing witness to the work they are all expected to perform. This may signal a shift in some expectations but not a radical departure from Israel's role as a priestly people.

The more troublesome shift occurs later, as this holy ground of inclusive covenantal responsibility finds Jesus as its definitive referent, eventually leading to the parable teller becoming the parable. How this happens is beyond the scope of this chapter. That it happened is critical, for with this transition, Jesus became for Christians their burning bush, no longer simply proclaiming a message about the covenanting God who includes whomsoever he includes but mediating and manifesting this divine identity and relationship as well.[52] To be sure, this shift intensified the conflict between the followers of Jesus and the emerging leaders of post, second Temple Judaism and contributed significantly to the eventual parting of their ways. Polemic grew sharper on both sides, especially after Jesus' death and following the fall of the second Temple. As Christians and Jews revisit this divide, especially now and alert to ways our post-Shoah reality requires us to rethink how we live with this history, two primary areas of caution stand out. First, any "displacement" reading of the relationship between Judaism and Christianity must be resisted. Not only does Christian complicity in the numerous forms of anti-Judaism and antisemitism require it ethically, but an authentic rendering of parables like "the landowner who . . ." requires it as well. Second, the revelatory significance of Jesus as the Christian burning bush leads to an important Christological caution. Any understanding of the revelatory significance of Jesus that consumes Jesus in the Christology must be challenged and resisted. To be sure, any such interpretation or Christology that "consumes" Jesus would be guilty of the heresy known as Monophysitism. Jesus' humanity would be lost. But more than Jesus' humanity is at stake. Jesus is a Jewish *ben berith*—child of the covenant. His Jewish identity and fidelity must likewise remain unconsumed by Christian interpretations of his revelatory power.[53] If Jesus is a burning bush, then the burning bush must remain unconsumed. The parable teller who became a parable must remain a Jewish parable teller even as he becomes a parable himself.

Grounding and Cultivating Covenant Life

Importantly, Jesus' parable is more than a cautionary tale, even in post-Shoah perspective. His story provides confessional ground for rethinking the historic relationship between Jews and Christians, ground that can be shared while recognizing the continuing divide that exists regarding Jesus and the tension over how inclusive the boundaries of this covenantal vineyard might actually be. Notice what Matthew shows Jesus doing in this episode. For those who hold him as the center of their faith life—that is any who followed him then and those who read this story as sacred Scripture—he is, directing their attention not to himself but to the owner of the vineyard, as well as to the vineyard and its care. The one who includes is the landowner. In other words, through the parable, Jesus conveys that the very purpose of creation is inclusive and grounded in the Creator, the Sovereign One of creation. The spirit of inclusion, which Jesus proclaims and embodies, is rooted for him in the One he serves. By locating the source of inclusion in the Sovereign One he served, Jesus provides a confessional model for his followers to embrace inclusion and a range of covenantal pluralism without having to be either a blatant or disguised form of appropriation passing itself off as inclusiveness. The source of inclusion for Jesus is God and God's intention for creation: the vineyard of covenant life, which Jesus, as a parabolic representative, invites others to enter.

In other words, the vineyard is bigger than Christianity. It is bigger than any religion even when, as in the case of the covenantal faiths (Judaism, Christianity, Islam—those with articulated agreements), they bear witness to that purpose and seek to serve the vineyard of covenant life. One who stands within such a faith tradition is a witness to a larger reality that embraces that person in faith, but neither that witness nor her faith tradition possesses that including reality. The reality of the vineyard is a reality *in which* they may participate; it includes them, not the other way around.

Still, as the parable and its figures make clear, covenant life is not an unbounded endorsement of just any well-intended human enterprise. Rather, the call of covenant life expresses a binding and sacred commitment to covenant relationship wherever and however one encounters that vineyard being cultivated. Like any vineyard, it will have boundaries—boundaries articulated in covenant fidelity. Yet covenant life will surpass any of the particular forms in which it is met and known. In other words, covenant life is abundant life! For example, covenant life is not restricted to its manifestations in marriage nor even to married life; it can exist in other partnerships, in friendship, and as the special bonds of teams and teammates. Neither is it limited to Christianity or Judaism or Islam, even though it can and should be known *through* each. And yet while covenant life transcends any particular form, it is never authentically encountered apart from its specific manifestations.

Furthermore, the story of the vineyard reminds us that *how* we embody covenant life matters. It is not just an invitation to a gathering; it is an invitation to work—to join the cultivation of a vineyard—a place that bears fruit for feeding others; a place that we might learn to see as truly the holy ground that God has entrusted to our common care. We are invited to join, to enter, a working and sacred partnership—a partnership in a specific, circumscribed place, hospitable and inclusive, but nonetheless with encounterable boundaries.

According to Jesus' parable, covenant life is also chosen life. People must choose to participate in the vineyard. We must choose, just as those who marry must choose the covenant life of marriage when they exchange their vows. Covenant life is chosen life—even as it is offered as a gift. Notice, however, what all is chosen: covenant life—mutual commitment and shared regard, bound up in promise and fidelity in particular relationships. It can and may have more than one manifestation, but it must be chosen, in its particularity.

This aspect, that covenant life must be chosen, that it must be actively received and embraced, is something conservatives have been saying to liberals through the years.[54] But the voice that comes from this parable, and often from liberals to conservatives, is that covenant life is always more than any of us think it is. Specifically, covenant life can be chosen by Jews, as Jews—just as it is offered to Gentiles, to include those of us who are Christians. It is as *included ones* that we bear witness thereby, to the grace of inclusion and the choosing of the connectedness of covenant life. Quite simply, it is not in our hands to restrict how it may be chosen and honored. Yet if we wish to be included, we must choose to accept the invitation and take our place in the vineyard.

The story, as it is passed on by Matthew, ends with Jesus saying, "[T]he first will be last and the last will be first." The last, who were once first, are not left out or behind. Rather, inclusion is so central that no matter who entered first, until all are included there is always the need to include more. The story ends in the unending, even unyielding, spirit of reaching out to the not-yet-included. The already-included are to make room for the not-yet-included; the not-yet-included continue to be the first priority. Once included, they join others in making room for the, as yet, still-not-included. The logic may be cumbersome, but it is important to point out that the dynamic of inclusion is not a simple matter of either-or.[55]

An interesting postscript arises from pondering the logic of reward in this story. As Jesus tells the story, the reward promised the workers is an equally shared, usual daily subsistence wage. The logic of the marketplace, that the laborers should be paid according to their comparative amount of work in the vineyard, is turned on its head. Those who worked least are paid the same as those who worked longest. Why? Perhaps the equally shared wage is not the sole reward for working in the vineyard after all. Furthermore, if the ones who have worked longest are paid last, then they have the opportunity to view the landowner's generosity played out in the valuing of the workers and their place in the vineyard equally. Consequently, they are brought into the logic of generosity as well as having a place in the vineyard, but only if they have eyes to see (and a willingness to join such an enterprise). Nonetheless, they are not punished if they do not recognize this dimension. They may grumble about it (which they do), but they are not excluded. The logic of inclusion remains.

In this fashion, Christians have confessional ground for inclusion, which in responding to the inclusive spirit they encounter in Jesus finds Jesus grounding inclusion in the larger reality of God and the covenantal vineyard of life that he serves. Inclusion is grounded in the original purposes of the sovereign landowner from the beginning. Inclusion is not derived from Christianity or Judaism or any religion. It is derived from the One who includes them all.[56] And its dynamic precedes them all. Therefore, inclusion need not imply that any recognition of the validity regarding another faith tradition must also subsume the other by identifying the other's truth claims as veiled forms of their own.[57] Or to say it more personally: I and my faith community are not the subjects (i.e., the includers) but the objects of inclusion (i.e., the included ones) who, in fidelity to our own faith experience, participate in the larger, more extensive project of creation that has embraced and included us through Jesus.

Even so, the parable retains cautionary power. The summons to embody covenant life is located by Matthew in the midst of conflict between Jesus and leaders of his own people. He is bound to the ones with whom he places himself in tension. His parable is rooted in real tension. Likewise, the summons to embody covenant life in a land of others (the summons at the burning bush) grounds its promise in real and contentious life.

We must not spiritualize the figurative power of the parable and remove it from the literal ground in which it lives and thrives. Similarly, covenant life must be cultivated in the contentious places in which we live and work. For Jesus, covenant life is rooted in the promise of *ha aretz Yisrael*. It is to be cultivated there, just as Moses recognized at the burning bush. That is, covenant life, however much it transcends its location in time, place, and figure, must remain firmly rooted in each.

APPROACHING POST-SHOAH HOLY GROUND

Now how do all these twists and turns help us deal with the questions that began these reflections: How do we live with God after Auschwitz; how without? What do we mean by God after the flames of the Shoah? Divine power, intervention, and deliverance? What ground can be holy in the shadows of Auschwitz, indeed even there? How should we approach it if we can identify and locate it? And what must we not attempt to say or do in our attempts to be faithful and honest in these critical times?

With the Shoah, we are once again called to face a burning bush that has not been consumed. However, this time we cannot speak of only the bush that survives. We must also ask about the 6 million branches that have perished in the burning. What of the 1.5 million tender shoots that were consumed? Surely the God who speaks from this gestalt of suffering and need, resistance and life, must be vulnerable to the anguished cries of the branches that have been cut off from the bush and its life. The God disclosed at the burning bush is revealed in the confirming interaction of covenantal presence. After Auschwitz, the broken branches cry out with their own silent yet evocative *hineni*. Authentic covenantal presence expresses and addresses their cries as well.

There are several dimensions to this. Clearly any simplistic understanding of God's relationship to history must be left behind. The thrust of modernity has led theological thinking in this direction already. The Shoah intensifies the quest. Does the burning bush story offer any help in this regard? At the heart of the story is the affirmation that God has heard the cry of his people in their oppression and therefore reaches out to Moses to act. Usually, we interpret this to mean that God has acted in history and intervened in the affairs of his people to deliver them. After Auschwitz, the notion of divine intervention is radically problematic.

As we more typically understand it, God intervenes by deliverance, election, salvation, judgment, or revelation by entering into the domain of history from some other realm in which God dwells. As a result, history is chosen, a people is elected for covenant or delivered from oppression, life is sanctified. And God binds God's own self to a historical relationship and to history as well. So bound, history becomes a functional constant with divine interventions becoming the historic variables. History is viewed and treated monolithically (whether given to Jews or Christians or both) and becomes the object of divine faithfulness. History is thereby functionally guaranteed and trusted because it is the object of God's loyalty.

However, the reflections in this chapter express an alternative model in which God is the constant, not history, with the divine intention for life remaining faithful to itself. History is not one general or monolithically conceived entity but always particular and plural. God is trusted not to guarantee history but to be faithful to the divine intention; history, especially in the shadows of the Shoah, is not an appropriate object of trust. In fact, history has proven otherwise. It is not worthy of such trust, though it may be the arena in which trust is risked. Furthermore, history, always particular, is a relational enterprise that unfolds in accord with how its relational activity happens. Each participant is an essential component in its specific unfolding. To say God acts in this kind of history is to locate and embrace God as a participant in a partnership that unfolds over time. Persons, peoples, nations can move toward or away from the divine intention that God seeks from the beginning. They can even participate in it. They can also drive others away from that intention, repelling them violently and/or drawing them into other partnerships, good and bad. History, and God's participation in it, is a partnership affair, an unfolding, relational process that, according to this model, God intends to be covenantal. Having committed to such a venture, intervention, apart from it, is not what God would or could do, even if individuals or any group might need intervention. Rather, the intervention would have to come from other freely participating partners in the enterprise.

When we read the burning bush episode according to the latter model, we can discover, as it were,[58] the story representing a moment in which Moses faced the revelatory significance of what was happening to his people, knowing that in order for God's intention for life to be served, he must act and only in his acting would God act in this divine-human partnership we call creation. More fundamental, God's act would be the calling forth that Moses heard as an interactive I AM-you are. The I AM remains as we resist and declare our own "I am" and as the silent voices of the Shoah's victims declare their violated yet covenantal presence as well.[59]

The "I AM" who could hear the cry of Moses's people could hear and act only as the "you are" of the responding "I am" heard the resisting cry of his people call him to intervene and give voice and presence to the One Who Is Absolutely.[60] Of course, in such a reading the great I AM is radically vulnerable, yet this is what the notion of creation is about in the first place. The One Who Is evokes relation that embodies the covenantal intentionality of creation that can unfold only in freely chosen partnership. Intervention is a human responsibility that expresses that partnership.

In similar fashion, the dimension of power is recast. Divine power is bracketed by the choice for creation with further discussion simply commentary on that prior decision. God has chosen otherness, otherness that sets itself apart from God with its own power to pursue life and relation in freedom. Creation is a radical risk for God, and as long as God remains faithful to creation and its relational intentionality, that risk pertains.

What, then, do we learn about God, the One Who Is Absolutely? To be sure, we have learned much more about what we cannot say. The Eternal One who wanted relation enough to risk it in this venture we call creation resists any explanation without remainder. Still, we can risk saying this Other who has chosen the otherness of creation and its attendant vulnerabilities is an embracing, covenanting Other who calls us into covenantal partnership with others who have been entrusted with a similar invitation. As a Christian and adopting the language of Jesus' parable, I can even claim my place in that vineyard, acknowledging that others came before me with their articulated covenant. I join them as an included one in a much bigger story than the one I can tell. And others shall come after me. I must make room for them and their place in this vineyard, as room was made for me. That is the holy ground of such an encounter and the holy ground we are all called upon to cultivate. Furthermore, that ground is bigger than my own faith tradition as well as that of others, for it is the promised ground of creation.

More daring, I may venture into the insights of Jesus' story about "the landowner who . . ." remembering the configuring and life-giving gestalt that Jesus called the "rule and realm of heaven" to claim that covenant life can happen, breaking into our world wherever we dare cultivate its promise, even in the midst of hell. But this healing gestalt cannot unfold without the partnership of others who dare intervene and make its happening possible. In the shadows of Auschwitz, the stakes are higher than ever before, and the risks of such a partnership the ultimate test of its promise. Likewise, the responsibility for it happening is unacceptable for those deprived of possibility and choice. For too many, this was the reality of the *lager*. Yet that such moments have happened even once saves such a belief from illusion and reminds us there is no place where grace cannot happen. Still, it cannot undo the evil that happened nor justify its occurrence by some greater plan. Any post-Shoah approach to this holy ground must proceed with the greatest sensitivity in this regard.

So when Christians like me ask, "How can I live with God after Auschwitz? How without?" we must answer, "Very carefully." There is much we can no longer claim or dare assert that once we may have believed. The holy ground on which we gather round the burning bush still requires that we remove our shoes and approach it carefully as we learn and relearn how to say "*Hineni*, here I am."

NOTES

1. Elie Wiesel's most recent reflections on the dilemma are recorded in the first volume of his *Memoirs: All Rivers Run to the Sea* (New York: Alfred A. Knopf, 1995), p. 84.

2. Elie Wiesel, *Night*, trans. Stella Rodway (New York: Bantam Books, 1960), p. 62.

3. "No statement, theological or otherwise, should be made that would not be credible in the presence of the burning children." Greenberg, Irving "Cloud of Smoke, Pillar of Fire: Judaism, Christianity, and Modernity After the Holocaust," in *Auschwitz: Beginning of a New Era?*, ed. Eva Fleischner (New York: KTAV Publishing House, 1977), p. 23.

4. Ibid., pp. 24, 28.

5. Even more, for Christians, God is intimately encountered in and through Jesus, their burning bush. This identification of Jesus with the burning bush, an explicit identification in the Gospel of John and perhaps alluded to at the end of the parable of the workers in the vineyard, will be taken up later in the chapter.

6. Most scholars agree that the Matthean ending "the first will be last and the last will be first" is not the original ending of the parable and was added by Matthew as a coda linking the parable to the themes of the larger unit.

7. *Midrash Rabbah* vol. 3 (London: Soncino Press, 1939), pp. 53.

8. Elizabeth Barrett Browning, *Aurora Leigh*, Book VII, ed. Margaret Reynolds (1857; Athens: Ohio University Press, 1992), p. 487, lines 821–24.

9. Even if Christians see the fence around the vineyard/garden to be more inclusively framed than does Judaism, the fence is clearly identified with the people of Israel (its boundary) and should remain so identified, making its prickliness (Israel's ethnoreligious particularity) even more significant—a kind of scandal for Christians. Thus there is room for disagreement and mutually distinguishable identities but with a distinct rationale for commitment to each other's service to the vineyard that they serve.

10. *Midrash Rabbah*, p. 55.

11. Michael Goldberg, *Jews and Christians: Getting Our Stories Straight* (Nashville, TN: Abingdon Press, 1985), p. 214.

12. See Michael Fishbane's discussion of the text's capacity to be the caller who calls its interpreter/reader to responsible presence and action. He notes that this awareness is conveyed in the traditional reference to the Hebrew Scriptures as *Miqra*, which means "calling out." Michael Fishbane, *The Garments of Torah: Essays in Biblical Hermeneutics* (Bloomington: Indiana University Press, 1989), p. 83.

13. Elie Wiesel, *Messengers of God* (New York: Random House, 1976), pp. 69–97.

14. Ka-Tzetnik 135633, *Shivitti: A Vision* (San Francisco: Harper & Row, 1987), p. 40.

15. Greenberg, "Pillar of Fire, Cloud of Smoke," p. 23.

16. Darrell J. Fasching has poignantly observed that "the command to welcome the stranger occurs in the Torah *thirty-six* times [italics are mine]—more than any other commandment." Dare we let this doubling of eighteen go unaddressed in its significance for the life of faithfulness in the lengthening shadows of our century? Fasching, *The Coming of the Millennium: Good News for the Whole Human Race* (Valley Forge, PA: Trinity Press International, 1996), p. 30.

17. Greenberg, "Cloud of Smoke, Pillar of Fire," p. 44.

18. Ibid., p. 23.

19. There is a double meaning carried by the phrase "coming to terms with." On the one hand, it implies looking for the best way to speak about some matter or concern, finding the most appropriate language to express the meaning one truly

seeks. On the other hand, it implies having to face up to a matter that is inescapable. There is a confrontational character to this latter implication. One must deal with a matter that has reached crisis proportion. Both sets of meaning are intended in this section as it addresses the gestalt one faces when asking about God and the Shoah. Old conceptions no longer hold; traditional terms may even break. Likewise, there is no place to hide from the searing questions raised by what happened. In the burning bush story, Moses must come to terms with what has happened to his people and with the God whom he encounters at the bush. That dynamic and its rendering in the narrative provide clues that our post-Shoah reading brings into bold relief, leading us to consider how the story helps us come to terms with God after Auschwitz.

20. See Arthur A. Cohen, *The* Tremendum: *A Theological Interpretation of the Holocaust* (New York: Continuum, 1981), esp. pp. 83–110.

21. See Richard L. Rubenstein, *After Auschwitz: Radical Theology and Contemporary Judaism* (New York: Bobbs-Merrill, 1966), esp. pp. 47–58.

22. See Irving Greenberg, "Religious Values After the Holocaust: A Jewish View," in *Jews and Christians After the Holocaust*, ed. Abraham J. Peck (Philadelphia: Fortress Press, 1982), pp. 63–86; idem, "History, Holocaust, and Covenant, Proceedings of an International Conference, Oxford and London, July 10–17, 1988" in *Remembering for the Future: The Impact of the Holocaust and Genocide on Jews and Christians*, (Oxford: Pergamon Press, 1989), pp. 2920–2926.

23. Peter C. Hodgson, *Winds of the Spirit* (Louisville, KY: Westminster/John Knox Press, 1994), p. 148. Drawing on the work of Karl Rahner, Hodgson reads the divine self-disclosure of *ehyeh asher ehyeh* to be "I am the One who lets being be."

24. Lawrence Kushner, *GOD was in this PLACE & I, i did not know: Finding SELF, SPIRITUALITY, AND ULTIMATE MEANING* (Woodstock, VT: Jewish Lights Publishing, 1994), p. 44.

25. See Lawrence Kushner, *The River of Light: Spirituality, Judaism, Consciousness* (Woodstock, VT: Jewish Lights Publishing, 1990), p. 121.

26. The imperfect tense/tension of the phrase *ehyeh asher ehyeh* could also be rendered "I am not yet who or what I am" and "I am not yet as I shall be," but they would not carry the ontological reality of promise as expressed in "I am who or what I am not yet."

27. Although there is a similar progression toward increased human responsibility in the divine-human partnership in the recounting of the plagues in Exodus 7–12, the presence of interventionist assumptions remains in the text and evokes resistance in the aftermath of the Shoah. See Burton L. Visotzky, *The Road to Redemption: Lessons from Exodus on Leadership and Community* (New York: Crown Publishers, 1998), p. 99.

28. Jewish reflection will undoubtedly find challenge in its liturgical rendering of this story in most Passover *aggadot*. They do not emphasize the role or work of Moses in the Exodus story but, instead, focus on the liberating action of God. Moses is not mentioned by name in the telling of the story, though his presence is surely felt. The traditional reason: to give complete glory to God for God's redemptive activity in the Exodus. God delivers. God acts. God redeems. Moses is simply the instrument. In the aftermath of the Shoah, this kind of traditional piety appears to be seriously challenged by the specter of 6 million silent witnesses to an absent deliverer. More searching, perhaps, is the muted cry of the children, yet un-

accountable to this way of rendering their story. Greenberg's depiction of the Shoah as an orienting/reorienting event is profoundly unsettling in this context. The root story of Exodus and how it is embraced and celebrated may be fundamentally undercut unless it denies the full scope of what happened in the Shoah or adjusts itself in the manner suggested here. Once an earthquake accompanied the giving of the Law at Sinai; now the very world symbolized by Sinai is shaken anew. See Greenberg, "Cloud of Smoke, Pillar of Fire," pp. 20–26.

29. Exod. 2:11–15 NRSV.

30. Even though he does not examine this specific set of texts, I am indebted to Ed Farley's treatment of the ciphers of redemption in *Divine Empathy* for this insight. He writes: "In communities of faith, the bespeaking of God begins with redemption. In its most inclusive sense, redemption means the transformation of human evil that corrupts the spheres of agency, the interhuman, and the social. In content, redemption means agential freedom, reconciliation, and emancipation." He adds, "In the sphere of human individuals, redemption has the character of 'founding.' " See Edward Farley, *Divine Empathy: A Theology of God* (Minneapolis: Fortress Press, 1996), pp. 124, 125.

31. I have been significantly influenced by Peter Hodgson's use of the term *gestalt* in his *Winds of the Spirit* as a configuring image for covenant life. He defines gestalt as "a pattern arranged, shaped, or structured from parts, producing a living, organic, plural unity—a unity of consciousness or of spirit—as opposed to a dead, mechanical identity." See p. 251.

32. While I am heavily indebted to the teaching of *tsimtsum* in this reading of the divine covenantal gestalt of God and creation, I am led in a different direction than the mystical trajectory of Lurianic kabbalism that is the context of this teaching. Instead, I have been drawn toward the radical implications of a covenantal reading of creation in which the first moment of creation is a divine embrace of otherness. Furthermore, I find Friedman's argument convincing that this choice is a processual one that is not yet complete but still unfolding in the ongoing evolution of human responsibility for caring for creation. See Richard Elliott Friedman, *The Disappearance of God: A Divine Mystery* (Boston: Little, Brown and Company, 1995). R. Kendall Soulen has developed a similar approach in *The God of Israel and Christian Theology* (Minneapolis: Augsburg Fortress, 1996). He argues for a covenantal theology of creation grounded in God's intention for and fidelity to creation. The blessing of life abides even in the face of sin and curse, and the covenantal intentionality of creation will eventually be consummated by the steadfastly faithful creator of that vulnerable enterprise.

33. Exod 3:8 NRSV.

34. The tradition of conquest, especially the recapitulation of Joshua 3–5, takes this approach in bold fashion. Joshua 3:10 puts it plainly: "The dispersal of the previous inhabitants of the land will be a sign of God's presence"

35. I have not quoted Micah 6 directly, although I intend to call upon Micah's words, if not his voice, in a new way.

36. See Isa. 42:6, 49:6, 51:4, 60:19.

37. See Fasching, *The Coming of the Millennium*, p. 30.

38. Greenberg, "Cloud of Smoke, Pillar of Fire," p. 28.

39. Clark Williamson posits a covenantal rule of faith to guide post-Shoah Christians in understanding what actions are entrusted to human beings in this

divine-human partnership: "It is only appropriate to ask God to do for us those things that only God can do; the rest is up to us. The rule is: if an action *can* be undertaken by God's covenant partners, it is they who will have to do it. And if some things should be done, *we should* do them." See Williamson, *A Guest in the House of Israel: Post-Holocaust Church Theology* (Louisville, KY: Westminster/John Knox Press, 1993), p. 224.

40. See Peter Hodgson, *Winds of the Spirit*, pp. 137–150, where he characterizes the gestaltlike configuration of divine action in and through the life and ministry of Jesus. Adopting his notion of gestaltlike configurations, we can speak of a covenantal project of creation that is called forth into being and life from the beginning by a divine Other who in the process of giving life takes on covenantal configurations of Being-in-relation with the other(s) and otherness of creation and its correlative being. Revising Paul Tillich's terminology, Hodgson suggests calling this divine Other the Power of Being (instead of the Ground of Being) which has the power to call forth life absolutely. For Hodgson, this One whom we know as God is a gestalt of configuring Otherness that draws forth life, presence, and responsibility. Hodgson, *Winds of the Spirit*, p. 47.

41. I will be rendering the Greek word *basileia* as both rule (or reign) and realm in order to emphasize not only the sovereignty of God who rules but the substantive reality, or gestalt, of life that unfolds when life is properly ordered and lived within the horizon of a covenantal partnership with the One Who Is Absolutely. Hodgson refers to the shape of *basileia* as a "gestalt of freedom." Hodgson, *Winds of the Spirit*, p. 259.

42. See Bernard Brandon Scott, *Hear Then the Parables* (Minneapolis: Fortress Press, 1989), pp. 7–62, esp. 42.

43. A denarius would have been a typical daily wage for this time period. But we should not be misled by this understanding. As Brandon Scott points out, this typical daily wage was subsistence pay for peasants. Any interpretation that focuses on the generosity of the landowner must deal with other features in the story. The wage of a denarius, itself, is not generous. See ibid., p. 291.

44. Most scholars concur that Matthew has provided this last sentence as a concluding coda, linking the parable with the other ones in the larger literary unit of Matthew 19 and 20.

45. According to Scott, the story really deals with only three characters: the householder (landowner), the first hired, and the last hired; the others (the later hired and the steward) drop out of view. Scott, *Hear Then the Parables*, p. 36. In our context, we must ask if this reading should be allowed to go unquestioned.

46. Ibid., p. 290.

47. I am intrigued by the notion that by taking the figure literally we are better equipped to comprehend the figurative meaning of the parable.

48. Rule and realm, while grammatically plural, configure a single reality, a gestalt, rendered in the Greek *basileia*. Consequently, I have used the singular form of the verb to call attention to this singular gestalt.

49. See Henry F. Knight "The Inclusive Call of Covenant Life," *New Conversations: Confronting and Combatting Christian Anti-Judaism* 15, no. 3 (Autumn, 1993): 32–36, where I explore the relationship of married life and marriage more explicitly.

50. See Soulen's *The God of Israel and Christian Theology*, Part II, pp. 109–177, for a provocative articulation of how such a revised theology might unfold.

51. See Hodgson, *Winds of the Spirit*, pp. 257, 259.

52. One can make the case, convincingly I think, that this transition is focally expressed in the Gospel of John as Jesus is portrayed speaking for God as the incarnation of the divine *logos*, saying, "I am." The transition is even more sharply expressed in John 15:5, with Jesus declaring, "I am the vine, you are the branches."

53. R. Kendall Soulen explains this dimension with great clarity, identifying a structural form of supersessionism that is not addressed if only the punitive and economic forms of supersessionism are challenged. At the structural level, Christian narrative emphasizes the humanity of the incarnation without dealing with the particularity of God's covenantal history with Israel as essential to the identity of Jesus as a Jew. See his *The God of Israel and Christian Theology*, Part I.

54. James W. Fowler in *Faithful Change: The Personal and Public Challenges of Postmodern Life* (Nashville, TN: Abingdon, 1996) suggests we adopt James David Hunter's categories of orthodox and progressive, instead of conservative and liberal, to characterize these polarities as mutually exclusive "tempers" of our postmodern age. See pp. 160–178. See also chapter 4 of James Davidson Hunter's *Culture Wars: The Struggle to Define America* (New York: Basic Books, 1991), pp. 107–132.

55. This is likewise Fowler's point above in his analysis of "the personal and public challenges of postmodern life."

56. Judaism provides this same insight with its understanding of the Noachide laws and in differentiating salvation from election. See Alan Segal, *Rebecca's Children: Judaism and Christianity in the Roman World* (Cambridge: Harvard University Press, 1986), p. 169; and David Novak, *Jewish-Christian Dialogue: A Jewish Justification* (New York and Oxford: Oxford University Press, 1989), pp. 26–41.

57. This form of inclusiveness is different from that identified by Alan Race in his threefold typology of Christianity's relationship to world religions where he distinguishes between Exclusivism, Inclusivism, and Pluralism. In each case, his referent is Christianity. Consequently, the including reality in his model of Inclusivism is Christianity. The covenantal inclusion described here is not restricted to Christianity and can even be termed a form of covenantal pluralism as well. See his *Christians and Religious Pluralism: Patterns in Christian Theology of Religions* (Maryknoll, NY: Orbis Books, 1983) for a fuller representation of his work.

58. See Fishbane, *The Garments of Torah* pp. 19–32, for a brief description of the *kivyakhol*, midrashic strategy that is being followed here.

59. The linguistic distinctions of Hebrew between *anochi* and *ani* reflect this relationship: the *I* (*anochi*) appropriate to God and the *I* (*ani*) appropriate to human beings. That is, the *I* of the human *I am* is derivative, known and constituted in response to a nonderivative and evocative *I AM*.

60. Hodgson, *Winds of the Spirit*, pp. 147–150.

5

Can These Bones Live?: From the Valley of Dry Bones to an Opened Tomb and Beyond

Ezekiel 37:1–14 and Matthew 28:1–20

People of faith who wrestle with the Shoah and its legacies of shame and despair often find themselves walking like the psalmist in a valley of dark shadows. Whether or not they can join him to affirm the steadfast loyalty of God and claim a life that overflows with blessing is another matter. Unconceivable devastation and death haunt this terrain, stalking those who venture into its shadows. The most precious professions of faith are challenged here. Indeed, many lie in ruin in this domain (like the bones in the valley we will be approaching via Ezekiel). Here we ask, How do Jews and Christians discover and then affirm the presence of God on the other side of encountering the full and devastating power of death? That is the enduring question that hovers in and over this valley. For Christians, this question inevitably leads to critical reflection on the core beliefs of their Easter faith. For Jews, it raises further questions about survival and rebirth, as they are focused in their shared identity as a people. It also reminds Jews that they are shadowed not only by the Shoah's aftermath of despair and the memory of near annihilation but also by the dead themselves. If they limit themselves by reducing their identity as Jews only to this tragic event, they risk becoming lost in the penumbra of the victims. However, if they do not attend to them with urgent vigilance, these dead will be lost forever as an impersonal and unembodied number (i.e., the 6 million). To be sure, Christian encounters with this valley must be credible not only to others within the various Christian traditions but also to their Jewish partners in the covenantal way. Furthermore, the matter of credibility, as an identity issue for Christians, also brings them face-to-face with the Resurrection of Jesus and the mission that grows out of that event. Jews, of course, as they reflect on the restoration of their people in the state of Israel, are challenged to reexamine the ties that bind all Jews to that parcel of promised and sacred land. What better texts, then, to encounter these issues than Ezekiel 37 with its vision of the valley of dry bones and the Resurrection story and final commission of Matthew 28?

We approach these texts by way of our own place in the world, a self-consciously entered valley in which the shadows of the Shoah mark its multitextured landscape. It is a treacherous place in which the valley of the psalmist with its steadfast hope clashes with the valley of despair known by the abandoned victims of destruction and death known by two names: *Churban* and Shoah. Here, their stories converge; and their landscapes comingle in tremors of confusion. Consequently, to sing with the psalmist "I will fear no evil" requires more than simple faith. Indeed, it is not unlike joining Ezekiel at the threshold of his vision to be asked, as he was: Can these bones live?

EZEKIEL'S VISION

Deported with other religious and political leaders some twelve years earlier, Ezekiel was living in exile in the Babylonian valley-plain between the Tigris and Euphrates rivers in a settlement called Tel Aviv. In fidelity to his role as a servant of the divine presence and a keeper of the covenant, he had been actively warning his people about the dangers they faced and their need to repent and change their ways, lest Jerusalem fall. With the fall of Jerusalem and the subsequent destruction of the Temple, his message turned to hope and restoration as he remained faithful to God and his people.

In this context, and in the third of four visions associated with his prophetic work, Ezekiel found himself transported by divine hand to a place of death and destruction with devastating implications: a valley strewn with a multitude of bones. Stripped bare of flesh, they were sun parched and unidentifiable, except that Ezekiel learned that they were the dry bones of the people Israel. Unburied, they lay where they were presumably slain. Ezekiel, a hereditary priest of the Jerusalem Temple, was face-to-face with the defiled landscape of his people. In every sense, this should not have been his place; and yet it was.[1] As his vision unfolded, Ezekiel was confronted by the searing question: Can these bones live? As reported in the biblical text, God, not Ezekiel, posed the question. He responded, "You know, LORD God [*Adoshem*]."[2] Ezekiel is then commanded to speak to the dry bones, telling them to hear the Word of God, saying:

I will cause breath to enter you, and will cause flesh to come upon you, and cover you with skin, and put breath in you, and you shall live, and you shall know that I am the LORD.

And so the vision unfolded with the bones coming to life and standing again as "a vast multitude." Ezekiel was then told that they were the "whole house of Israel" who "are cut off completely." To them, he was to say:

Thus says the LORD: "I am going to open your graves, O my people; and I will bring you back to the land of Israel. And you shall know that I am the LORD, when I open your graves, and bring you up from your graves O my people. I will put my spirit within you and you shall live, and I will place you on your own soil; then you shall know that I, the LORD, have spoken and will act," says the LORD.

The vision is followed by an oracle depicting the restoration as a reunification of Israel in the Promised Land in a covenant of peace.

Can These Bones Live?

The recurring refrain of Ezekiel's vision, even though it is asked only once, is the question, Can these bones live? As the divine question posed to Ezekiel, it is the *peshat* of the vision—its givenness, its plain meaning, its sine qua non. Whether rendered in the Hebrew (*Hatihyena haatzamot hayeveshot haelu?*) or in English, it punctuates the whole passage. In its confronting otherness, that question addresses Ezekiel throughout the entire vision.

To begin with, the vision reverses the expected way of encountering the question. Facing a valley of death and destruction, it is not the human voice of Ezekiel that asks about life after death or meaning in the face of despair. It is God. When we ponder why Ezekiel should be the one being questioned instead of being the one to pose the question, we encounter several possibilities. Perhaps Ezekiel is being tested. Perhaps Ezekiel is in shock and needs to be called out from his despair to face what has happened. Perhaps the responsibility for life in the face of this destruction lies not in divine but in human hands. Perhaps God needs Ezekiel in order to respond to what has happened. Perhaps the bones themselves cry out to Ezekiel, and he hears them, in their stark and silent otherness, posing the question as if to speak on God's behalf.

According to the text, the question is posed by God, not Ezekiel. Furthermore, Ezekiel is addressed as "son of man" (*ben adam*), calling to mind the context of creation and humanity's place in the larger scheme of things. To paraphrase Psalm 8, what is the child of *adam* that God should pose this question to him? *Ben adam* is created as a representative figure, reflecting both the image of creation as a child of clay and the image of the creator who breathed life into all creation. What does it mean for Ezekiel to be asked, "Can these bones live?" when addressed as *ben adam*? As we confront Ezekiel, we meet as well a representative figure, a priestly *ben adam* who stands between his people and God, representing the whole House of Israel including those left behind and those taken in exile. It is Ezekiel, a figure whose name means "vision of God," who is being asked, in effect, his *ayecha*: Where are you; can these bones live?

But we must not allegorize too quickly. Ezekiel is not simply a representative figure for us. He is the son of a priest, and himself a priest, who has been deported with other religious and political leaders to Babylon following the first deportation of 598 B.C.E. He is a displaced person who is seized in a vision in which he is called upon to face a valley of dry bones. Moreover, he is led to, and around, a valley of death that ordinarily would be off limits to a priest. But in his vision, he is called upon to attend to the dead whom otherwise he would not directly encounter. In other words, before he can be a representative figure for us, we must recognize who he is in his own right, a representative figure for others whose bones lie desecrated and abandoned in an undesignated valley-plain as well as others who share his exile. And in the presence of the bones of those whom he represents, he is asked, "Can these bones live?"

What does all this mean? Let us return to the text and the question with which we began. First, the question, which one might expect to be on the lips of any survivor or refugee looking on from a distance, is posed by God to Ezekiel, not to God. What might this mean? Does it mean that God does not know? Does it mean that Ezekiel is being tested? If so, what a bizarre test. Perhaps it means that the question itself is of divine significance and is meant to evoke Ezekiel's prophetic-priestly presence. Perhaps it simply means that God is not yet sure about Ezekiel. In this regard, it could be a plea from God for Ezekiel to act with decisive power and presence, in effect declaring "yes" and calling forth life immediately. As it is, Ezekiel's response (You know, LORD God—*Yaddah attah adonai YHWH*) is capable of being read in several ways: as a humble deferral to divine power; as a despairing expression of priestly resignation; or as a failure to grasp the situation and act decisively as God might hope. Whichever way we read it, God confronts Ezekiel precisely at this limit with a summons in which life is at stake in the face of death. God calls Ezekiel, dare we say in a summons that grows out of the recognition of the hopeless situation. "Prophesy," speak to these bones. And give life to them.

The text does not explain how the summons happened, only that it happened. Still, we know that the summons grows out of the recognition and full acknowledgment of the bones. The prophet-priest must attend to them first before he can speak any words of life to them. And the text tells us what he sees: They are lying exposed, very dry, vulnerable to time, decay, and the prey of others. That is, Ezekiel must allow the dead to be who they are and what they are; he must recover them as they are, in order for them to call out for new life and for Ezekiel to respond on their behalf.

What does it mean for Ezekiel to call forth life from these bones? How does Ezekiel call forth their life? At the textual level, he is instructed to give them flesh and bone and sinew by the power of his words, but not his words alone. His words must bear in representative fashion the divine Word that calls forth life.[3] He is to name these bones in such fashion that he restores their flesh and blood. Then he is to call for the breath of life carried by the four winds. The language, of course, is reminiscent of Genesis. God creates by speaking life into existence. And like in the creation stories, flesh and bone are not enough. Without breath, they are empty forms, without life. How does Ezekiel do this? If there were magic words, the text does not report them. Indeed, the text is silent on what Ezekiel says—only that he acted and spoke prophetically.

Perhaps our post-Shoah perspective is helpful here in supplying some possible scenarios. When the dead have lost their identity, their flesh and sinew, their particularity, it can sometimes be restored by telling their stories and giving back to the nameless and faceless skeletons the stories and voices that gave them life in the first place. Indeed, one of the strategies of post-Shoah testimony is to restore to the dead their identity and dignity by telling their stories with care and attention to the detail (flesh and sinew) of their lives. In so doing, they are rescued from oblivion. Furthermore, this strategy may also supply a clue to the shift in the vision from dry, unburied bones of slain victims in a valley to the dead who have received burial (v. 12) in proper respect to their humanity. Of course, one can read the shift allegorically and note that the bones in the valley and the buried corpses in their graves are one and the same, the exile community.[4] This identification is ambiguous and suggests a subtler linkage between them.[5]

Whose Bones? These Bones!

Whose bones? The text tells us only that they are the whole house of Israel, but only after Ezekiel speaks to them his words of life. What does this mean? Who, indeed, is the whole house of Israel? Is it a representative designation? A literal one? Does it include all Israel past and present? and future? How encompassing is "whole"? The text, itself, appears not to give an answer,[6] unless the timing of the identification as the whole house of Israel is an important clue.

The question God poses is asked of "these bones," but whose bones are "these"? The text tells that they are very dry and strewn across the valley. They were the bones of victims. Indeed, according to the flow of the text, the designation that these bones are the whole house of Israel comes after Ezekiel has spoken words bearing life for them. Should we not conclude that before they can be allegorical or figurative, they must literally be the decayed bones of slain victims denied the dignity of burial and left forgotten and unattended where they fell? Their individual identities are lost; their identification as the whole house of Israel follows confronting them forthrightly in their specificity as victims and in Ezekiel's speaking words that bring them flesh and sinew and eventually breath. Only then are they designated as the whole house of Israel.

This point is important. We dare not view them representatively as the house of Israel if we do not view them in their unsettling particularity as victims first. Any focus on the survivors in exile must not forget the fallen who were left behind—or else they would be doubly victimized, losing their humanity not once but twice. This is also true for how we address post-Shoah Judaism and Israel. The surviving community must be called to life with words that bear life. But not at the expense of the fallen in the valley of the whirlwind. The victims cannot be offered as sacrifices by their own people even for the sake of their own survival. Words of life must be spoken to them *as victims in their valley*. Their bones must be given new flesh (with their stories) and given the breath of life (voice). Only then can they be images of the whole—representative figures, reclaimed from death's dominion. More problematic, of course, is that most of their bones have been crushed and scattered and turned to powder. In order to be reclothed with flesh and sinew, their skeletons must be reconstituted from ash and clay by *ben adam*. Their stories must be located and reconstructed, if necessary piece by piece, in order to be linked together and told.

Having faced the specificity of these bones, we may also ponder what kinds of bones lie in the valley confronting Ezekiel. Perhaps they are not only human but also institutional and cultural "bones" as well. After the destruction of Israel, the bones in the shadows of Moriah and Zion would be mixed with the sun-bleached ruins of the Temple. Pottery shards from family tables and other remnants could be expected as well. Would they not also include the torn fabric of Law and tradition? While the text is ambiguous, its message is clear: In their specificity they can be seen as the whole house of Israel, and we must risk confronting as much of that particularity as we can. For these other "bones" are ruins of the whole house of Israel as well.

The same logic helps us as we ponder the valley in which these bones are strewn. Where is it? Does it lie in Israel or Judah or Babylon? Indeed, the commentaries do not always agree. Some identify it with the valley-plain where Ezekiel and fellow exiles reside. Some would locate the valley in Judah, just below Jerusalem. Asking "Which valley?" is like asking "Whose bones?" Are they those who were slain in the destruction of Jerusalem and the Temple? Are they the allegorical symbols of the exiles in Babylon who are represented as if they were lifeless skeletons trapped in a foreign land? These questions and possible responses are inseparable. The text itself does not specify the location by name. To complicate matters, the same Hebrew word is used for the plain in Chebar (Babylon) and the valley of dry bones—*biqah*. But that does not necessarily imply that the same geographical space is intended. As with the bones, the text does not provide a simple answer. The text simply specifies that these bones are the whole house of Israel. And perhaps for this reason some scholars assert that the valley is allegorically filled with the dry bones of the living exiles. But the text and its vision also portray the valley-plain as the scene of a previous battle or massacre. Those who lie there were slain (*harugim*, verse 9).

In the vision's landscape of destruction, we are asked to face the utter devastation focused in a field of what once was filled with corpses and now victims of a double violence. Walther Zimmerli's description is potent in this regard: "These bones have been lying about unburied for a long time, naked, already picked clean by the birds of the sky, stripped of their skin and flesh and sinews, bleached and dried out by the heat of the day."[7] When we recall that the meanings of allegory grow out of the particularity of the *peshat*, we recognize that the valley in the vision can be the plain below Jerusalem, while it can also be seen as the plain between the rivers of Chebar and the dwelling place of exiles themselves shattered by the devastation they have witnessed from a distance. Thus we can say that those who were slain there represent the whole house of Israel, for in the specificity of their being slain, the house of Israel as it was embodied in the Temple and Jerusalem was shattered. The whole house of Israel collapsed, both as focused in the Temple as well as in significant others living in exile in Babylon. As Zimmerli's interpretation makes clear, both the dead and the surviving remnant in exile are humiliated by such a scene—though each in very different and unsettling ways. Zimmerli adds that Ezekiel is being led very carefully to explore this valley of bones "to be impressed . . . that this is not simply a symbol of death, but death in all its fullness—the great death."[8] We would simply add that the terrain of this valley is multilayered in its implications and can authentically locate the devastation of Israel wherever Israel dwells in representative specificity.

Coming to Terms with What Happened

How we come to terms with this valley is not simply dependent upon whether we are working from the Hebrew text or translation. In this case, the "plain meaning" of the text, its *peshat*, is hidden in the phrase "these bones" (*haatzamot heleh*), with the emphasis on the particularity of the bones, not the word bones per se (which can be conveyed in Hebrew or in English) . The *peshat* is not simply the plain meaning of the text and its vision; it is its givenness, its otherness, as well. In order to come to terms with this vision and its valley, we must face what actually happened there, letting the bones be the bones of those who perished and were left unattended—who in "the now of the vision" demand Ezekiel's attention. Ezekiel was confronting the bones of Jerusalem along with the ruins of Jerusalem and the Temple. In this way, through its very particularity, Ezekiel was confronting the destruction of the sacred center of Israel's world (the whole house of Israel, which he served as a priest); the destruction in Judah reached to Chebar as well. In short, Ezekiel's vision confronted him and the exiles with whom he lived with the inescapable givenness of what happened in the *peshat* of "these bones." By itself, an allegorical identification of the dry bones with the exiles separates them from the literal bones that were slain in the fall of Jerusalem and the destruction of the Temple. In doing this, that tragedy is softened by reducing the crisis to one of meaning for the exiles only. Clearly that is not the case. The "whole house of Israel" has been destroyed. And the victims include those literally slain by the Babylonians as well as those whose identities and futures are also stolen from them, including the dead!

Post-Shoah this point is critical. We know too well this kind of scenario. The Nazi attack on European Jewry resulted in the loss of nearly 6 million lives, nearly two thirds of Europe's Jewish population. Eastern European Jewry with its characteristic *shtetl* life was wiped out. This devastation directly affected every Jew in Europe and elsewhere. Jewishness itself was attacked. Elie Wiesel has put it succinctly: "Not all victims were Jews, but all Jews were victims."[9] And yet the particularity of the 6 million who perished in the Shoah matters and must not be sacrificed in the symbolic significance they hold for the "surviving remnant" of world Jewry. As we look at Ezekiel's valley, we cannot forget this.

To be sure, there is an allegorical or figurative linkage in the text, as Zimmerli points out.[10] But it must grow out of and be held in tension with the plain meaning of the text, its *peshat*, which in this case is captured in the words "these bones." Too easy an allegorization bypasses the slain in the Palestinian valley to reach the spiritually slain in the plain of Chebar. Coming to terms with the overall significance of what happened in the exile and the destruction of the Temple requires honoring the particularity of what happened in each valley with its distinctive landscapes of destruction. Together this is the devastation of *Churban*. Coming to terms with our post-Shoah exile in the valley of its aftermath requires no less attention to the particularities of our time and place.

A Compelling Vision

There is a compelling otherness that seizes Ezekiel in this vision, taking him deeper and deeper into the images of his vision.[11] Ezekiel cannot not look at what has happened to his people and to all that represents the sacred in his world. The double negative is instructive. He cannot avoid seeing what he sees. He cannot not look. He is compelled. Ezekiel is being led through a place that in every normal respect would be unclean and out of bounds to him as a priest. In coming to terms with Ezekiel's vision, we must not overlook how Ezekiel, a prophet-priest, is led to a valley filled with dry bones. As a priest, this is not a place where he would be called upon to be present. Indeed, the opposite would be the case. Put boldly, that place should not be his place. Regardless of the fact that he is led there in a vision—not in actual fact—this would be a startling image to encounter. For one thing, Ezekiel is taken, by the One he serves, to this unclean place of death to attend to slaughtered kin whose bones are shamefully left unattended and therefore had become unidentifiable. Could any other experience be more compelling, especially if Ezekiel were to hear himself called to priestly presence in such a place? And when we remind ourselves that among these dry bones would be the ruins of the Temple and the sacrificial system he served, we glimpse something of how compelling and even transfiguring the experience must have been for him.

Of course, it should not be difficult for us to understand how compelling the landscape of destruction can be, even for a priest. For Ezekiel, the valley of dry bones was strewn with people he served and quite possibly cherished and, most probably, stones and other ruins from the Temple to which he was devoted. This valley contained the house of Israel that was his priestly and natural home. It lay shattered in that valley. And Ezekiel was drawn to it in spite of any halakhic admonition to avoid death.

Those who are compelled to wrestle with the Shoah know a similar sense of urgency about their study. We cannot not face the Shoah. It stalks us, not the other way around. The otherness of the Shoah has grasped our consciousness and compels our engagement. Ezekiel's vision is also compelling for those who meet objections to the work of reflecting on the Shoah, asking: "Why are you preoccupied with such destruction? You must move on." If Ezekiel's vision is trustworthy, we must not overlook that the very bones of the house of Israel summoned this prophetic priest. The way to life, in exile, lay in facing the death and destruction that he and his companions, in exile, survived. For us, in post-Shoah exile, the way forward, if it is to be life giving and responsible, may similarly depend upon our facing the bones (even as ashes and powdered bones) in our post-Shoah valley as well. If we attend closely to Ezekiel, we may be challenged by his hearing the God of creation address him, even through death and its silent witnesses, by way of a question: "Can these bones live?"

Placing Ezekiel

In this vision, Ezekiel sees a valley filled with the "very dry bones" of the entire house of Israel. He could be imagining the future, but as the full text of his book demonstrates, he is not. He is seeing Israel after its destruction. The Temple has been destroyed; Jerusalem razed. In important ways he is a survivor, albeit from a distance, since he is also a refugee. In a vision, he sees the entire house of Israel devastated. And yet as a survivor/refugee he looks on at the devastation. Thus, in this sense, not all Israel lies in that valley, unless—and the *unless* is the prophetic key—unless the full significance of the valley is comprehended in priestly, representative fashion.

Ezekiel, speaking prophetically as a priest, bears the mixed responsibility of passing on the sacred tradition that in narrative and law bears the identity and that shapes Israel's identity as Israel. At the same time, he is called upon to warn the people who bear that identity and adjust it accordingly from his side of survival. Both continuity and discontinuity, fidelity and change, characterize his life and work. His place, after the devastation, is overlooking the destruction as well as looking into the future and the aborning present for the sake of the whole house of Israel—a prophetic-priestly role of urgent proportion. Neither task, the priestly nor the prophetic, can be collapsed into the other; otherwise, the fundamental task of Israel's survival after devastation is compromised. Perhaps this tension is necessary for our time as well.

Ezekiel saw the destruction of his beloved homeland and people as a refugee, in a vision while living in exile. He was a survivor—at least of the initial occupation and forced deportation. Still he looked on the utter devastation that followed from a distance. His ambiguous role may be instructive, especially for a generation that looks back—some as survivors, some as children of survivors; some as bystanders, some as children of bystanders; some as perpetrators, some as children of perpetrators. But all from a distance, in time and space.

Throughout his prophetic career, Ezekiel is addressed as *ben adam* (son of man). Indeed, he is so addressed ninety-six times. Why? Joseph Blenkinsopp suggests a functional explanation, that God is emphasizing Ezekiel's prophetic function.[12] Perhaps so; however, the appellation also recalls the creation imagery of Genesis, reminding Ezekiel, prophet and priest, and those addressed by his story, that he bears the legacy and responsibility of creation as it has been entrusted to human beings from the beginning. Ezekiel, the prophet-priest, is a representative person. What better representative appellation than *ben adam* as he stands as a representative image of the human being from the beginning. Similarly, *ben adam* calls to mind the eschatological image of creation's consummation and humanity's final fulfillment as evidenced in its use in the apocalyptic imagery of the Book of Daniel.

The Divine Command—Prophesy to These Bones

In the face of this vision, Ezekiel was summoned to act. He spoke to his people in the face of their annihilation as a distinctive people. Thousands had been killed. Their religious and political leaders had been removed from the land that was the literal sign of their covenant with God and their place in creation. And finally the Temple and its city, Jerusalem, had been destroyed. Not only had the core symbols of Israel come unraveled; but also their very foundations had been destroyed. The resulting crisis was seismic. Literally and figuratively, it was world shaking. The house of Israel had collapsed. Those in exile could only look on from a distance, horrified and fundamentally disoriented by the devastation. This was *Churban*. How could they sing as a witness people in these circumstances? This was the valley in which the exiles found themselves, a valley they could never separate from the valley below Jerusalem and Moriah/Zion. How could Ezekiel and his people survive? How could he, a priest, come to terms with what happened and fulfill his vocation to honor and serve the glory (*kevod*) of God?

The daunting task before Ezekiel was how to speak words of life and hope to a broken and exiled people while facing the full scope of devastation and the power of death to destroy everything that mattered. How would the prophet-priest address this complex valley of death and remain a faithful steward of the God he served?

In one sense, the path to new life and restoration began before the final scene of destruction unfolded. Early in the exile, Ezekiel spoke poignantly of God's removal of the divine presence and favor from the Temple. In the face of unfolding events, he began to disassociate the One he served from the holy precinct of the Temple in the name of fidelity to this self-same One. Traditional meanings were relativized in service to the One those traditions served. As the sacerdotal house of the Temple collapsed, Ezekiel drew strength and vision from the imagery of this place in mystical ways. The once portable presence/*kevod*/glory, with an ark as its focus, was on the move again in word and story. And its portability and power would be tested in the extreme as Ezekiel found himself called upon to speak its words and focus its power on the demise that followed his warnings. Fundamental themes and categories were restored, but with important and necessary adjustments to life before them and behind them. Covenant, chosenness, divine presence, Israel (as people and land) had to be reconfigured. But we are ahead of the story.

What did Ezekiel do? First, he did not find life *in* the valley. It was filled with dry bones, *very* dry bones. Because of their presence, that valley was unclean. It was defiled by what happened to them in their death and in the abandonment that followed. He may have found meaning earlier in the crisis situation of his people. Indeed, he saw divine judgment, and he bore witness to that judgment because of their infidelity to God. But in the destruction of the *Churban*, he saw lifelessness, abandonment, defilement—and it was "very dry." In other words, there was no meaning to be found *in* the valley of dry bones. Like Ezekiel's prophetic words of life, meaning and its gift of life had to be brought to the valley. This was essential testimony after the *Churban*. It remains essential post-Shoah.

So then, what did Ezekiel do? At first, nothing declarative. When faced with the bones and the question, Can these bones live? he answered, "You know, O LORD [*Adoshem*]." The response was ambiguous. Indeed, the Talmud records an interpretation that he waffled, explaining that God hoped he would respond immediately: "Yes!" Instead, he hesitated. And for that, claims this interpretation, he was buried in exile. His bones were not returned to Israel with the restoration.[13] Still, he allowed himself to be led into a defiled, unclean place filled with the lingering remains of death. There he listened for divine instruction. There he heard a summons to attend to what he saw. There he accepted, in an agnostic but not faithless manner, the prophetic task of speaking words of life to the dead. He acted as a priest in an unclean valley of death. And in doing so, he restored the house of Israel. Once again, he did not literally venture into this place, but in the context of all that had been lost in the *Churban*, he clearly ventured into the realm of despair and lifelessness that attended the vision that he saw.[14] Of course, we must be careful of too easy an identification of the dry bones, graves, and house of Israel with the exilic community in Babylon. It avoids the difficulty Ezekiel and his contemporaries would have had with a literal valley of bones, bespeaking the destruction of the house of Israel. Indeed, that is the heart of the crisis of the *Churban*. In that valley, Ezekiel is summoned, first to attend to the shattered house of Israel, scattered before him.

In full attention to these bones, he is called deeper into what he sees, recognizing that he is implicated as well, as are all others in the surviving exile community. One could even note that the form of the verb to hear (*shimu*, an echo of the *shema* reminding those in prayer to remember their identity in standing before God) is grammatically built from the second-person plural—"let us hear." And so, Ezekiel and the other survivors are called to attend to what happened and to remember who they are and who God is, even in this valley in the presence of these bones. Facing these bones, Ezekiel is summoned by God to act. The divine command: "Prophesy over these bones and say, 'Hear the Word of the LORD.' " What is Ezekiel called to do? Not only must he attend to the dead; he must honor them with direct address, calling to them as God has called him. And the first word is like that addressed to him and addressed to his people from the beginning: "Hear the Word of the Lord!" [*shimu d'var Adonai*— again, the grammar reminds us that this is a command that addresses Ezekiel as well]. Direct address to the bones is tied to Ezekiel's speaking over them as well. Ezekiel's words—"Hear the Word of the LORD"—direct attention, including his own, to the Word of the Eternal One who speaks words of life-giving power to the dry bones. And as the flesh and sinew were restored by divine address, God called upon Ezekiel to speak to the wind/breath on behalf of the Eternal: "Come O breath from the four winds and breathe into the slain that they may live again." Ezekiel speaks first to direct attention to the Word of God; then Ezekiel, on behalf of God, speaks the summoning words of life. In other words, the prophetic-priestly action of Ezekiel is a representative work of partnership for the sake of the life of the shattered house of Israel. Earlier God proclaims to Ezekiel that any restorative action is neither for the sake of Israel nor dependent upon any action of theirs. Rather, it is for the sake of honoring the divine name. We should not see this action on behalf of God's people as contravening this point. Instead, it supports the representative reading of this action: Ezekiel is called to act on behalf of God and his people. And God acts through Ezekiel in order to restore God's witness people, who are restored to their representative role and place (literally and figuratively) in the world.

Restoration and New Life

According to the text, Ezekiel announces renewed life brought to the dry bones strewn in the valley before him. By attending to them in their particularity, he remembers who they are and whose they are. Thereby he clothes them with their "flesh and sinew." Still they are not alive; they require the inspiration of breath. They must find their voice. Thereupon, Ezekiel, as he is divinely instructed, calls upon the spirit of life to come from the four winds and breathe on them so that they in turn might breathe with life. As they rose up, God declared them to be the whole house of Israel, which sees itself as "completely cut off." At this point, Ezekiel is directed to speak to those who have been reborn, describing the power of God to call forth life from death by opening their graves so that the dead might be reborn and return to the land of Israel where God will establish them once more as God's people. Apart from a magical reading of this material, several points can and should be made. New life is announced, in anticipatory fashion, calling forth that which is promised. The vehicle is language. And Ezekiel, the prophet-priest, is called upon to speak to the dead words of life. Moreover, he himself is called to summon the spirit of life that it might enliven those whose flesh and blood are restored. As he is summoned, he, too, calls forth.

How does this happen? The text does not explain, testifying only that it does. Does it occur with the full encounter of those that are lost and by telling their story? Does it occur with the full encounter of those in despair, confronting them with their own gravelike existence, that they have died before their time? Does it occur with giving the slaughtered and lost their voice and place without glorifying their lives or their death? Does it occur because Ezekiel the priest is able to identify the divine presence outside the boundaries of the Temple and the Promised Land with prophetic power? Does it occur because the prophetic words of Ezekiel are joined to symbolic actions that mediate the very life his words promise and evoke? If we read the text attentive to its own dynamics, these dimensions all emerge as very real possibilities. Moreover, the new life evoked by Ezekiel among the exiles is, in part, tied to the new life called forth by God in Ezekiel himself as he comes to terms with the devastation in the valley—both the valley in his vision and the one where he lives in exile. In dramatic fashion, he is called to be his people's priest, standing at the threshold as their representative and God's. And as he is restored to priestly and prophetic duty, he passes on the new life he has found among his people who are likewise restored to their priestly and prophetic task as witnesses to life in spite of the death and destruction each has known. Once more, they are placed on a hill, a light to the nations, even in exile—even though they dwell in a valley.

There is a transcendent and ethical character to this summons. According to Levinas, it is the "I" of *these bones* who in their absence cry out "Here I am" as Cain's blood cried out to God long ago. Their "I" is reconstituted in learning and telling their story, returning to them their flesh and sinew—yet still without the breath of life. Ezekiel in calling to the four winds recognizes what is missing and calls upon forces outside his voice, representing for him the very source of life, which is other to all creation. Only then can these bones live. They rise up, and Ezekiel is only then directed to speak to the graves of the dead and the gravelike reality of exiles. Interestingly, the breath of the slain and abandoned appears to be dependent upon the exiles breaking forth from their graves. In other words, if life is to be lived, it must be lived for others.

We must be careful here. In identifying the survivors with the house of Israel, we must not dishonor nor disregard those who were slaughtered and forgotten in the valley. Still we are "pierced to the soul," to use Emil Fackenheim's words by this vision. As he points out, the subject matter is nothing less than death and resurrection. Even Christians, ready to distinguish between resuscitation and resurrection must be prepared to concede that in this valley, where death and destruction reign, the new life envisioned here breaks the power of death.[15] Fackenheim goes on to clarify the need for caution, explaining that from our vantage point after the destruction of 1933–1945 and the founding of the state of Israel in 1945, "Ezekiel's image of death and resurrection comes easily to mind. It could come too easily."[16] He contends that Ezekiel's valley falls short of representing the reality of the Shoah, noting that the dead in Ezekiel's valley were killed in battle.[17] His point: The dead in Ezekiel's vision were allowed the honor of fighting for their freedom and their lives. For the most part, the victims of the Shoah were not. Furthermore, as he points out, they were denied "the peace even of bones . . . for they, the others [Nazis and their agents], ground their bones to dust and threw the dust into rivers."[18] Even so, we cannot overlook the fact that the dry bones were the unidentifiable remains of victims who were abandoned and left unburied. Their identity and memory were destroyed as well as their lives. They were defiled, left to decay and be forgotten. In limited measure, then, the missing bones of the Shoah are given presence, albeit fragile and limited, by the dry bones of Ezekiel's vision.

While the devastation of Ezekiel's vision falls short of the destruction experienced in the Shoah, we can see how, together in their abandonment, their victims cry out to be remembered with flesh and sinew. But how can anyone call forth life in the presence of such a place as the modern valley of shadows we know as Auschwitz? If Ezekiel's vision is instructive, it cannot happen without recovering the particularity of the parched skeletons strewn before him. They must regain flesh and blood—their flesh, their sinew, their blood. And they must be animated with life; they must breathe anew.

Post-Shoah, we have a partial glimpse of what this might mean. Stories must be recovered and told. Each individual narrative matters, for in each telling of one story, the whole house of Israel is reclaimed. Furthermore, these words must be spoken and, in more than one place and time, given breath and told in the breathing, lest they lie lifeless in an unread text or on unpursed lips. Their stories must be told to live in the life of the whole house of Israel.

After the destruction of the sacerdotal system by which Israel knew the presence of God, new forms[19] were necessary in order for the divine presence to continue to be served. That was a vital part of the priestly-prophetic task of Ezekiel and the role of his visions. After the *Churban*, the presence had to be rediscovered, refocused in ways that conserved and reformed at the same time. Likewise, after the Shoah, with the shattering of European Jewry and all things Jewish, Jewish identity had to be conserved and reformed. This time, while there was no literal priesthood to take up the task, there were survivors and leaders who have had the courage to look forthrightly at the valley of dark shadows that they walked. They accepted the prophetic and priestly task of speaking words of life to the shattered house of Israel. Furthermore, the Modern State of Israel was formed in 1948, and Jews returned to take responsibility for a sacred homeland once again. The people Israel was restored with its identity essentially linked to the victims of this last destruction. Nonetheless, what to conserve and what to change remain in debate. Perhaps Ezekiel has instructive words, life-bearing words, for this work, too.

Throughout his book and especially in his priestly-prophetic role, God addressed Ezekiel as *ben adam*. The Hebrew designation may be more important to retain than the English "son of man," especially for Christians. In its otherness, its *peshat*, it recalls the context of creation and suggests that at the heart of Ezekiel's work lay the very intentionality of creation. Ezekiel was not just priest and prophet of Israel; he served creation and its covenantal goal as well. As Israel was set apart and restored, this primal dimension of restoration was renewed as well. The goal of creation infuses the identity of Israel reborn. Its identity bears the reflection of this prophet-priest who represents it: *ben adam*.

Yet Israel finds itself reconstituted in the Promised Land as a representative people set apart in the midst of others who did not seek their presence. It is precisely in this context that Israel is given new life. That gift, with its representative role, is precarious in profound ways. Nevertheless, that has been Israel's identity through the ages. And that task remains; however, the stakes are raised substantially, just as the international stakes for cooperation among nations is likewise increased. Nations now have the capacity to inflict mass murder at the push of a button without ever having to face the ones they have chosen to obliterate. Having lived through such loss and overcome near annihilation, Israel dare not succumb now and, by seeking to win at all costs, lose what it has so preciously held in trust for four millennia. Wisdom's caution is still Ezekiel's warning. However, equally urgent, Israel dare not forget what other nations can do and have done when they choose to destroy others. That, too, is a tenet of post-Shoah wisdom. How, then, shall their set-apartness be conceived by Jew and Gentile alike?

Representative Particularity

To be sure, the particularity of restoration is a critical and tangled issue. In this episode of Israel's life and throughout Israel's history, God's fidelity to a "chosen people" is played out. Israel is selected from all the people of the world for a special role in God's intentions for all creation. In the Shoah, selection and chosenness were turned on their heads. As a result, chosenness will forever after have a problematic ring to it for Jews, if not for *goyim*. Indeed, the very notion of chosenness has a problematic ring apart from the Shoah. It is manifest in how Jews relate to Gentiles and how Gentiles relate to Jews. Likewise, it is sharply focused in the unique issues of Christian-Jewish relations. And politically it permeates Israel's relationship to the "Promised Land" and the others who claim the same land as home.

Yet Ezekiel may still be instructive for this complexly woven tapestry. To be sure, the vision of God's faithfulness to Israel and Israel's restoration informs perspectives present in Israel today. For example, a verse preceding the vision narrative, from chapter 36:24 ("I will take you from among the nations, and gather you out of all the countries, and will bring you into your own land") and citing the restoration of the land to Israel, is emblazoned on the wall of the president's home in Jerusalem.[20] As well, the vision of the valley of dry bones and the command to speak words of life to its scene of death is also cited in Yad VaShem. Fackenheim singles out this line of reason and raises important questions about reading too much into the founding of the State of Israel. He writes: "Whether in terms of future, Messianic time or of a world-to-come beyond time, 'Resurrection' connotes redemptive finality. But much though we might yearn to take either recourse, confined as we are to that Ezekiel passage on the wall, we cannot, dare not, ascribe redemptive finality to the State of Israel."[21] As "monumental" an event as the founding of Israel is, the Shoah relativizes any eschatological hope associated with the State of Israel.[22] As one who himself has made *aliyah* and existentially invested his life in the future of Israel, he explains that it is not Israel that is resurrected from the remains of the Shoah but the hope of Israel—a wounded, still vulnerable hope against hope. And that hope is representative in all its particularity for those who see life through the lens of the divine-human partnership of covenant life.

There is a further qualifier at work as well. According to *Ezekiel* 36:22, [23] God restores Israel not because of anything Israel does but in spite of what Israel has done, at the initiative of God to serve God's own identity. Many Christian commentaries focus on the gracious character of God at this point. We must be very careful not to overlook the representative implications of this witness when we recognize the graciousness of such action. God spares Israel so that she might bear witness to the One Israel serves. Any talk of election, even if unearned and gracious, must bring this representative character to the fore. Chosenness cannot be forgotten nor avoided. But its particularity is representative and must be carefully placed in its service of witness to the covenantal intentions of creation.

Admittedly, this is a fragile and complex affair. Our insistence on the givenness of *peshat* anchoring any allegorical reading of the text applies in poignant ways to the restoration of promise for the people Israel in the land of Israel, for the particularity of Israel folds back on itself in compounding fashion. To begin with, Israel, as a displaced people, reclaims her place as a representative people among other nations and peoples. As a storied and set-apart people, Israel represents the promise with which all peoples have been endowed as children of God and seeks to demonstrate its accountability and responsibility for that gift—but only as a clearly identifiable people set apart in this way. Moreover, Israel does not simply fulfill a spiritual role that can be inhabited abstractly. It is indwelled in the flesh and sinew of place. That is, for the promise to be representative, it must happen somewhere in the midst of others. That place is *eretz Yisrael*. The land of promise for Israel is that "promised" land, a given both of Israel's history and sacred narrative. Furthermore, their "promised" land has never not been occupied by others, even at the beginning. That land is contested. And as contested land, the full promise of creation is tested there as it could be in no other place. That, too, is a given. Furthermore, new life on the other side of violence can represent the full promise of creation only as the actual perils of contested space are transformed into new possibilities for cooperation among the contending parties in that same land. The convoluted character of Israel's reality is expressed in the following, albeit awkward way: Israel's promise in its promised land can be realized as promise for others only as that land and its several inhabitants bear promise for new ways of living together. Yet for all its complexity, there is a profound simplicity. The representative particularity of this people, in this place, like that of "these bones," is radical particularity. The choice, however, is between exclusivism at the expense of others in a zero-sum game or a radical, yet representative, particularity for the sake of the whole. And that choice, post-Shoah, for Israel is laden with risk.

Chosenness Revisited

Ezekiel and Israel are called and set apart. They are "chosen" in order to bear witness—Ezekiel to Israel and Israel to the nations. They are representative figures. From our modern vantage point their representative role is most significant. Neither one in their "chosenness" is set apart for salvation or for a gift that others are not to enjoy. Rather, they are set apart for the sake of the larger whole in which they participate—the covenantal existence intended for all creation. Covenant life is not intended only for Jews, or only for Jews and Christians. Nor is it restricted to their witness. It precedes their existence, just as the rainbow precedes and signals for every Jew the Noahide bond between God and all creation. As we look at modern Israel's relationship to the nations, this places a burden on their people, one, to be sure, they have known before. However, the burden is complicated by the very quality that should make it less problematic for their neighbors. Their chosenness does not bestow a special ontological status withheld from others. They are not set above or apart from others by virtue of any moral or spiritual quality they may or may not possess. Rather, Israel's election gives unique embodiment to the ontological promise shared by all. Quite simply, their task is to bear witness. Yet Israel's citizens are not of one accord in what their witness is. In fact, in Israel, debate is sharp over who is truly a Jew and entitled to the rights and privileges accorded Jewish citizens of Israel. At the same time, not a few Israelis view the very notion of witness to be a problem, especially when applied to a nation–state. Personal moral categories and religious expectations regarding the people Israel are applied to the political state of Israel, leading to double standards among nations. As a result, instead of being treated like any other nation, Israel is often held to unrealistic expectations for any modern state and, being set apart, echoes as yet another victimization. Not surprisingly, there is much ambivalence toward the notion of chosenness.

Nevertheless, with chosenness understood as a representative expression of Israel's particularity, we are invited to reexamine exclusive notions of covenant. Covenants, if they are likewise representative, embody in particular relationships a quality of life lived in relation, each for the other. Seeing each covenant as representative of a larger reality helps us to recognize that each covenant participates in a covenantal quality of relationship to which God's covenant with Israel bears witness. To be sure, covenant life is known by way of discrete covenants, and each covenant can even expect exclusive devotion on the part of the human partner to the Holy One whom they know covenantally. Still, none of the human covenant partners need to view their covenant, exhausting the character and graciousness of covenant life. This is not unlike the unique relationship that any child (in the right circumstances) in one family can experience with his or her mother or father. While the devotion they give to their parent is limited to that parent, the parent may be passionately committed to each child with whom the other shares the parent. Of course, as the stories of Genesis make so powerfully clear, the sibling side of sharing such devotion has been a problem from the beginning. Nevertheless, the covenantal obligation of God for creation need not be exclusive in order for human partners to know unique and representative covenantal bonds with the Eternal One.[24]

What, then, are the implications of representative particularity when we incorporate the logic of attending to "these bones" in paying attention to "other bones"? The question "Can these bones live?" comes to us from beyond ourselves, from beyond the bones, yet through them, asking Can they live? As we face their very real particularity, they represent the whole of which they are a part. Yet the whole in which Israel participates—even the whole house—is more, too. A witness people, they represent the covenantal promise and reality for all peoples, all creation. Hence, other bones and other valleys can in fidelity to the text and Ezekiel's vision compel us—only as "these bones" compel us. We can let Ezekiel's valley and its bones guide us in how we attend to valleys with names like Wounded Knee, Little Big Horn (the Grassy Green), Gettysburg, My Lai, Babi Yar, Srebrenicza. In each of these places, the way toward restoration and healing (*tikkun*) begins with attending to the defilement and destruction in its particularity, using their names, telling their stories, and speaking their life in the presence of others, for others. Indeed, this is a critical moment as Israel is being restored as a witness people; restoration is not simply for the sake of Israel but also for the sake of others. Israel is to show the way forward for others—facing their dry bones and reclaiming their place in the world; changing that place from a place of defilement to one of honor; speaking life to their bones and then to those whom they represent; then opening the closed graves of their dead, even including those who dwell among the living.

Can These Bones Live? The Returning Question

When the world around us collapses, what saves us from despair? When suffering surmounts our capacities to cope, what prevents us from giving up and restores our hope? When life "falls apart" and the center no longer holds,[25] what restores or allows us to survive and recover meaning and life anew? For Jews and Christians who wrestle with the Shoah, these questions chip away at the horizons of our worlds. Indeed, they can even attack our core beliefs and threaten our identities as people of faith. "Who knows what beast slouches toward Bethlehem waiting to be born?"[26]

When Jews speak of restoration and hope, especially post-Shoah hope, they often echo the sentiments of the prophet-priest Ezekiel, pointing toward the rebirth of modern Israel. Elie Wiesel's statement is not atypical:

From his exile, Ezekiel speaks to all generations, and particularly to ours, for, more than his own contemporaries, we have witnessed the frailty of social structures and the irresistible power of spiritual courage and dreams.

For once upon a time some of us did indeed see a deserted land covered with dry bones.

And yes, we could testify to man's ability to transform memories of tragedy into necessary hope.

Indeed, no generation can understand Ezekiel as well—as profoundly—as ours.[27]

When Christians speak of hope beyond despair and life in the face of death, we speak of resurrection. Our horizon of meaning grows out of an event called Easter. In the face of utter devastation, in the shadows of the Shoah, even the language of resurrection is threatened (if not shattered, which it certainly is for some)—not the least because it has been implicated in the destructive legacy itself. How, then, can Jews as Jews and Christians and Christians face the utter threat the Shoah poses and remain true to each of our identities while allowing room for the new life that must surely follow? Or to use the words of our texts, what words of prophesy can we speak for ashes and pulverized bones, as well as dry bones, to live?

The midrashic return to the text recognizes the recursive character of the question, Can these bones live? It is the abiding *peshat* of Ezekiel's vision. And the question even addresses this commentary, as if its words were bones, skeletons without flesh and sinew, much less breath and voice.

Can these bones live? That is the returning question that enlivens Ezekiel's vision as well as our own post-Shoah encounter with it. It is addressed to the remains of the victims in the valley where they were slain. It is addressed to the exiles in Chebar, in the settlement they called Tel Aviv. And it is addressed to victims of our Shoah-carved valley in our own time. It is addressed even to the skeletons of broken dreams and stories of those of us who, in post-Shoah exile, look on from a distance by way of midrashic commentary. In each case, the question calls upon us to face the particularity of "these bones." Can these bones live?

FROM THE VALLEY OF DRY BONES TO AN OPENED AND EMPTY TOMB

For Christians, the question, Can these bones live? does not end with Ezekiel's witness. It addresses Jesus' life and death as well as those of his followers. Indeed, it attends the Crucifixion and empty tomb of Jesus in ever penetrating ways. At the heart of Ezekiel's vision is testimony that the power of death, which appears to hold sway in this valley of devastation and death, is not equal to the power of God. Namely, God has the last word, through the prophetic partnership of Ezekiel; and that word is life. While death is not vanquished from life, it is shown to be subject to the divine word of life spoken courageously by God's representatives from the other side of despair. At the heart of Christian claims about resurrection beats a similar affirmation. After the Shoah, Christians dare not overlook this. How, then, might our encounter with the representative prophet-priest Ezekiel help those of us who are Christian follow our own representative figure, Jesus of Nazareth, to show us how to live on the other side of despair in the darkened valley of post-Shoah exile? Still haunted by God's question to Ezekiel we turn to the concluding chapter of Matthew's Gospel and his account of the Resurrection of Jesus.

Return to the Tomb—Encountering the Question

Matthew's story of the empty tomb is familiar. The day after the Sabbath the two Marys had returned to the tomb where the body of Jesus had been placed after the Crucifixion. While there, they were surprised when their world was again shaken by an earthquake. A figure appeared, like lightning, as the stone at the entrance to the tomb was rolled away. To their astonishment they were faced with an empty tomb and the announcement, by a messenger of God (an angel), that Jesus had been raised from the dead. Hurriedly they left to tell Jesus' disciples, and on their way, they encountered the risen Jesus themselves who reassured them in their confusion and sent them along their way. At the direction of the women the disciples went to a mountain earlier identified by Jesus where they were also joined by their risen teacher. He met them as he had the women and sent them forth to make disciples of others and to baptize them in the name of the Father, the Son, and the Holy Spirit while assuring them of his abiding presence until the end of the age.

However, let us not be too hasty in thinking we know this story as well as we think. Rather, let us take our time and approach it with Ezekiel's eyes and the question that haunted him and shook his world. For example, before Jesus' tomb could be proclaimed empty, Mary and the other Mary had to return to it, expecting to come to terms with the body of their beloved Jesus that was buried there. Jesus had been placed there. When the women arrived the stone was in place. With the earth-quake the tomb opened, but there was no body inside. An attendant in white announced that the one they sought, Jesus of Nazareth, had been raised from the dead. They were told to go to the disciples and tell the others to go to Galilee, where they would meet their risen Lord. Typically, Christians speak of this scene referring simply to the empty tomb. What if instead of simply reading "empty tomb," we read "(*al tiqre*) an opened and empty tomb"?

What does an opened tomb "open" for us that the phrase "empty tomb," by itself, does not? Several possibilities come to mind. One of the ways a tomb can be opened is by asking of the bones buried there, "Can these bones live?" The very question breaks the power of death in such a place, expressing the reality that God, who is sovereign of life and death, may yet do more with the less of death. And when the question is posed *to* the human partner not *by* her, an interesting set of relations/dynamics arises. On the one hand, it is not in human hands to effect, whereas on the other, it depends upon human response for the action to be completed and known. Moreover, if the human partner is receptive, even if agnostically so, there is still work to be done by that partner in preparing the way for life to come forth. Indeed, divine expectation is signaled by such a question. The human partner is expected not to accept death as the last word in life. Again, it is as if the human partner is asked, "Where are you?" and the human response is a *hineni* of covenantal readiness for life to be brought forth even out of death. "Can these bones live?" "You know, O Lord. What am I therefore to do?" Indeed, before claiming any encounter with a resurrected Jesus, one must respond to the real albeit tacit and unexpressed question, "Can these bones live?" How the two Marys respond makes all the difference.

The first recognition is that Jesus whom they sought is not in the grave. He is not where they left him. From the beginning of their relationship with him, he has moved forward, confounding them and not remaining where his disciples left him. And here, even in death, that dynamic continues. He is not there; instead, there is a messenger who proclaims his Resurrection.

What can we learn from this initial encounter at the tomb? What happened? Whom did they meet? What did they meet? The text, in announcing Resurrection, only describes bits and pieces of what happened. But there are clues. First, the text begins with absence, as did the original encounter. And the absence was an opening. Jesus was not where the women left him. The messenger who was attending the opened grave provided a double message: He is not here; he has been raised. Furthermore, he goes on before you. In the text, the messenger at the tomb is clothed in white as if he were performing a ritual function. Indeed, some scholars see the traces of ritual action read back into the story here. The point remains, regardless: The sheer fact of an empty tomb is not enough. It must be interpreted. It was opened. What happened to Jesus? He has been raised from the dead.

Importantly, there is more. He is going on ahead, returning to Galilee—there you will see him. At least that is what the messenger announces. The proper vantage point for understanding what has happened will be back in Galilee. And so the women are instructed. Their mission: Go, tell the disciples that he will meet them there. They have not been "clean cut off" as they had thought. And so they departed, excited and not a little overwhelmed. Then suddenly, along the way, Jesus hailed them and they grasped him, clutching at his presence. But he reassured them, telling them not to fear but to tell the disciples that he would meet them in Galilee. The risen one had confirmed the message about himself.

The narrative movement is important. The encounter was first with Jesus' absence at an opened and empty grave. Then with a messenger who

Can These Bones Live? 145

bore witness to what happened, interpreting his absence for them. Jesus had been raised. The women were instructed to tell the disciples and tell them to meet him in Galilee. Then they departed, but they were not left alone, for they encountered the very one who had been taken from them as he greeted them on the way. Acting on his behalf, even after death, they met him while taking his message to others.

Here the story of coming to terms with the opened and empty tomb is interrupted by a report of the actions of the chief priests and some of the guards. In order to head off any trouble following the discovery of an empty tomb, the guards were to report that his disciples had stolen Jesus' body. The chief priests would back up the guards' testimony if necessary, and trouble would be averted. Scholars point to the probable presence of a counterstory circulating about Jesus' body being stolen and that this interruption is directed toward that countertestimony. After the Shoah, there is more at stake in how we attend to this portion of Christian witness.

What, then, do we make of this aside about the chief priests paying the guards at the tomb of Jesus to say that the disciples came and took his body? After Auschwitz, we surely know what we dare not do with it: use it to indict Jews in general for the Crucifixion of Jesus or as a basis for teaching contempt. While many post-Shoah Christians might prefer to read this account omitting these five verses, that would be irresponsible and a theological dodge, not to mention confessionally dishonest. Instead, the *al tiqre* strategy of midrash may be helpful here. That is, "do not read" these verses as a contemptuous action that invites a contemptuous response. Instead, read them otherwise [28] (*kivyakhol*, as it were), describing an act rooted in several alternative motives that can range from jealous blockage of the Easter message to explicit, even if misguided, concern for the larger population of the city, swollen with pilgrims who had come for *Pesah*. At one end of the spectrum, the action could be viewed as rooted in selfish motives and overt resistance to the news of an empty tomb. At the other end, the action could suggest a legitimate, though still problematic, concern for social order. That is, if word got out that the tomb of Jesus was empty, then chaos and possibly rebellion would follow. As a result, thousands would be slaughtered. The chief priests, acting for the sake of those they served, might, in this spirit, work out an arrangement with the guards that saved their people—ironically, providing a ransom to the authorities in question for the many who would be spared! The point: the *al tiqre/kiveyakhol* strategy allows the text and its witness to be faced (with conservative and liberal options) in its plain sense but without having to adopt the reading strategy of blame and contempt that has accompanied this passage for too many, for too long.

Back to the story. The eleven remaining disciples go to Galilee, as instructed, to the mountain "to which Jesus had directed them."[29] There they encountered Jesus, with some worshipping him and some doubting.

Again, the meaning of the encounter requires some interpretation, even by the one whom they mourn. In what appears to be a midrashic extension of Daniel 7, Matthew describes Jesus as claiming divine authority to guide them and do what he has done. Then he charges his followers to go even further than before and to make disciples of all nations (*panta ta ethne*) and to baptize them in the name of the Father and of the Son and of the Holy Spirit. He concludes: Do all that I have told you and remember that "I am with you always to the end of the age."[30]

A Critical Pause

Rereading the Matthean text and accompanied by God's question to Ezekiel, "Can these bones live?" we are tempted to reply quickly yes. However, Ezekiel's hesitation could prove helpful; and it need not indicate the absence of trust or hope. Rather, a thoughtful and critical pause could signify the presence of caution born of mature and thoughtful faithfulness. It could also arise out of respect for the place where one is standing. Or both. So let us pause and ask just what are "these bones" with which we are faced? What have the women placed in the tomb? What have the disciples placed there? And what have we placed there as well? By asking "What," we recognize that more than Jesus' body has been placed in that grave. It includes his way of life that he embodied with others, along with the hopes and dreams that he kindled as well. And since commitment to others was a constitutive feature of his life, then we are right to identify all this with him. Consequently, not "just" Jesus lay in his tomb but Jesus as he lived his life for others, especially Jesus who lived for those who followed him and the two who returned to his tomb. To ask, "Can these bones live?" is to confront not just Jesus but his relations with others as well. More specifically, the Jesus in his tomb is the full reality that he embodied in his life and ministry. That is the identity of who and what was placed in his tomb.

These Bones, This Body—A Covenantal Gestalt

As with Ezekiel's vision, attention to the very particular character of the bones placed in Joseph of Arimethea's tomb helps us understand what has taken place in this event. Indeed, any talk about the Resurrection of Jesus' body requires asking about "that body." Thorwald Lorenzen's comments are instructive in this regard:

The "body" of Jesus' earthly life was much more than the physical body at the point of his death. To limit the "body" of Jesus to the corpse in the tomb would be a serious reduction. His "body" was himself, his identity, his mission, his affect on the world. It included all of his life; a life shaped in relationship to God, to human beings, to nature, and to history.[31]

Peter Hodgson makes a similar point in referring to the Resurrection presence as a gestalt. He explains:

> What is risen is not the corpse of a dead man but a gestalt, a sociohistorical dynamic that coalesced in and around a specific human being and with which this human being is still identified.[32]

In other words, "these bones" must include all that *this* Jesus embodied in his life and ministry. More than existential impact is conveyed in this observation. We dare not overlook the otherness of Resurrection, both with regard to its not fitting regular epistemological categories as well as its association with the identifiable otherness encountered in the one named Jesus. I have referred to this (elsewhere in this volume) as a covenantal gestalt that Jesus identified in his teachings with the rule and realm of God and that his disciples experienced in his presence. That unfolding and inbreaking gestalt was a compelling and configuring presence, which in its identification with Jesus was also placed in his borrowed tomb. Likewise, that same identifiable gestalt was encountered in profound ways following his death, transfiguring the abandonment, denial, and rejection that accompanied his Crucifixion. As the reconstituted covenantal gestalt of Jesus, the Resurrection should be seen as happening not only to Jesus but also to his disciples as participants in that gestalt. Nevertheless, the event retains its dimension of otherness, in effect, calling the disciples out of their despair to renewed life. While Resurrection asserts itself as an act of God, it requires the participation and cooperation of those with whom the covenantal relationship is embodied. That is, the Resurrection is a vulnerable triumph that does not intrude into the tragedy, undoing the suffering that has happened. Rather, it unfolds as the covenantal partnership that the tragedy of Golgotha cannot sever. Covenant life as mediated in this life prevails even in the face of its rejection.

For Christians, this is the testimony of Easter and its good news. However, if we stop here and identify this testimony and good news as the whole story of Easter faith, then we fail to account for the lost children of Israel, whether we mean the lost of Jesus' generation to whom he was steadfastly committed or the children lost to the Shoah (Greenberg's burning children of Auschwitz) who cry out in their silence to our generation.

There is not just a compelling presence enlivening the covenantal gestalt of resurrection; there is also a summoning presence whose otherness demands our attention, again and again. For Jesus, it was the lost of his generation whom he sought to restore to the fellowship of his people. For us, the lost cannot be other than the 6 million lost to the Shoah, especially the 1.5 million children. Only in attending to them and restoring them to their place as the children of Israel (i.e., the people of God) can we tend to others who, like them, need our solidarity and care.[33] In other words, the covenantal healing of Resurrection is unfinished. The Resurrection of Jesus, while bearing the fruits of creation's promise, is good news, yet it remains a representative moment of that promise and, as such, restores those who follow Jesus to the work of restoration and healing that he embodied. We are both sent and summoned by the reality of the not yet.

Coming to Terms with What Happened—A Recurring Task

R. Kendall Soulen's commentary on the Resurrection is helpful as we linger here wondering what to make of this event. Following the lead of many New Testament scholars, Soulen distinguishes between Resurrection and the appearances that follow, differentiating critical moments in this unfolding event. There are first the bare moment of Resurrection, then succeeding moments of recognition, forgiveness and reconciliation, restored fellowship, and finally the sending forth. And each moment is a "meeting" of some kind; throughout, the experience is relational. However, in and of itself, Resurrection stands apart as the given component, the *peshat* of this experience, which is encountered in and through the unfolding consequences of it. First is the recognition of the configuring gestalt of Jesus and the rule and realm of God that he embodied. There is a gestaltlike otherness that gives rise to the recognition without which the rest cannot unfold. In making this point, Hodgson is mindful of the problem of identifying the Resurrection as solely a moment of revelation rooted in the experience of the women and the other disciples only. To be sure, their experience and knowing are essential; whatever the Resurrection is, it does not occur without it. Nevertheless, the Resurrection is more than the subjective or intersubjective experience of those who are grasped by it.

Recognition does not complete the experience, either, for it is followed by a moment of forgiveness and reconciliation wherein the relationship with Jesus and with one another is discovered to be unbroken by their previous denial and abandonment. The configuring gestalt that the disciples witnessed in Jesus, restoring life to others, now reconfigures their world. Even tragic death in which they were complicit could not undo what he gave them. Lastly, the disciples were compelled by this enlivening and reconfiguring presence to reach out and extend its embrace to others in the name of the very one whom it embodied. This was good news indeed. The power of God they met in Jesus was conferred even after their failure to uphold their part of the relationship. The enduring power of covenantal fidelity as they met and knew it in Jesus was disclosed to be stronger than death as well as the torturous crucifixion that Jesus suffered. His passion for life overflowed even this bitter cup and blessed them still. That was an essential part of the Resurrection for them and their testimony afterward. To be sure, this gift remained vulnerable, dependent as it was (and remained) upon their participation in it (through recognition, trust, and their sharing of it). Soulen's summary is succinct:

God vindicates Jesus' trust in the triumph of blessing over curse, life over death, communion over isolation.[34]

The act is representative of the final consummation of creation's goal; hence, it is also its promise. In this sense, it is a triumph over death yet without triumphalistic bravado that is blind to the suffering and anguish of an as yet unfulfilled promise. The story and its consummation remained unfinished. And yet, because of what the disciples encountered after an "opened and empty tomb," they are empowered with new life and hope.

After Auschwitz, the tension between the peril of creation and its covenantal promise is brought to intensive crisis. For many of God's people, the covenantal promise of creation has been lost beyond repair, lying with the powdered bones and ashes in our post-Shoah valley. Consequently, any authentic restoration requires facing those bones and their shadows. And if Emil Fackenheim is correct, any restoration of the house of Israel vis-à-vis the modern State of Israel is a restoration of hope, not of the dead. In other words, the work of restoration and resurrection is starkly vulnerable and includes the burden of resistance rooted in the belief that the lost lives of Israel's children are still of infinite value and not beyond the reach of our covenant fidelity to them. In this regard, we note a convergence of Fackenheim's 614th commandment[35] and Jesus' unrelenting attention to the lost of his generation. Fackenheim proclaims the haunting command that reverberates through the death of 1.5 million Jewish children not to give Hitler a posthumous victory and thereby render their deaths meaningless. For Christians, after Auschwitz, Jesus' commitment to Israel's lost and marginalized must include these same missing children. To make disciples of and for Jesus includes seeking people who will reach out to these lost, these bones, that they may have life on the other side of their death. Only in this fashion, confronting and honoring their particularity, can they become representatives of the lost of other groups and situations.[36] The paradox of Christian belief in Jesus' Resurrection, especially if it is divine confirmation of his life and ministry, is that Christians may not give up on these lost lives of Israel (these bones). Can these bones live? The answer remains vulnerable as does the hope.

The Great Commission Revisited

What do we make of the threefold baptismal formula by which Jesus charged his disciples to reach out to others? How do we read his charge to mission with its reference to ritual action and anticipatory echoes of later Christian doctrine regarding the Trinitarian nature of God? In this reading, baptism and mission are reconfigured. The charge to make disciples of the nations and to baptize in the name of the Father, Son, and Holy Spirit are viewed as ways to incorporate others into the extending reach of Jesus' ministry of inclusion to others, embracing those outside the covenantal community and incorporating them into that community in the name of God as well as the name of the one who represents God and the originary offer of relation, all in the power of promise to bind the One to the other.[37]

Regarding baptism, we can be sure that it was known and understood as a ritual action of restoration and inclusion by which persons sought to be cleansed from their sin and renewed and embraced in the community of God's people. Indeed, Jesus' ministry began with his own baptism at the hand of John the Baptist. In the light of Matthew's review of Jesus' life and ministry, we can be sure he built on a familiar action. Where he pushed the boundaries was in reaching out to others who were marginal at best and separated from their own people and their sacred mission as a witness people. For this reason, we would be wise to focus not on the ritual act as much as the inclusive embrace of others that it represented. By it, those far off were brought near. By it, those separated from their people were restored to community. By it, the not yet included were included.[38] And lest an essential connection be broken, this movement of extension and inclusion reaches from its base in and with the witness people, Israel. Again, the allusive and extensive dimension of *remez* remains linked to its *peshat*.

Clearly, the threefold formula "in the name of the Father, Son, and Holy Spirit" would not have been put forth in Matthew's narrative as a doctrinal understanding of essential Christian belief since that development came much later as result of the work of Augustine in the late third and fourth centuries C.E. Rather, even if the phrase is an editorial gloss added later, it is consistent with the relational intentionality Jesus sees in the heart of God. Post-Shoah this recognition allows and invites us to frame that character covenantally as revealing the very nature of God who has incorporated otherness into the reality of Godself such that otherness is not undone but preserved in and through the power of God's covenanting spirit that we glimpse through the capacities of promise and steadfast fidelity to hold the relation of one and other together. In this manner, differentiation is not undone but upheld in a unity that on our side of the relationship remains an eschatological (and even vulnerable) hope. Such a reading can be instructive for Christians engaged in dialogue with their Jewish siblings. It grounds a goal that does not seek to undo our differentiation, for that would be to oppose the generating dynamic of creation. Instead, the goal is directed toward understanding, respect, and cooperation in the covenantal mission of creation, which each partner is called to pursue in his or her distinctive ways. As we move toward that eschatological horizon we recognize that it is an embrace of life in its fullness and diversity with the hope for a unity that honors the richness that has been its blessing from the beginning. The cup of life truly overflows.

Of course, the tension between Jewish and Christian participation of this divine project remains, but refocused, redirected from its attention to mutual condemnation and contempt for the other toward disagreement regarding the scope and manner of differentiation in an honest conflict of interpretation regarding the life of faith and the rule and realm of God.[39] In the past, however, Christians have interpreted their mission as a responsibility to convert followers to Christianity. Instead, this reading has emphasized the importance and role of representative particularity as it participates in the larger entity to which it points. This is true for mission as well. As a representative people, the followers of Jesus are sent to incorporate others into the covenantal reality of God's rule and realm that they represent while inviting others to join them in bearing this witness. With regard to Jewish siblings, they may be viewed as cowitnesses to the larger reality that includes them all in their particularity. Indeed, as the text reports it, Jesus' disciples are sent to all the nations (*panta ta ethne* in Greek),' which in the context of Matthew's portrait are those who are "other" to Jews; they are those who dwell outside Israel's covenantal identity and world and, for Jesus and his followers, are yet to be embraced in covenantal witness and care.

RETURN TO THE VALLEY

Our midrashic journey from the valley of dry bones to an opened tomb takes us back to the valley of dark shadows where we began, with images from each place haunting the other. Our work remains unfinished and critical. The shadows are revealed for what they truly hide: piles of bones and mountains of ashes in land defiled by violence and the disregard for life. Like Ezekiel, we face the task of restoring promise to a defiled place. The words that he faced stalk our return as well: "Can these bones live?" In their presence, we take up the psalmist's words, recognizing that the cup of blessing that we have been given is held in trembling hands. It has been dropped and cracked before. It has been spilled by careless hands. This time it has been shattered. Painstakingly, it has been pieced together by stained and wounded hands. Each shard bears the marks from where it has been repaired before—more than once. And it has taken many eyes and hands to find missing pieces, refit the parts, and restore its shape—at least as much as can be done, for that work is still in process as well. Nevertheless, when held up for others, the cup overflows with promise and life for those who dare drink from its jagged lip.

Clearly, this reading is tempered by the Christian lenses I wear, even when attempting to view the world through an other's eyes. The words of this commentary form a verbal cup of blessing that overflows with my own Christian hopes. Nevertheless, I am called over and over again to attend to the "very dry bones" in this valley in which we continue to dwell. And I dare not silence the question that addresses me still: Can these bones live?

NOTES

1. In 1985, Elie Wiesel spoke to President Ronald Reagan about his intended visit to the military cemetery in Bitburg, Germany, pleading with him not to go there because it was not his place. A strong sense of defilement of memory and place marked his words. Here, I wish to echo his sensitivity but in order to emphasize the irony and power in Ezekiel's priestly-prophetic work and presence.

2. The actual text employs the divine name preceded by *Adonai*. Wiesel renders the expression *Adoshem*, combining *Adonai* with *HaShem*. See Elie Wiesel, *Sages and Dreamers: Biblical, Talmudic, and Hasidic Portraits and Legends* (New York: Summit Books, 1991), p. 84.

3. There is a paradoxical character to the prophetic word and divine Word that is uttered in partnership, one with the Other. The prophets' words are human and cannot be those of God; and yet God's Word is uttered in and through them. Moreover, without the utterance of the prophetic words of a faithful partner, the divine Word is not made known.

4. Many scholars take this approach, Christians and Jews alike. For example, see Herbert May's commentary in *The Interpreter's Bible* vol. 6, George Buttrick and Samuel Terrien, eds. (Nashville: Abingdon Press, 1956), pp. 41–338, as well as J. H. Hertz's notations in *Pentateuch and Haftorahs* (London: Soncino Press, 5745–1985), p. 1015.

5. We must be careful to avoid a one-to-one correlation between the Shoah and the *Churban* and in doing so implicate the Jews of Europe as being prophetically warned to change their ways, lest they be destroyed. They were not so warned; nor do we wish to imply that what befell them was somehow linked to anything that they did. It was not. The association here is allusive and not meant as precisely parallel.

6. In taking the particularity of the victims lying exposed to the elements and the object of their oppressors' disdain, one is able to recognize the greater expanse of victimhood that extends beyond these bones but not apart from them. For example, when the numbers of the Shoah's Jewish victims are recalled, they represent nearly two thirds of European Jewry. Still, all Jews, especially European Jews, were victims of the Shoah. Though not all of them perished in the death camps, those who did represent the others who died on the way or somewhere else but as a consequence of the same intentionality. Moreover, the 6 million who died in the Shoah were not the only victims, since Judaism, Jewish memory, and even the Jewish dead were targeted as well. Memory and the dead were victims too, oftentimes with the dead being slain twice. In this case, graves may need to be "opened" so that those who were twice killed can be restored their dignity and place in Jewish memory and properly buried. With this dynamic in mind, we have alternative readings that we can suggest, *kivyakhol*, for the shift in the vision from a valley of dry bones to graves and their dead. In this way the shift to allegorical representation does not ignore the specificity of the literally slain.

7. Walther Zimmerli, *Ezekiel*, trans. James D. Martin, ed. Paul D. Hanson, with Richard Jay Greenspoon Vol. 2 (Philadelphia: Fortress Press, 1983), p. 259.

8. Ibid., 2:260.

9. Elie Wiesel, *Memoirs: All Rivers Run to the Sea* (New York: Alfred A. Knopf, 1995), p. 66.

10. Zimmerli, *Ezekiel*, 2:258.

Can These Bones Live?   153

11. Walther Eichrodt explains, "[T]he experience of the vision begins with Ezekiel being *seized* [italics added for emphasis] by the hand of YHWH as in 1:3 and 8:1." Eichrodt recognizes a compelling otherness—a summons from beyond that drives Ezekiel into his vision. See Walther Eichrodt, *Ezekiel*, trans. Cosslett Quin (Philadelphia: Wesminster Press, 1970), p. 507.

12. Joseph Blenkinsopp, *Ezekiel* (Louisville, KY: John Knox Press, 1990), p. 171.

13. Wiesel, *Sages and Dreamers*, p. 92.

14. Wiesel captures the richness of his relationship to what happened. "Although he lived the tragedy from a distance, he agonized over it as if it were his own." Ibid., p. 96.

15. To be sure, there is a theological distinction between resuscitation and resurrection; but not here, lest the shadows of supersessionism creep once more into this valley.

16. Emile Fackenheim, *The Jewish Bible After the Holocaust: A Re-reading* (Bloomington and Indianapolis: Indiana University Press, 1990), p. 67.

17. While the text does not explicitly name a battle, it implies fighting of some kind, whether in battle or in defense against a massacre. More precisely, their death is a consequence of violence.

18. Fackenheim, *The Jewish Bible After the Holocaust*, p. 67.

19. The Synagogue, for example, emerged as one of the institutional forms capable of giving voice and focus to the life of Jewish faith in the exilic period. It provided an alternative path of study and prayer outside the sacerdotal system of the Temple.

20. Fackenheim, *The Jewish Bible after the Holocaust*, p. 49.

21. Ibid., p. 67.

22. Ibid., p. 68.

23. "It is not for you, O house of Israel, that I am about to act, but for the sake of my holy name."

24. See chapter 4 in this volume for further elaboration of an inclusive reading of covenant life.

25. William Butler Yeats, "The Second Coming," *Selected Poems and Two Plays of William Butler Yeats*, ed. M. L. Rosenthal (New York: Collier Books, 1962), p. 91.

26. Ibid.

27. Wiesel, *Sages and Dreamers*, p. 82.

28. The adverb *otherwise* carries an interesting double entendre in this context. On the one hand, it suggests the logic of *al tiqre*, suggesting an alternative reading. On the other hand, to read this text *otherwise* suggests an understanding of the other that is integrated with some measure of wisdom—perhaps the very point of a post-Shoah reading.

29. Interestingly, these instructions are not preserved in the Matthean narrative until they are so mentioned.

30. Matthew's Gospel began by informing his readers that Jesus was called Emmanuel, God with us; he concludes in similar fashion, returning to the theme that has subtly punctuated the entire narrative.

31. Thorwald Lorenzen, *Resurrection and Discipleship: Interpretive Models, Biblical Reflections, Theological Consequences* (Maryknoll, NY: Orbis Books, 1995), p. 181.

32. Peter C. Hodgson, *Winds of the Spirit* (Louisville, KY: Westminster/John Knox Press, 1994), p. 271.

33. Once again, the allegorical reference (*remez*) of Scripture grows out of the givenness of its plain meaning (*peshat*). Rowan Williams in his brief, but insightful, meditation on Resurrection speaks of the task of giving voice to the voiceless as an act of the Resurrection community. His caution is apropos here, especially if we link the mission of Resurrection with the priestly-prophetic work of Ezekiel:

> To speak for the victim, for the forgotten and killed, requires not only the Spirit's truthfulness, to give us the awareness of this "memory of suffering," but also an opening of our mouths: boldness to speak, to venture into the uncomfortable world of assertion and counter-assertion, debate, accusation and defence. Identification with the suffering is not only a matter of inner sympathy, nor is it only a matter of action. It means also the hard work of intelligent interpretation of the needs of the "voiceless."

Rowan Williams, *Resurrection: Interpreting the Easter Gospel* (Harrisburg, PA: Morehouse Publishing, 1982), p. 69.

34. R. Kendall Soulen, *The God of Israel and Christian Theology* (Minneapolis: Augsburg Fortress, 1996), p. 165.

35. "Thou shalt give Adolf Hitler no posthumous victories." See Emil Fackenheim, *God's Presence in History: Jewish Affirmations and Philosophical Reflections* (New York: Harper Torchbooks, 1970), p. 84.

36. Again, the allusive meanings of *remez*—allegory—must grow out of the plain meaning/givenness of *peshat*.

37. The liturgical echoes in this passage, whether or not they were added to the text later, are extended nonetheless by those acting in the liturgical now of hearing them read in worship.

38. See chapter 4, "From the Bush to the Vineyard (and Back)," for a more thorough exploration of this dynamic.

39. The hermeneutical task need not be to remove the differentiation between God's people and the world but to rethink the way we name and approach that differentiation. *Clean* and *unclean* may be recast as *clean* and *not yet clean*, *included* and *excluded* might yield to *included* and *not yet included*. Israel and the new Israel might be designated *Israel proper* and the *extended commonwealth of Israel*. In this fashion, the hermeneutical tension could be creative and life-serving, not destructive and life-diminishing.

6

Looking Back over the Journey: Theological Implications for Post-Shoah Faithfulness

As we approach the close of this hermeneutical experiment, we pause for one more glance back, to identify and claim some of the truths discovered along the way. They emerge in the process of attending to the world mediated by the text and reconfigured in the encounter with it and our Shoah-tempered perspective. Whether or not they are anything more than one post-Shoah Christian's confession will be up to others to confirm or challenge. This is the nature of midrashic authority, just as it is the way of all Christian witness. Whether or not an individual confession takes its place within the boundaries of Christian witness, the Body of Christ, is finally not up to the individual who bears his or her witness. It must be confirmed by others within the larger body. Consequently, these insights are offered here as one expression of the kind of personal credo, which can orient and guide Christian fidelity in the shadows of extreme violence and devastation.

MIDRASHIC THEOLOGY

At the heart of this project is a recovery of Jewish literary tradition (that is, the way of midrash) as a resource for Christian theology. It is at once a breakthrough to a critical methodology capable of moving beyond the impasses of modern theology[1] at the same time that it is a return to the confessional roots of Scripture. Midrash offers an alternative way of being critically faithful in the modern world without relying on the Enlightenment traditions of rationality and human autonomy that have been seriously undercut by the tragic events of the last sixty to seventy years. The midrashic option pursued here adopts the interpretive strategy of viewing and reading Scripture as a multivalent and multivoiced text that mediates an overarching, though at times ambiguous, narrated tradition as well as a lived partnership of covenantal regard for life in its myriad aspects. In this regard, it shares a great deal with narrative theology but includes as well the enigmas and anomalies that overflow the storied cup of tradition. Midrash is thus a way of embracing narrative, as narrative, while also engaging those aspects of our lived experience that do not fit within the plot structures of our narratives.[2] In other words, while strongly rooted in biblical narrative, the midrashic way is not reduced to narrative. Likewise, while textually based, midrash is not restricted to the text but linked to it in a dialectical relationship, mediating the larger, narrated[3] world in which the text participates at the same time it points to it: *PaRDeS*. That is, midrash configures its world in several voices and textual forms, some direct and many indirect. Together, they portray a richly textured world punctuated with challenges and problems that arise when actual, lived experience fails to fit within the interpretive frameworks of previous renderings. In this fashion, midrash is both conservative and creative, profoundly serious and liberatingly playful. Midrashic Christian theology finds in this rich but latent resource within Jewish tradition a way of moving forward that is both responsible to and with the past at the same time it is responsible for the future.

Throughout this volume, I have maintained a distinction between midrash per se and a midrashic approach to theology. Nonetheless, midrashic theology, like midrash, is a form of threshold thinking. Each mediates encounter with the literal qualities of the text in such fashion that they break open the text's figurative dimension and configuring power for renewed participation and further discovery of what the text offers. Similarly, as threshold thinking, midrashic theology participates both in the self-referential world configured by the text and the lived world of experience that the text represents and addresses.

Midrashic theology also moves beyond the debate encountered between so-called Christocentric and Theocentric approaches by challenging the configuring dynamic of "centric" theologies of any kind. They tend toward univocal systems even when complexly nuanced. They indicate a preference for a singular, unifying thread of meaning to tie the larger texts of tradition together. A midrashic way of doing theology recognizes the multivocal and multivalent character of the biblical tradition and proceeds with sensitivity to the richness of an ecologically configured way of viewing life. Instead of a single center, many centers interact in a greater wholeness, signaling a fundamental appreciation for the generative rhythms of differentiation and integration that empower life. Indeed, this very dynamic expresses an unfolding wonder vis-à-vis creation and contributes to a reconfiguring of the call and power of creation itself.

CREATION REVISITED

Configured explicitly in such texts as Genesis 1–11 and Psalm 8 as well as tacitly throughout Scripture, the spirit of creation also animates the interpretive dynamics of midrash. Each serves the emergence of a more significantly differentiated and integrated expression of life. Behind this dynamic, the eyes of faith behold the wonder of creation as a sacred embrace of otherness, a divine choice for life in a fundamental commitment of the Holy One for the many others of creation and its radical expression of otherness. Relation and relationship are chosen in an ultimate embrace of life that the language of faith calls creation. And midrash, serving this dance of life, builds on the rhythms of differentiation and integration[4] in recursive fashion, recapitulating the work of creation in the very acts of interpretation that fund our lives.

In a literal but not fundamentalist sense, the power of creation is revisited. That is, when the notion of creation is used as a lens for viewing life, it is capable of providing critical as well as conservative and confessional perspective from which to engage the unfolding complexities of life, even modern ones. Its power is the orienting power of a lens. Just as a lens has the power to reflect and refract light, an interpretive framework like creation has capacities for orienting those who view life through its interpretive window. Its power to focus can provide needed clarity in confusing times and circumstances. Likewise, its focusing power can help identify important ground on which to stand. As well, its power to refract can provide valuable assistance in seeing what too often goes unnoticed in the day-to-day moments of our lives. And its power to concentrate light can generate energy and passion in the service of many projects and desires.

In these reflections, the dynamics of differentiation and integration are seen at the service of the unfolding richness of life. At the level of human experience, such dynamics call forth a choice for relation and an ongoing commitment to that choice in a relationship that faith identifies as covenantal. Life is to be lived in service of others. From the beginning, the Holy One has chosen life for the other/others. Furthermore, the Holy One invites the choosing of life in service of the other to be recapitulated in each choosing other who follows. As a radical embrace of otherness, creation would imply that even that which would oppose and deny this dance of life (a radical other to the One who chose life at the beginning) would be risked as well. In other words, the shadow side of the wonder of creation is also its radical risk—hence, the urgent significance of the other's role in creation as creation.

COVENANTAL REGARD FOR THE OTHER

Life is fundamentally relational, but from this perspective, life is not *just* relational. It needs a reciprocating choice for otherness that leads forward to the increase of otherness. Life fundamentally requires a commitment to the differentiated other that in valuing otherness respects the other's relative autonomy. In other words, the intentionality of life lived for the other is covenantal. As human beings recognize their place in life, they discover themselves peculiarly qualified to exercise choice in life's regard. If life is thoroughly relational, then responsibility for those myriad relationships is called for, with particular manifestations representative of the whole. Furthermore, when that responsibility is understood within the context of a covenantal ecology of the whole, the focus is not on covenant per se but on life, relationally configured and embraced through the prism of covenantal regard for the other.

We must be careful with our phrasing here. Life is served—covenantally. The glue in this mix is promise and fidelity. And its form is covenantal, but the end is not covenant. The goal is life in its differentiated and integrated richness lived and steadfastly honored in relationship. At the heart of this project has been a refocusing of attention from a substantive concern for specific covenants to the covenantal character of life when life is lived and cared for with sustained commitment to its relationships. This orientation does not focus on the establishment of covenants per se but on the fundamental gift of life and its rich, relational intentionality that covenants bring to particular and shared expression.

Midrashic theology, as it rehearses the same dynamics, likewise serves the dance of life. It too unfolds covenantally, accountable to others, modified by others, and respectful of others. Midrashic theology even recognizes and engages the text as an other with whom it relates covenantally. Moreover, the expanding reach of covenant leads to a rethinking of more traditional Christian, doctrinal matters. They have been hinted at throughout the text but can be more specifically identified and summarized here.

COMING TO TERMS WITH JESUS

At the heart of any Christian confession is the figure of Jesus. Christians in some fashion are each called upon to come to terms with him as Christ and Savior. In the shadows of the Shoah, this aspect of Christian fidelity emerges as a significant challenge. The post-Shoah Christian is not simply accountable to the demands of Auschwitz but also to the traditions of the Church as well as to the realities of that Christian's relationship with this central figure in his or her world. The Transfiguration of Jesus to Christ is an essential component of each Christian's confessional experience. Yet, in the shadows of Auschwitz, that Transfiguration must be reexamined. Nonetheless, it remains essential, even if reconfigured. Our encounter with the Sinai traditions and the story of Transfiguration in Matthew makes this clear. As a consequence of that encounter, how Christians relate to Jesus as God's representative figure has far-reaching implications. However, even putting the observation this way already prefigures the change in perspective that follows from the encounter.

In the shadows of Sinai and Auschwitz, Jesus may no longer have credibility as the key figure in a triumphalistic or supersessionary theology. But he can have central and representative power as the full embodiment of the divine intention for creation without participating in the structural (even if unintended) violence of previous understandings. Indeed, looking back at the face of Matthew's transfigured Jesus, it is my claim that we meet

the Representative One for Christians who represents God's covenantal intentions for life as well as God's own covenantal embrace of life revealed and concealed in the very act of creation and articulated for Israel at Sinai;

the Representative Other in whose face Christians meet and face up to the covenantal claims of otherness, whether encountered in others or in themselves;

the uniquely Representative One for Christians who represents the covenantal image of God, reflecting and fulfilling our place in creation as creatures constituted in such fashion.

In this sense, for post-Shoah Christians, he can be Emmanuel, God with us, as Matthew presents him, this time through Shoah-tempered lenses.

Of course, one cannot speak of Jesus as God's representative without also speaking about the work he does as that representative. In theological terms, Christology and Soteriology are interrelated. How then does a post-Shoah Christian come to terms with the issue of Salvation?

Historically, the Church has articulated the saving work of Christ using four complementary models: Exemplar, Substitute (or Satisfaction), Conqueror (Christus Victor), or Abiding Presence. And more recently, a fifth model has emerged: Liberator. The exemplar model clearly emphasizes the Galilean ministry and teachings of Jesus. The substitution/satisfaction models are oriented toward the Passion and Crucifixion of Jesus, whereas the Christus Victor model emphasizes the Resurrection. The emphasis on abiding presence is oriented more philosophically to the whole of Jesus' life, and the liberation model focuses on Jesus' liberating actions regarding the poor, disenfranchised, and oppressed.

Salvation has been viewed primarily as an expression of one of these models complemented by the others. What is fundamental to all of them is that the Jesus story itself is the orienting narrative for how Christians come to experience and understand that which they call Salvation, with Christology providing their theological grounding. Our midrashic experiment invites the recognition of an alternative: a covenantal approach that, most importantly, would be grounded not in Christology but along with it in the covenantal intention for life that began at creation.

In other words, unlike much Christocentric theology, both Christology and Soteriology would be rooted in a covenantal theology of creation, although Christology could still be the primary point of confessional entry into this orientation. That is to say, Salvation is viewed as a derivative doctrine, in this case, from a covenantal understanding of creation. Ontologically, Salvation is not of the same order as creation; it is restorative. Any claims that Salvation is primary, that is, a first-order doctrine, would be implying that the divine goal of life from the beginning has been Salvation. Of course, many have claimed exactly that. Still, that would mean that the brokenness of creation was likewise a primary, albeit instrumental, goal, for it would be the prerequisite of Salvation. And after Auschwitz, that simply is unacceptable.

To treat any rupture in creation as intended by God, or any suffering as instrumental to a greater divine plan, is problematic. God chose life—life in relation—a fragile and precious project that has time and again been threatened and thwarted by the misuse of the freedom that accompanied the divine choice for life in relation. We call that estrangement *sin*, but not sin only. Our estrangement may also include the consequences of sin: oppression and violence done to others who often bear no responsibility for what has happened to them. Their suffering is equally a contradiction of God's intention for creation, but it is not necessarily sin. From a covenantal perspective, Salvation, a return to the relational wholeness and health intended for creation, is an act, a movement, a process of restoration and/or inclusion that brings about a rejoining of the original purpose to those estranged from it, which for human beings is not just any kind of relation but an entrusted partnership we identify with the term *covenant*. Salvation, from this vantage point, also includes the restoration of the freedom necessary for life in relation, covenant life, to be chosen or rejected. Put positively and confessionally, the goal of creation is creation, not redemption. Redemption is the restoration of creation.

Forgiveness should be viewed in a similar way. Just as there is more than one way to look back, there is more than one way to forgive or seek forgiveness. If Salvation is to be truly restorative, forgiveness, when called for, must be based on memory, fully facing and facing up to one's past. It must therefore be distinguished from forgiveness that is based on forgetfulness. Indeed, in the name of true reconciliation, the former must resist the latter. Furthermore, neither forgiveness nor Salvation is the end toward which we are to live in covenantal fidelity. From a covenantal perspective, they serve the larger goal of the restored relationship.[5]

RENDERING GOOD NEWS

Looking back at Sodom through the midrashic eyes of Abraham and Jesus led us to recognize the essential nature of hospitality for anyone hopeful of living in accord with God's intentions for life. Indeed, Jesus linked the presence of hospitality with the good news of the dawning of God's kingdom in such ways that we are invited to recognize the relationship between hospitality and Christianity's fundamental message to be essential. Whether one views the good news of Christianity in relationship to Salvation or the fulfillment of God's purposes for creation, our exploration invites us to see the essential connection between hospitality and the good news of and about Jesus. Indeed, hospitality is nothing less than the interpersonal embodiment of the rule and realm of God. Its presence is good news, for the breaches in creation are repaired when hospitality is practiced and strangers are welcomed, the excluded are included, the wounded are healed.

Moreover, in recognizing the essential connection between the proclamation of good news with the presence of hospitality, post-Shoah Christians are given guidance in where and how they may go forth as emissaries of grace in a world marked by violence and hatred. First, they are sent looking for hospitality, not for persons to confront or convert. When found, they are to proclaim its greater significance; and when absent they are instructed to move on. After Auschwitz they must be prepared to recognize that there are places where such grace is missing absolutely and not necessarily because of anything for which the victims of its violence may bear any responsibility. In this regard, where hospitality is absent, post-Shoah disciples of Matthew's Jesus will do well to move on, but toward those in need of the hospitality being sought, knowing that the closer one moves to the victims of such situations, the more they must embody in their hospitality the very good news they seek to proclaim.

Still, there is a credibility crisis with this good news. What saves it from being the disguised usurpation of the other's identity? What saves it from the glorification of human misery or of the missionary conquest of triumphalistic preaching and theology? Again, our midrashic experiment grounds us in a different reading of the saving work of Jesus. It is restorative work meant to bring others into the responsible stewardship of creation.

For Christians, the life, ministry, and continuing impact of Jesus of Nazareth are the focused embodiments of covenant life and care that orient me, and others like me, to the divine intention for creation. Through these embodiments we can know covenant life to be extensive as well as intensive, including and inclusive, steadfast and ever lasting. The Passion Story is pivotal in coming to terms with this. Typically, Christians focus on the suffering Jesus underwent, focusing on the sacrificial character of his life and death. In doing so, meaning is assigned to his death as an act of expiation or propitiation, to use terms Christians often hear in their liturgies; or satisfaction or substitution, to use terms from the traditional models of Atonement. The emphasis, of course, is on the meaningfulness of Jesus' death as a substitute payment to God or a representative offering to balance one sinless life against all others who accept such a gift. In either case, the meaning is in Jesus' sacrificial death, with Christians referring to this act as Christ dying for our sins. Moreover, it is the good news the Church proclaims in Jesus' name. In the face of what we know about suffering in our age, viewing Jesus' suffering, much less anyone's, as having intrinsic meaning is problematic and serves the glorification of victimization. Our encounter with the Gethsemane story helps us see another way, viewing Jesus' Passion as a radical commitment to covenant life that retains the power to heal and transform even in the face of rejection and death. Liberated from the lens of viewing Jesus' Passion as a sacrificial requirement of God, Christians are free to see Jesus' choices for life, particularly covenant life, that manifest his commitment to covenant relationship as he chooses to take his message to the city he deeply loves yet that is filled with danger, as well as to disciples whom he expects to deny, fall away, and even betray him. In the face of abandonment, rejection, and most probably death, Jesus still chooses life, covenantally bound to those who resist him. The point: Jesus' Passion need not glorify suffering and victimization. Instead, without changing any of what happened, a covenantal reading of this material recognizes a radical passion for covenant life *in the face of* death and abandonment, even in the face of covenant life's greatest threat—betrayal. To choose covenant relationship in such circumstances is to break the cycle of rejection and betrayal (i.e., the power of death) at its point of violation.

Salvation, from this perspective, is the embrace of covenant life, as it includes me and others in its fundamental and relational promise of life—forgiving, fulfilling, empowering, restoring, and challenging us to participate in the ongoing work of creation. As a Christian, I view this as good news. It is an embrace that Jesus embodied and extended to those who followed him—and that, in his name, has been extended to me. The good news of post-Shoah faith is the good news of inclusion in God's covenantal embrace of life in and through God's representative one, Jesus. Yet it is not an embrace that undoes the pain of radical destruction and humiliation. Instead, it confronts it again and again in profound sadness and grief, needing the response of partners in hospitality to make it real.

After Auschwitz, it is the Christian's task to render the good news of covenantal hospitality where it is practiced and to embody it where it is absent. In moving beyond inhospitable ways with others, Christians do well to remember that they are included ones as they reach out to welcome and include others. As hosts, we recall that we are "guests in the house of Israel,"[6] to use Clark Williamson's phrase. In this regard, there is still more work to be done and even contention ahead. For as included ones, followers of Christ cannot help but see the excluding dangers of the categories of *clean* and *unclean*. And as Gentiles our hospitality will move outside these distinctions. Even post-Shoah this will remain a problematic distinction for us, including some and excluding others. Our contribution to the abundance of covenant life may be to contend with our Jewish siblings not to convert them but in order to make this a creative, life-yielding tension revealing for each of us an even larger view of God's ways. But in the process, we may find ourselves called to move beyond the distinctions between *saved* and *unsaved* as well. After Auschwitz, that may be good news we are yet to hear.

REFOCUSING MISSION

What kind of mission is associated with hospitality? Clearly we cannot wander about simply doing hospitality; that, in effect, puts the shoe on the other foot. Instead, we can venture forth—calling attention to the full significance of the hospitality we meet along the way. Proclaiming the fulfillment of creation's goal in each instance, it is embodied in the hospitable embrace of others. Like a seed, hospitality grows and spreads as it is recognized for what it is, welcomed and embraced for the future, and passed on to others. In a world marked by violence, the occurrence of hospitality is good news indeed. When seen as an enacted parable of the intention of creation punctuating ordinary life, hospitality becomes an encounterable gestalt of meaning and hope we can refer to as the rule and realm of God unfolding in our midst. The implications for Christian mission are profound.

Jesus identified the vineyard in Matthew 20 with God's purposes for creation, what he called the rule and realm of heaven (God). It has been identified here with covenant life. Inclusion in its divine embrace is nothing less than the fulfillment of God's intention for creation. The one who includes is the landowner—over and over, Jesus directs his listeners to attend to the landowner in the story, not to him. In other words, through the parable, Jesus conveys that the very purpose of creation is inclusive and grounded in the Creator, the Sovereign One of creation. The spirit of inclusion, which, for Christians Jesus embodies, is rooted, for him, in the One he serves.

Accordingly, we are called to participate in God's mission of creation by joining our sovereign covenantal partner as well as inviting others (individuals, groups, communities, institutions) to join us, in an ever-increasing covenantal regard for life. As Christians, we do so in and through the one who included us, the Jew, Jesus of Nazareth. And we do so as we meet him in the apostolic witness of Scripture, in the testimony of significant people in our lives, in our own experiences of study, worship, and service in the Church and beyond.

More specifically, through Jesus, Jews marginalized in their own communities (women, tax collectors, prostitutes, lepers, and other untouchables) as well as Samaritans and some non-Jews (e.g., the Roman centurion) were included in Jesus' embrace of covenant life. He extended the reach of covenantal care to many believed beyond reach. He included those thought to be outside the covenant community. In other words, he included the unincluded, even the excluded. This is the story, at least, in part, that Christians, as included ones, tell about the inclusive embrace of covenant life that for us is embodied and grounded in Jesus.

Nevertheless, as included ones, we must be clear about this covenantal project that includes us. It is mediated representatively by Jesus, a covenantally faithful partner in this fundamental enterprise of creation. Jesus comes to his covenantal fidelity as a Jew; that is, Jesus is a faithful child of Israel. His covenantal partner is the God of Abraham, Isaac, and Jacob; the God of Sarah, Rebecca, and Rachel. As Christians, then, we can affirm that the covenantal purpose of creation is revealed in and through Israel even when we confess that the same purpose is not restricted to Israel, for Israel's election is to bear witness, as a priestly people, to the abiding covenantal intentionality of life that forever includes Israel, even as it surpasses Israel. Furthermore, we make the same qualification regarding the Church: The covenantal project that includes Christians is not to be exclusively and restrictively identified with the Church, for creation's goal surpasses the Church even as it includes the Church.[7]

As we look at the restorative work we are called to do, we should not overlook the issue of forgiveness and its place both in the good news we bear and in the work we are commissioned to undertake. In the shadows of Shoah, we should distinguish between forgiveness based on memory and forgiveness based on forgetfulness. In the name of true reconciliation, the former must resist the latter. And in the spirit of divine hospitality, the good news of post-Shoah Christianity is that forgiveness is possible—but we must be ever more careful in how we embody this part of our work with others.

The goal of covenant life, and therefore the goal of our mission, is neither Salvation nor forgiveness, restoration nor liberation, but fidelity—faithfulness, loyalty to the covenantal intention for life. To be sure, the covenantal purpose in our lives and in the world is often imperiled, even blocked. It is a fragile and precious project, at once threatened and thwarted by the very freedom it requires. Salvation and forgiveness, restoration and liberation, each in their ways, serve this larger vision by addressing the crises, which prevent creation's promise from being experienced and fulfilled. When we step through any of these doorways in pursuit of the relational wholeness that fulfills the promise of creation, we participate in the stewardship of creation that has been our vocation from the beginning. In this way, the particular mission of post-Shoah Christianity is joined to the mission of God in which we are all invited to participate.

To be sure, this is not something any one of us can give ourselves, as life is not something any of us can give ourselves. That is one of the critical points of the creation story. Such a gift must come from an Other who, in the power of covenantal embrace, can break through another one's solitariness and restore their own world as well as their shared world and even God's world—if we have the eyes to see and an openness to receive and participate in such a gift.

FACING GOD ANEW

In each midrashic encounter, we have been called upon to face God in more enigmatic ways. At the Jabbok, we learned there are some things we cannot name and some we can. Jacob, through his intimate wrestling with issues of integrity and fidelity to every significant other in his life, encountered the deeper significance of his wrestling and named the place of encounter while leaving the one he encountered unnamed by him. Jesus, wrestling with his issues of integrity and fidelity, chose to be faithful to the covenant commitments of his life and world even in the face of their rejection by those he cared for most dearly in his life. Looking back at the destruction of Sodom and Gomorrah, the gaze of Abraham and Jesus focused on the presence of hospitality as the determining factor in their understandings of divinity encountered in the workings of history. Standing simultaneously in the shadows of Auschwitz and at Sinai as well as on an unnamed Galilean peak, our eyes are turned toward a transfiguring encounter with the Summoning Other of Sinai. Root experiences are revisited and even reconfigured in the images of God borne by faithful and unfaithful people alike. Summoned by the burning bush of his people's suffering, Moses discerned the very identity and call of God in his being called to responsibility and partnership in liberating his people and leading them to a land of promise and peril to take up the work of covenant life. The Covenanting Other, the very One Who Is Absolutely, speaks in and through this burning experience as *I AM–you are . . . for others, for your people*. And the same Eternal One reaches out through a story of a vineyard capable of including others within the divine covenantal embrace. Then staring at a valley filled with carnage and destruction we are asked by the One we seek to ask: Can these who are lost absolutely be recovered and given new life? The response of faithful agnosticism suggests an openness and commitment even to the dead that remains critically open to life. Likewise, approaching the opened and empty tomb of Jesus leads to the covenantal gestalt known in and through Jesus as capable of transfiguring even the ignominious death he risked and endured. And in each case, more is learned about the limits of our knowing and the ways of a God beyond easy theologizing.

Every step of the way, the very gift of the hospitality of creation (to support life chosen and cared for by those given its freedom) is discerned as ever precious and fragile, as well as the fundamental choice of that One we know as *I AM–you are . . . for others*. At every step, creation is at stake, and we are at stake, as the divine host of life awaits our response to this divine gift of life in hospitality to the other.

Whether wrestling with questions of personal integrity, or matters of fidelity to our most fundamental promises and relationships, or the invitation to take one's place in a covenantal vineyard, the identity of God has been relationally rendered, but always through the indirection of metaphor and allusion. God's relationship to history and human behavior has been similarly configured, and divine agency is affirmed but hidden in the mixed agency of covenantal fidelity. In the midst of covenantal configurations, something more is mediated, revealing a sacred dimension undergirding life in relational fashion. In the midst of history, God's hospitality, like ours, requires the response of the other to be fully embodied and enjoyed. Still, we are able to know this One as the Other before whom and in whom we have our being.

As Christians, we know this Covenanting Other through the embodied hospitality of Jesus, in whom and through whom we refocus our attention on the significance of hospitality to the other. Hospitality becomes the human face, the metaphoric veil through which we glimpse the God of history and creation. Likewise, hospitality to the other becomes the torn veil through which we look back at the shadowed ground of Auschwitz.

God, in hospitality, lets being be; God, in hospitality, lets creation be and history unfold. Similarly, hospitality becomes the lens that refracts and focuses our view of Jesus as he remains for Christians the face of the invisible God. Only now we approach him through our own prism of post-Shoah anguish and shame. Divine hospitality to life becomes the rubric through which we see the Creating and Covenanting God at work in history, making room for our partnership in the project we call creation, beckoning our participation, even imploring it, yet never once violating our part in crossing the threshold at which the invitation is offered to take our place in the Eternal One's domain. Furthermore, we are addressed in this domain by One who remains neither object nor subject of any part of creation but present as dimension and other, agent and process, beyond all differentiation or integration. Finally, we stand, in that hospitality, in the presence of One whom we know addresses us *I AM–you are . . . for others.*

THE PROVIDENCE OF HOSPITALITY

In our time, hospitality may very well be the most appropriate way, biblically as well as critically, for depicting God's way with creation, both as creator and as sustainer. Its movement is active and other oriented but without being intrusive or manipulative. Human freedom—the freedom of the other to be other—is respected and never violated. The hospitable host actively prepares to embrace and entertain the other. Indeed, the host anticipates the coming of the other. Nonetheless, the other must respond in order for the preparation to move fully to the embrace of welcome and hospitality to be realized.

As hospitality unfolds, the host sets a table, feting the guest in the host's domain, sharing with the guest a token of the host's abundance. Ritualized at table with food and drink, the shared exuberance is not restricted to its ritual expression. Such is the nature of the graces of life, which Jesus likened to the inbreaking rule and realm of God.

In the end, hospitality is distinguished by the rest and safety provided by the host. Importantly and perhaps essentially, this rest and safety are vulnerable entities. In Sodom, for example, Lot was forced to confront an angry crowd out to do violence to his guests. Yet, in standing up for his guests, he had to be defended by them and pulled to safety by their action. Moreover, his own protective actions betrayed the sanctuary of his own home as he offered his daughters to the crowd and its violence. Portrayed in ambiguous circumstances as well as by imperfect though representative persons, the vulnerable character of hospitality is accentuated even more.

Seen through the metaphoric lens of hospitality, providence emerges as a much more vulnerable notion of God's ways with creation. Even so, as Abraham, Lot, Jesus, and others demonstrate, hospitality is not a tentative act. In its responsiveness, it is highly active, but always with respect toward the other and the other's freedom to be other. Reframing divine providence in terms of hospitality should not be mistaken, however, as a simple substitution of vocabulary for traditional approaches to this issue that distinguish the differences between divine and human freedom. The vantage point of hospitality and what it means to remain steadfastly committed to it makes a profound and fundamental difference.

THE RISK OF HOSPITALITY

There is another side to hospitality, which we must not overlook or ignore, especially in the aftermath of the Shoah. In responding to life hospitably, life does not always reciprocate the gesture. More specifically, there are others who do not welcome otherness in their lives and in whose presence anyone other to them is fundamentally threatened. Hospitality to them is not simply dangerous; it can be perilous in the extreme. After Auschwitz we cannot simply advocate a naive approach to the other with an equally naive understanding of the virtue of hospitality. With this critical recognition, then, how does one proceed, remaining committed to the movement of hospitality in life yet alert to its violation and the perils of its practice?

The risk of hospitality must not be understated. Openness to the stranger can and may lead to death. When one is open to the other without qualification, then one risks facing an other who does not choose to regard all others as worthy of his or her recognition as such. After the Shoah, this risk must be seen for what it is—the specter of death on the horizon of choosing unqualified openness to the other. For Christians, if they read the Passion of Jesus as a radical embrace of covenant life, as I have, then St.

Paul's admonition that the cross of Jesus is a stumbling block for Jews (1 Cor. 1:23) takes on new and troubling meaning. That is, the risk of hospitality, when radically embraced, can lead to crucifixion. Radical hospitality, in this reading, is the stumbling block signified by the cross of Jesus. After the Shoah, it remains so, but not just for Jews. It is a stumbling block for anyone who would regard covenant life as the divine intention for creation. After the Shoah, we know that the risk of hospitality can lead to staggering and tragic results. If the good news proclaimed by Christians is tied in an essential way to this risk, then after Auschwitz, we must ask, "What makes that news good?" or else we risk falling over it later.

The risk and ultimately the cost of radical hospitality are not unknown to Israel. Indeed, it is possible to read the Book of Job as a lament in this regard. That is, if creation unfolds as an ongoing act of hospitality, then given the suffering and evil that creation has endured, how can Job ever hope to fathom God's anguish? How can Job, who has reached his limits, know such grief as that, for Job grieves for only his family, not for all the families of creation? Radical hospitality is a high-risk venture, and the cost can be beyond imagination.

According to Matthew, Jesus embodied this risk in his Passion. His embrace of the other included the other who could and would betray, deny, and crucify him. He withheld his hospitality from no one in his company. However, as Matthew reports the commissioning in Matthew 10, he describes a different and more circumspect approach. Here, Jesus instructs his disciples to look for others who are hospitable to them. When met with hospitality, they are to articulate its significance, to extend and deepen it by declaring how it fulfills the very intentions of God for creation. Still, Matthew reports Jesus' awareness of the danger of this task, warning his disciples to be "wise as serpents and gentle as doves."[8] His caution immediately follows the commissioning and is accompanied by a depiction of conflict and persecution, which includes the resistance of synagogues and their leaders. With our understanding of the conflictual circumstances of Matthew's time near the end of the first century, we are most probably encountering aspects of that conflict in this report. Nonetheless, we may discern a critical and abiding word of caution. Jesus advises his disciples to exercise discretion and good judgment as they undertake their mission. As we read the material post-Shoah, we can likewise practice similar care, attempting to be "wise as serpents and gentle as doves" for the sake of hospitality. Retaining the spirit of caution and openness, which Jesus advocates, we can resist the negative portrayal of Jewish leaders in the text while retaining the wisdom that comes from knowing hospitality's violations. Such an approach suggests that at times it may be appropriate to withhold the invitation to hospitality or be wary of responding too quickly to an overly facile gesture of it. At other times, circumstances might require qualifying the invitation. Nonetheless, the practice of such discretion would always occur within the larger movement toward hospitality, with the moment of recognition taking on increased significance in the light cast by the pyres of Auschwitz.

Our recognition that hospitality, as a fundamental goal for life, can be thwarted by failing to be careful in our search for its presence compounds the risk it seeks to transform. Including all others indiscriminately, can lead to a diminishment of hospitality especially when large numbers of those so included exclude and give exclusion increased power and presence. This is fearfully clear in the case of Nazi Germany. As a result, we are driven back to Jesus' admonition to his disciples when he sent them forth to look for hospitality. They were commissioned to look for places where they would be welcome *as guests*. As guests, they were then charged to proclaim their good news, the significance of their host's action and the inbreaking of God's ways in their midst. Embracing the rejecting other was reserved for other times and other places, with the accompanying recognition that in the case of a rejecting, imperial power, the rejection risked in that situation was a one-time life or death affair, no matter how much the dynamic of radical inclusion informed the overall movement toward that occasion. In this way, we should be careful not to confuse the radical hospitality of Jesus with an indiscriminate embrace of all others.

Christians must live in the tension between this radical act of hospitality and more strategic acts, as guests in the worlds of others must.[9] Even so, radical hospitality still holds the key for how Christians view God's ways in the world. If hospitality to the other is God's way with creation and essential to the covenantal vocation of human beings, then it can only be embraced in spite of and with full awareness of its risk. Furthermore, the risk of hospitality will remain a stumbling block, not in a pejorative sense but as a warning to the perils of taking such a path. In this way, radical hospitality does not cease to be a stumbling block even after it is risked; but it is chosen (not coerced or proscribed) and confessed with the full awareness of what is being risked. The way of hospitality becomes, then, a high-risk venture sustained by the promise of life that it serves, but ever vigilant to the dangers along the way. Only then can such hospitality be a cornerstone of fidelity to a fuller expression of covenant life. And even then, it risks otherwise.

RELATING TO DOCTRINE (INCARNATION AND TRINITY)

While midrashic theology is not dogmatic, it is more than capable of bridging the narrated world of text and doctrine. Two doctrinal touchstones invite brief commentary in this regard, indicating how these bridges might be built and traversed: Incarnation and Trinity.

At the core of Christian identity is the fundamental belief in the Incarnation, that God is somehow fully present in the life of Jesus of Nazareth. The portrait derived in this study from the Gospel of Matthew is a representative figure who represents the human promise of covenant faithfulness to others and to God while demonstrating for humanity the steadfast faithfulness of a covenanting God. The entire Gospel is seen as a portrayal of the meaning of Matthew's view of Jesus as Emmanuel: God with us. And in this particular reading, that incarnate solidarity is shared representatively.

We may similarly build our bridge to this doctrine from the other texts we have considered. In their midrashic wrestling, Jesus can be, for Christians, the human face of God, the mortal veil through which we see the Holy One of Israel. Or, adopting the language of the call of Moses, Jesus can be viewed as the Christian's burning bush, in and through whom (but not, in the end, consuming him) we meet the God of our ancestors addressed by a summoning voice that proclaims: *I AM–you are . . . for others*. Or looking back at destruction through the eyes of Abraham and Jesus, we might see that the covenantal dynamic of creation is nothing less than the divine movement of hospitality. In this way, post-Shoah Christians may dare claim that the presence of God may be met in the open-ended and vulnerable gesture of hospitality that they encounter fully embodied in Jesus. He is the very image of divine hospitality, who in his own creaturely fidelity and hospitality reflects the hospitality of the Creator as well as creation itself at the same time he fulfills the promise of the same in his creaturely action.

The doctrine of the Trinity can pose serious difficulty when its affirmations become hardened and rigid categories of being and knowing, which, in turn, undo the very insights they seek to preserve: that relation lies at the heart of God's being. That is, relation actually reflects God's own essential reality. More specifically, when tied to the dynamics of Incarnation, covenantal language can provide a way of recovering this relational quality. Jesus, seen through the lens of covenant life, becomes the one in whom the fullness of covenant life was pleased to dwell: as covenanter (covenanting one), as covenanted (covenanted one), and as the embodied power of promise to bind each to the other in the unity of covenant. The triadic embodiment of covenantal reality brings together the latent but very real ecology of covenant life and the relationship of the two doctrines, demonstrating a more dynamic way of approaching them.

RETURNING TO THE TEXT

Of course, there is much more to be developed with regard to the theological implications of this midrashic experiment. But the goal of midrash is not some final and abstract articulation of clarified beliefs. Along with the critical reflection of theology, they have their place in the service of that return. In the end, however, the midrashic goal is to return to *PaRDeS*. The way forward is by way of return to the world of the text along with the story and the divine-human partnership it mediates to those who choose to respond. For Jews, that partnership is captured by the multivalent word *Torah*. For Christians, its counterpart is the covenantal relationship that they know in and through Jesus, in the Body of Christ, which has been approached here as a covenantal partnership of abundant life, which we meet in the hospitality of creation and the life and teachings of Jesus. To be sure, theology and its abstractions have their place, but in the rhythm and service of life, in partnership with the text and its narrated world of an even greater partnership that still includes those who dare respond to its summoning address. *Hineni.*

NOTES

1. Mark I. Wallace characterizes such a rhetorical approach as a postmetaphysical strategy that provides critical leverage and confessional ground for confronting the loss of the absolute as well as the tyranny of the relative, two important characteristics of the modern age. See Mark I. Wallace, *Fragments of the Spirit: Nature, Violence, and the Renewal of Creation* (New York: Continuum, 1996), pp. 48–53, 189–198.

2. As Wallace points out, wisdom literature bears this function in keeping the witness of Scripture whole and open to life as it is lived at the margins of its worlds.

3. Note the distinction between narrative and narrated world.

4. Robert Kegan has done pioneering work with regard to the dance of differentiation and integration as it is recapitulated in the dynamics of human development. See *The Evolving Self: Problem and Process in Human Development* (Cambridge: Harvard University Press, 1982); and more recently, *In over Our Heads: The Mental Demands of Modern Life* (Cambridge: Harvard University Press, 1994).

5. Miroslav Volf, *Exclusion and Embrace: A Theological Exploration of Identity, Otherness, and Reconciliation* (Nashville, TN: Abingdon Press, 1996), p. 91. Volf, writing about the ethnic division and hatred in Bosnia Herzegovina, identifies forgiveness as a doorway to the embrace of restored relationship, not the goal of the work of reconciliation.

6. Clark M. Williamson, *A Guest in the House of Israel: Post-Holocaust Church Theology* (Louisville, KY: Westminster/John Knox Press, 1993).

7. See R. Kendall Soulen, *The God of Israel and Christian Theology* (Minneapolis: Augsburg Fortress, 1996), for an insightful analysis of the structural as well as punitive supersessionism that lies within "standard" readings of salvation history as the goal of creation (Part I). He puts forth an optional reading of the canonical story (Part II) bearing much similarity to the position articulated in this presentation. His chapter "The Scriptures: Curse and Redemption" is particularly focused on the central theme of the Scriptures being the consummation of creation with its attendant blessings for all; salvation/redemption is thereby a restorative act in this larger commitment to creation.

8. Matt. 10:16.

9. Jesus, in his practice of hospitality, has helped his disciples see that the guest is always another's host, whereas the host is always another's guest. After Auschwitz, this takes on added significance as Christians and Jews—and Christians, vis-à-vis Jews—learn to integrate this recognition.

7

The Return to *PaRDeS*: A Concluding Midrash

After the parable teller had died, his disciples returned to what they had done before he had come into their lives. Three of them (Peter, James, and John) were deeply grieved. Remembering his stories, they went out one day (I believe it was a Sabbath) to a mountain overlooking Galilee. From there, on a good day, they could see the Kinneret (Sea of Galilee) where they had fished and then later sailed with Jesus. From there they could see the hills they walked, the villages they had visited (and sometimes disturbed). From there they could look south into Judea. From there, on a clear day, they could almost see Jerusalem.

As they talked they used the places they saw in the distance and the geography that stretched out before them to get their bearings. They remembered and talked, recalling Jesus' stories and parables, Torah, and the Prophets to reconstruct his story. One of them remembered the parable of the workers in the vineyard, and each responded with his version of the tale and interpretation of its meaning. As they spoke, they marveled at how this very parable—about a vineyard and so much more—was like their own Scriptures: a garden to be tilled and turned until it bears its fruit and feeds those who labor in it. One of them remembered that the parable worked in silent, unsettling ways, reminding him of Elijah's experience in the cave on Mount Horeb, where he heard the voice of God in full and fragile silence. Another said he was led a different direction, more like Moses approaching the burning bush, overwhelmed with the presence he had encountered. Yet they all agreed, the parable was bold and challenging, forcing them to step back and take second and third looks at themselves and their worlds. Peter, deeply moved by his friends and what each of them remembered, told them so and suggested they find some way of saving the moment and their insights. As they talked further they were overcome. The best they could describe it afterward was that they were once more caught up in the reality that embraced them when Jesus preached and taught, what he called the rule and realm of heaven. He had brought it near to them in word and deed; once more it enveloped them. Indeed. Jesus was with them, yet he was gone, killed by the Romans, though just as surely his followers were implicated in his death as well.

Nevertheless, they were convinced that the very One whom Jesus served had descended upon them in the same way God had spoken through him when he had taught them before. It was like the burning bush and the still small voice were not just stories but happening anew in their midst. And they were overwhelmed. It was as if Jesus were telling them anew:

> The rule and realm of God are in your midst. Its promise and power are in *your* hands. Take it and use it—responsibly and with love. For whom you include in your embrace, God includes. (And whom you exclude may be excluded as well from the same divine embrace that extends through you.) Nonetheless, just as God's love is conveyed by you it is borne by others, who like you, hear the divine summons of life. Act wisely and with care; but do not remain here. Go.

And they went down the mountain to the valley below, then set their faces on Jerusalem.

Selected Bibliography

Allison, Dale C. *The New Moses: A Matthean Typology.* Edinburgh, Scotland: T & T Clark, 1993.

Bauman, Zygmunt. *Modernity and the Holocaust.* Ithaca, NY: Cornell University Press, 1989.

Blenkinsopp, Joseph. *Ezekiel.* Louisville, KY: John Knox Press, 1990.

Browning, Elizabeth Barrett. *Aurora Leigh.* Book VII. Ed. Margaret Reynolds 1857. Athens: Ohio University Press, 1992.

Brueggemann, Walter. *Genesis: Interpretation—A Bible Commentary for Teaching and Preaching.* Atlanta, GA: John Knox Press, 1982.

Burnham, Frederic B., ed. *Post-Modern Theology: Christian Faith in a Pluralist World.* New York: Harper & Row, 1989.

Cohen, Arthur. "In Our Terrible Age: The *Tremendum* of the Jews." In *The Holocaust as Interruption,* ed. Elisabeth Shussler Fiorenza and David Tracy. Edinburgh, Scotland: T. & T. Clark, 1984.

———. *The* Tremendum: *A Theological Interpretation of the Holocaust.* New York: Continuum, 1981.

Cohen, Norman J. *Self, Struggle & Change: Family Conflict Stories in Genesis and Their Healing Insights for Our Lives.* Woodstock, VT: Jewish Lights Publishing, 1995.

Cunningham, Lawrence S. "Elie Wiesel's Anti-Exodus." *America,* April 27, 1975, pp. 325–327.

Eichrodt, Walther. *Ezekiel.* Trans. Cosslett Quin. Philadelphia: Westminster Press, 1970.

Fackenheim, Emil. *God's Presence in History: Jewish Affirmations and Philosophical Reflections.* New York: Harper Torchbooks, 1970.

———. *The Jewish Bible After the Holocaust: A Re-reading*. Bloomington and Indianapolis: Indiana University Press, 1990.
Farley, Edward. *Divine Empathy: A Theology of God*. Minneapolis: Fortress Press, 1996.
Fasching, Darrell J. *The Coming of the Millennium: Good News for the Whole Human Race*. Valley Forge, PA: Trinity Press International, 1996.
———. *Narrative Theology After Auschwitz*. Minneapolis: Fortress Press, 1992.
Fishbane, Michael. *Biblical Interpretation in Ancient Israel*. Oxford: Clarendon Press, 1985.
———. *Biblical Text and Texture: A Literary Reading of Selected Texts*. Oxford: Oneworld, 1998.
———. *The Garments of Torah: Essays in Biblical Hermeneutics*. Bloomington: Indiana University Press, 1989.
Fishbane, Michael, ed. *The Midrashic Imagination: Jewish Exegesis, Thought, and History*. Albany: State University of New York Press, 1993.
Fowler James W. *Faithful Change: The Personal and Public Challenges of Postmodern Life*. Nashville, TN: Abingdon Press, 1996.
Fox, Everett. *Genesis and Exodus: A New English Rendition with Commentary and Notes*. New York: Schocken Books, 1990.
Freedman, H., trans. *Midrash Rabbah Exodus.*: Vol. III. London: Soncino Press, 1939.
———. *Midrash Rabbah: Genesis*. Vol. II. London: Soncino Press, 1939.
Friedman, Richard Elliott. *The Disappearance of God: A Divine Mystery*. Boston: Little, Brown and Company, 1995.
Garber, Zev. *Shoah: The Paradigmatic Genocide—Essays in Exegesis and Eisegesis*. Lanham, MD.: University Press of America, 1994.
Goldberg, Michael. *Jews and Christians: Getting Our Stories Straight*. Nashville, TN: Abingdon Press, 1985.
Greeley, Andrew, and Neusner, Jacob. *Common Ground: A Priest and a Rabbi Read Scripture Together*. Cleveland, OH: Pilgrim Press, 1996.
Greenberg, Irving. "Cloud of Smoke, Pillar of Fire: Judaism, Christianity, and Modernity After the Holocaust." In *Auschwitz?: Beginning of a New Era?*, ed. Eva Fleischner. New York: KTAV Publishing House, 1977.
———. "History, Holocaust, and Covenant." In *Remembering for the Future: The Impact of the Holocaust and Genocide on Jews and Christians*. Proceedings of an International Conference. Oxford and London, July 10–17, 1988. Oxford: Pergamon Press, 1989.
———. "Religious Values After the Holocaust: A Jewish View." In *Jews and Christians After the Holocaust*, ed. Abraham J. Peck. Philadelphia: Fortress Press, 1982.
———. "Voluntary Covenant." In *Contemporary Jewish Religious Responses to the Shoah*, ed. Steven L. Jacobs. Lanham, MD: University Press of America, 1993.
Hall, Douglas John. *Professing the Faith: Christian Theology in a North American Context*. Minneapolis: Fortress Press, 1993.
Hartman, Geoffrey H., and Budick, Sanford, eds. *Midrash and Literature*. New Haven, CT: Yale University Press, 1986.
Hodgson, Peter C. *Winds of the Spirit*. Louisville, KY: Westminster/John Knox Press, 1994.

Hunter, James Davison. *Culture Wars: The Struggle to Define America.* New York: Basic Books, 1991.
Jacobs, Steven L. *Contemporary Christian Religious Responses to the Shoah.* Lanham, MD: University Press of America, 1993.
———. *Contemporary Jewish Religious Responses to the Shoah.* Lanham, MD: University Press of America, 1993.
Ka-Tzetnik 135633. *Shivitti: A Vision.* San Francisco: Harper & Row, 1987.
Kegan, Robert. *The Evolving Self: Problem and Process in Human Development.* Cambridge: Harvard University Press, 1982.
———. *In over Our Heads: The Mental Demands of Modern Life.* Cambridge: Harvard University Press, 1994.
Knight, Henry F. "Choosing Life Between the Fires: Toward an Intentionalist Voice of Faith." In *Remembering for the Future: The Impact of the Holocaust and Genocide on Jews and Christians.* Proceedings of an International Conference. Oxford and London, July 10–17, 1988. Oxford: Pergamon Press, 1989.
———. "From Shame to Responsibility and Christian Identity: The Dynamics of Shame and Christian Confession Regarding the Shoah." *Journal of Ecumenical Studies,* 35, no.1 (Winter 1998): pp. 41–62.
———. "The Inclusive Call of Covenant Life." *New Conversations: Confronting and Combatting Christian Anti-Judaism* 15, no. 3 (Autumn 1993): 32–36.
Kushner, Lawrence. *GOD was in this PLACE & I, i did not know: Finding SELF, SPIRITUALITY, AND ULTIMATE MEANING.* Woodstock, VT: Jewish Lights Publishing, 1994.
———. *The River of Light: Spirituality, Judaism, Consciousness.* Woodstock, VT: Jewish Lights Publishing, 1990.
Laytner, Anson. *Arguing with God: A Jewish Tradition.* Northvale, NJ: Jason Aronson, 1990.
Levenson, Jon. *The Death and Resurrection of the Beloved Son.* New Haven, CT: Yale University Press, 1993.
Littell, Franklin. *The Crucifixion of the Jews: The Failure of Christians to Understand the Jewish Experience.* New York: Harper & Row, 1975.
Lorenzen, Thorwald. *Resurrection and Discipleship: Interpretive Models, Biblical Reflections, Theological Consequences.* Maryknoll, NY: Orbis Books, 1995.
Lynd, Helen Merrell. *On Shame and the Search for Identity.* New York: Harcourt, Brace & World, 1958.
Metz, J. B. *The Emergent Church: The Future of Christianity in a Postbourgeois World.* New York: Crossroad, 1987.
Migliore, Daniel L., ed. *Princeton Seminary Bulletin: The Church and Israel: Romans 9–11*, Supplementary Issue, no. 1 (1990).
Moore, James F. *Christian Theology After the Shoah: A Re-interpretation of the Passion Narratives.* Lanham, MD: University Press of America, 1993.
Moore, James F., special edition ed. *Shofar: Jewish-Christian Dialogue After the Shoah,* vol. 15, no. 1 (Fall 1996).
Neusner, Jacob. *The Midrash: An Introduction.* Northvale, NJ: Jacob Aronson, 1990.
———. *What Is Midrash?* Philadelphia: Fortress Press, 1987.
Nicholls, William. *Christian Antisemitism: A History of Hate.* Northvale, NJ: Jason Aronson, 1993.

Nicholson, Ernest. *God and His People: Covenant and Theology in the Old Testament.* Oxford: Clarendon Press, 1986.
Novak, David. *Jewish-Christian Dialogue: A Jewish Justification.* New York and Oxford: Oxford University Press, 1989.
Ochs, Peter. "Returning to Scripture: Trends in Postcritical Scriptural Interpretation." *Cross Currents* 44, no. 4 (Winter 1994/95): 437–451.
———. *The Return to Scripture in Judaism and Christianity: Essays in Postcritical Scriptural Interpretation.* New York: Paulist Press, 1993.
Ogden, Schubert. *Is There Only One True Religion or Are There Many?* Dallas: Southern Methodist University Press, 1992.
Ogeltree, Thomas W. *Hospitality to the Stranger: Dimensions of Moral Understanding.* Philadelphia: Fortress Press, 1985.
Oliner, Samuel P., and Oliner, Pearl M. *The Altruistic Personality: Rescuers of Jews in Nazi Europe.* New York: Free Press, 1988.
Patte, Daniel. *The Gospel According to Matthew: A Structural Commentary on Matthew's Faith.* Philadelphia: Fortress Press, 1987.
Pellegrino, Charles. *Return to Sodom and Gomorrah: Bible Stories from Archeologists.* New York: Random House, 1994.
Plaskow, Judith. *Standing Again at Sinai: Judaism from a Feminist Perspective.* San Francisco: Harper & Row, 1990.
Race, Alan. *Christians and Religious Pluralism: Patterns in Christian Theology of Religions.* Maryknoll, NY: Orbis Books, 1983.
Reuther, Rosemary Radford. *Faith and Fratricide: The Theological Roots of Anti-Semitism.* With an introduction by Gregory Baum. New York: Seabury Press, 1974.
Ricoeur, Paul. *Figuring the Sacred: Religion, Narrative and Imagination.* Trans. David Pellauer. Ed. Mark I. Wallace. Minneapolis: Fortress Press, 1995.
Ricoeur, Paul, and LeCoque, Andre. *Thinking Biblically.* Chicago: University of Chicago Press, 1998.
Robbins, Jill. *Prodigal Son/Elder Brother: Interpretation and Alterity in Augustine, Petrarch, Kafka, Levinas.* Chicago: University of Chicago Press, 1991.
Rubenstein, Richard L. *After Auschwitz: Radical Theology and Contemporary Judaism.* New York: Bobbs-Merrill, 1966.
Rubenstein, Richard L., and Roth, John K. *Approaches to Auschwitz: The Holocaust and Its Legacy.* Atlanta, GA: John Knox Press, 1987.
Schneiders, Sandra. "Does the Bible Have a Post-Modern Message?" In *Christian Faith in a Pluralist World,* ed. Frederic B. Burnham. New York: Harper & Row, 1989.
Scott, Bernard Brandon. *Hear Then the Parables.* Minneapolis: Fortress Press, 1989.
Segal, Alan. *Rebecca's Children: Judaism and Christianity in the Roman World.* Cambridge: Harvard University Press, 1986.
Senior, Donald. *The Passion of Jesus in the Gospel of Matthew.* Wilmington, DE: Michael Glazier, 1985.
Soulen, R. Kendall. *The God of Israel and Christian Theology.* Minneapolis: Augsburg Fortress, 1996.
Spong, John Shelby. *Liberating the Gospels: Reading the Bible with Jewish Eyes.* San Francisco: Harper, 1996.

Steinsaltz, Adin. "The Downfall of Rabbi Eliezer." In *The Strife of the Spirit*, ed. Arthur Kurzweil. Northvale, NJ: Jason Aronson, 1988.
———. *The Essential Talmud*. Trans. Chaya Galai. New York: Basic Books, 1976.
Stemberger, Günter. Introduction to the TALMUD and MIDRASH. Trans. and ed. Markus Bockmuehl. Edinburgh, Scotland T & T Clark, 1991.
van Buren, Paul. *The Westminster Tanner-McMurrin Lectures on the History and Philosophy of Religion: The Change in the Church's Understanding of the Jewish People*. Salt Lake City: Westminster College of Salt Lake City, 1990.
Visotzky, Burton. *The Genesis of Ethics: How the Tormented Family of Genesis Leads Us to Moral Development*. New York: Crown Publishers, 1996.
———. *Reading the Book: Making the Bible a Timeless Text*. New York: Schocken Books, 1996.
Volf, Miroslav. *Exclusion and Embrace: A Theological Exploration of Identity, Otherness, and Reconciliation*. Nashville, TN: Abingdon Press, 1996.
Wallace, Mark I. *Fragments of the Spirit: Nature, Violence, and the Renewal of Creation*. New York: Continuum, 1996.
Waskow, Arthur. *Godwrestling*. New York: Schocken Books, 1978.
Westermann, Claus. *Genesis 12–36: A Commentary*. Trans. John J. Scullion. London: SPCK, 1985.
Wiesel, Elie. *Against Silence: The Voice and Vision of Elie Wiesel*. Ed. Irving Abrahamson. New York: Holocaust Library, 1985.
———. *Memoirs: All Rivers Run to the Sea*. New York: Alfred A. Knopf, 1995.
———. *Messengers of God*. New York: Random House, 1976.
———. *Night*. Trans. Stella Rodway. New York: Bantam Books, 1960.
———. *Sages and Dreamers: Biblical, Talmudic, and Hasidic Portraits and Legends*. New York: Summit Books, 1991.
———. *The Trial of God*. Trans. Marion Wiesel. NY: Random House: 1979.
Williams, Rowan. *Resurrection: Interpreting the Easter Gospel*. Harrisburg, PA: Morehouse Publishing, 1982.
Williamson, Clark M. *A Guest in the House of Israel: Post-Holocaust Church Theology*. Louisville, KY: Westminster/John Knox Press, 1993.
Williamson, Clark M., and Allen, Ronald J. *Interpreting Difficult Texts: Anti-Judaism and Christian Preaching*. Philadelphia: Trinity Press, 1989.
Zimmerli, Walther. *Ezekiel*. Trans. James D. Martin. Ed. Paul D. Hanson, with Richard Jay Greenspoon, Vol. 2. Philadelphia: Fortress Press, 1983.

Index

Abraham, xvi, xxiv, 1, 7, 34 n.11, 39, 40– 49, 51–52, 55, 58–59, 69, 86, 94, 100, 102–3, 160, 164–65, 167, 170; contending with God, 45–46, 48
Aggadah, xiv, 15, 119 n.28
Akedah, 91
Al tiqre . . . elah (do not read . . . but), 12–13, 16–18, 143, 145, 153 n.28
Allen, Ronald J., 33 n.7
Antisemitism, 5–6, 21, 25, 33, 33 n.6, 36, 54–55, 77, 90, 92, 111
Atonement, 159, 161–62, 171

Babylon, 124, 126, 128–30, 134
Baptism, 73, 83–84 n.21, 149–50
Baum, Gregory, 33 n.6
Ben adam, 22, 125, 132, 137
Bet Midrash, 34 n.23
Blenkinsopp, Joseph, 132
Bones: dry bones, xxiv, 123–24, 126, 128–31, 133–36, 138, 141–42, 151, 152 n.6; other bones, 128, 141; these bones, xxiv, 123–34, 136, 139, 141–44, 146–47, 149–52, 152 n.6
Booths, 72–73

Browning, Elizabeth Barrett, 87, 118 n.8
Brueggemann, Walter, 45–46, 59–60 n.4
Burning bush, 86–94, 96–97, 99, 102–3, 110–12, 114–17, 118–19 nn.5, 19, 165, 170, 173; summons at the bush, 97, 101

Chebar, 124, 126, 128–30, 134, 142
Christocentric, 78, 156, 159
Christology, xvi, 4, 63, 76– 80, 84, 112, 158–60; constitutive Christology, 78; left hand of Christology, 4; representative Christology, 78, 80, 84 n.28, 158–59, 169–70
Churban, 124, 130, 133–34, 137, 152 n.5
Church, xiii, xx, 4, 5, 20–31, 33, 53, 109, 158–59, 162–64, 171
Cohen, Arthur, A. 37 n.61, 47, 60 n.15, 82 n.2, 93, 119 n.20
Confessing Church, 25
Confessional identity, xxiii-xxv, 6, 7, 9, 17–19, 21, 32, 52, 63–66, 80, 92, 112, 114, 155, 157–60, 171 n.1
Consummation, 149, 171 n.7

Contempt, xiii, xxiii, 6, 21, 28–29, 32, 79, 145, 151
Covenant life, 5–9, 11, 14–16, 18, 24–25, 26–32, 40, 55, 68–70, 74–75, 79–81, 86, 88, 96, 100–101, 103–4, 108–15, 117, 120 n.31, 139–41, 147, 160–65, 167–71
Covenantal crisis, 18, 27–28, 81, 96
Covenantal fabric of life, 5, 6, 42, 47, 64, 69, 93
Covenantal fidelity, 14, 86, 148, 160, 164, 166
Covenantal gestalt, 94–95, 99–100, 102, 109, 120 n.32, 146–48, 165
Covenantal legacy, 8, 24
Covenantal orientation, 16, 30–31, 64
Covenantal partnership, 6, 11, 14, 18, 44, 48, 58, 80, 83 n.15, 86, 89, 93–96, 98–102, 110, 117, 120–21 nn.39, 41, 140, 147, 163–64, 171
Covenantal perspective, 32, 160
Covenantal presence, 70–74, 89, 92, 96, 99–100, 102, 115–16
Covenantal purpose of creation, 5, 31, 37 n.63, 79, 102, 109–10, 116, 120 n.32, 139, 159, 162, 164
Creation, xvi, 5–6, 14, 21, 23, 30–31, 40, 43, 55, 57, 64, 69, 77, 79, 81, 84 n.29, 86, 95–96, 99–100, 102–3, 108–10, 112, 114, 116–17, 120 n.32, 125, 127, 131–32, 136–41, 148–50, 156–71
Credibility crisis, 123–24, 161
Critical faith, 28–29, 33
Crucifixion, xx, 22–25, 29–30, 36 n.52, 81, 142–43, 145, 147, 148, 159, 168
Cunningham, Lawrence S., 36 n.56

Dabar aher (another interpretation), 12
Darshan, 12
Derash, xvi, 10, 13–17
Displacement theology, 4–5, 9, 53, 55, 76, 79, 108–9. *See also* Supersessionism

Easter, xiii, 79, 85, 101, 123, 142–47, 154 n.33, 174
Eckardt, Roy and Alice, 82 n.2
Ehyeh asher ehyeh, 95, 102, 119 nn.23, 26
Eichrodt, Walther, 153 n.11
Election, 35, 87, 115, 138–41, 151, 164
Eliezer, R., 34 n.23
Elijah, 66, 72–77, 79–81, 173
Emmanuel (God with us), 63, 71–73, 78–80, 153 n.30, 159, 170
Empty tomb, xxiv, 142–45, 149, 165
Epistemology, 12, 30, 65, 67–69, 71–72, 82 n.8, 103, 147
Esau, 1–4, 8–9, 33 n.1
Exegesis, xiv, 10, 16
Ezekiel, xxiv, 123–43, 146, 151, 152 n.1, 153 n.11

Facelessness, 50–51, 127
Fackenheim, Emil, 17, 35, 50–51, 64, 69–70, 75, 81, 82 n.3, 127, 136, 138, 149, 153 nn.16, 17, 23, 154 n.35; 614th commandment, 70, 149
Farley, Edward, 120
Fasching, Darrell J., 118 n.16
Fishbane, Michael, 13, 16–17, 34 n. 22, 61 n.28, 118 n.12, 122 n.58
Fleischner, Eva, 60 n.12, 82 n.6
Fowler, James W., 122 nn.54, 55
Fox, Everett, 34 n.13, 46

Garber, Zev, xiii–xviii, xx, xxv n.2, 34–35 n.31, 36 nn.46, 53
Gestalt, 88–90, 93–96, 99–100, 102, 104–9, 111, 115, 117, 119 n.19, 120 nn.31, 32, 121 nn.40, 41, 48, 146–48, 163, 165. *See also* Covenantal gestalt
Gethsemane, xvi, xxiv, 1, 9, 21–28, 30–33
God, 85–117 passim; divine name, 86, 95, 102, 110–11, 135, 152 n.2; I AM-you are, 91, 95, 96, 102, 116–17, 165–66, 170; presence of, 67–68, 70, 74–75, 77, 79, 83 nn.9, 15, 96, 103, 118–19 nn.5, 19, 23, 24, 25, 26, 120, 123, 137, 170. *See* Providence
Goldberg, Michael, 71, 84 n.24
Gomorrah, xxiv, 39, 40–41, 43, 52–53, 55, 58–59, 60 n.5, 165
Good news, 53–56, 147–48, 160–64, 168–69
Greenberg, Irving, 18, 28, 32, 36 n.58, 46, 60 n.12, 64, 70, 77, 79, 82 nn.2, 6,

Index

83 n.14, 84 n.31, 85, 92–94, 101, 118 nn.3, 15, 119–20 n.28, 147
Guilt, 2, 5–7, 9, 47, 98

Halakhah, xiv, 3–4, 15–16, 18, 35 n.45, 131
Hall, Douglas John, 84 n.28
Hanson, Paul D., 152 n.7
Hartman, Geoffrey H., 10–11, 34 n.15
Healing (*tikkun*), 18, 26, 53–54, 83 n.15, 141, 148
Hermeneutics, xiii, xvi, xix, xxiii, xxiv, xxv, 10, 12–14, 17–19, 28–29, 37 n.63, 55, 66, 80, 84, 107, 154 n.39, 156
Hertz, J. H., 152 n.4
Hineni (here I am), 86, 88–89, 92, 93, 102, 115, 117, 144, 171
Hodgson, Peter C., 95, 119 n.23, 120 n.31, 121 nn.40, 41, 147, 148
Holy Ground, 85–86, 88–89, 103–4, 108, 110–11, 113, 115, 117
Hospitality, xxiv, 39, 42–43, 48–59, 60–61 nn.19, 22; 68, 83 n.9, 98, 100–101, 160–71, 171 n.9; risk of, 56–58, 167–69
Hunter, James David, 122 n.54

Image of God, 8, 70, 77–78, 92, 159
Incarnation, 78, 122 nn.52, 53, 169–70
Inclusion, 6, 105, 107, 110, 112–14, 122 n.57, 150, 160, 162–63, 169
Ish (pl. *Anashim*), 2–3, 6–9, 14, 23, 44, 48
Israel: people of, xiv, xxiv, 2, 4, 8, 15, 17, 23–24, 27–28, 30–32, 33nn.1, 5, 34 n.12, 35 n.44, 44, 53, 65, 67–71, 74, 79–80, 84 nn.28, 30, 86–98, 100–111, 118 n.9, 120 n.32, 120–21 n.39, 122 nn.50, 53, 124–42, 147–51, 153 n.23, 154 nn.34, 39, 159, 162, 164, 168, 170, 171 nn.6, 7; state of, 124, 137–38, 149

Jacob, 1–4, 6–9, 20, 22, 25, 29, 33 n.1, 44, 165
Jacobs, Steven L., xx, xxv n.2, 36 n.46, 83 n.14

Jesus: hospitality of, 53–59, 160–65; parable teller, 103–7, 109–15, 117, 173–74; Passion of, 21–33, 168–69; representative of God, 72–80, 158–60, 165–66
Job, 168

Kabbalism, 120 n.32
Karen, Robert, 34 n.10
Ka-Tzetnik 135633, 91, 118 n.14,
Kevod (glory), 67, 133
Kingdom of God, 54–55. *See also* Rule and realm of God/heaven
Kivyakhol (as it were), 12, 16–18, 76, 145, 152 n.6
Kushner, Lawrence, 95, 119 n.24, 25

Laytner, Anson, 44, 60 n.6
Levenson, Jon, 84 n.21
Lindbeck, George, 35 n.35
Littell, Franklin, xx, 36 n.55, 82 n.2
Lorenzen, Thorwald, 146, 153 n.31
Lot, 41–42, 49– 51, 167
Lot's wife, 41–45, 51
Lynd, Helen Merrell, 34 n.10

May, Herbert, 152 n.4
Metz, Johann Baptist, 40, 59 n.2, 65, 82 n.2
Midrash, xiv–xvi, xix– xx, xxiii–xxv, 9–21, 29, 33 n.2, 34 nn.14, 15, 22, 23, 25–31, 35–36 nn.33, 35, 39, 40, 41, 45, 46, 47, 37 n.63, 43–44, 46, 75, 81–82, 83 n.19, 145, 153 n.28, 154 n.33, 36, 155–58, 170–74
Mission, xxiv, 5, 40, 52, 59, 81, 144, 147–51, 163–64, 168
Monophysitism, 112
Moore, James F., xx, xxv n.2, 29, 36 n.46, 37 n.60, 60 n.9
Moses, 63, 65–68, 70–81, 84 n.22, 86–103, 115–16, 118–19 n.19, 119 n.28, 165, 170, 173

Neusner, Jacob, 10, 11, 15, 20, 34 nn.14
Nicholls, William, 36 nn.50
Nicholson, Ernest, 79, 84 n.30
Night, 26, 35 n.43, 85

Noachide laws, 122 n.56
Novak, David, 122 n.56

Ochs, Peter, 60 n.11
Ogden, Schubert, 78, 84 n.27
Oliner, Samuel P. and Pearl M., 50, 60
Otherness, xxiii–xxiv, 7–9, 13, 18–20, 55–57, 83, 95, 100–102, 116–17, 121 n.40, 129–31, 147, 150–51, 152 n.3, 157–59, 167–68

Parable, 11, 103–8, 110–11, 121 n.47, 163, 173
PaRDeS, xvi, 13–17, 19–21, 35–36, nn.33, 45, 47, 156, 170, 173
Parkes, James, 4
Patte, Daniel, 36 n.51
Peck, Abraham J., 119 n.22
Pellegrino, Charles, 60 n.5
Penuel Peniel, 3, 4, 80
Peshat, xvi, 13–14, 18–20, 125, 129–30, 137, 139, 142, 148, 150, 154 n.33
Plaskow, Judith, 83 n.15
Polanyi, Michael, 82–83 n.8
Prosch, Harry, 82–83 n.8
Providence, 47–48, 93–96, 100, 119 n.26, 120–21 nn.39, 40, 166–67, 169–70

Race, Alan, 122 n.57
Remez, xvi, 13, 16, 20, 150, 154 nn.33, 36
Repentance, 6–7, 52, 55
Representative particularity, 138–41, 151; Election, 35, 87, 115, 164
Restoration, xxiv, 52, 83 n.15, 124–25, 133–39, 141–42, 147–51, 160, 164
Resurrection, xxiv, 71, 81, 83–84 n.21, 124, 136, 142–49, 153 n.15, 154 n.33, 159
Reuther, Rosemary Radford, 4, 33 n.6, 36 n.48
Ricoeur, Paul, 14–16, 35 n.32
Ritschl, Dietrich, 15
Robert Kegan, 171 n.4
Root experience, xxiv, 63–69, 70–72, 80–82, 165
Roth, John K., xi–xii, 34 n.11

Rubenstein, Richard L., 34 n.11, 64, 93, 119 n.21
Rule and realm of God/heaven, 104, 106, 108, 110–11, 117, 121 nn.41, 48, 147–48, 151, 163, 174

Salvation, 23, 70, 78, 86, 115–17, 120 n.30, 122 n.56, 140, 159–65, 171 nn.5, 7
Schneiders, Sandra, 34 n.24
Scott, Brandon, 71–72, 83 n.18, 106, 108, 121 n.42, 45
Seder, 22, 24, 26, 33, 35 n.43, 36 n.53
Segal, Alan, 33 n.1, 122 n.56
Shame, xxiii, 3–9, 21, 26, 33 n.1, 44–45, 52, 55, 61 n.24, 77, 84 n.25, 88, 98–99, 102, 166
Sin, 6, 49, 53, 120 n.30, 150, 160
Sinai (Mount Horeb), xvi, xxiv, 17, 63–75, 77–82, 86, 103, 158–59, 165, 173
Sod, xvi, 13, 14
Sodom, ix, xxiv, 39–53, 55–56, 58–59, 60 n.5, 160, 165, 167
Son of man, 22, 125, 132, 137
Soulen, R. Kendall, 35 n.44, 122 nn.50, 53, 148–49, 154 n.34, 171 n.7
Steinsaltz, Aidin, 34 n.23
Stumbling block, 168–69
Supersessionism, xv, xvi, xxiii, xxiv, 5–6, 18, 21, 23, 30–32, 35 n.44, 53, 66, 74–79, 109, 122 n.53, 153 n.15, 159, 171 n.7

Temple, 22, 27, 111, 124, 128–33, 135, 153 n.19
Text: intertextual, 16–17, 35 n.39; world of the text (PaRDeS), xxv, 12–15, 17, 20, 35 n.35, 169, 171. See PaRDeS
Theology of the cross, 57–58. See also Hospitality, risk of
Tillich, Paul, 29, 30, 121 n.40
Torah, xiv–xv, xvi, 12, 17–18, 20, 60, 63, 66, 69, 73–75, 80, 84 n.29, 92, 101, 118 n.16, 170–71, 173
Transfiguration, 63–65, 71–81, 158
Trinity, 149, 169–70

Triumphalism, 5, 16, 149, 159, 161
Tsimtsum, 120 n.32

Valley of dark shadows (Ps 23: 1), 123, 137, 151
Valley of dry bones, xxiv, 123–24, 126, 128–31, 133–36, 138, 151–52
Van Buren, Paul, 4, 5, 33 n.5, 34, 82 n.2, 178, 179
Vineyard, xvi, 86–87, 103–15, 117, 118 nn. 5, 9, 163, 165, 173
Visotzky, Burton L., 119 n.27
Volf, Miroslav, 171 n.5

Wallace, Mark I., 35 n.32, 171 n.1
Waskow, Arthur, 33 n.4
Westermann, Claus, 60 n.19
Wiesel, Elie, xix, 2, 21, 25–26, 33 n.3, 35 n.43, 36 nn.49, 54, 41, 47, 60 n.14, 85, 91, 118, 130, 141, 152 n.1, 152 n.9
Williams, Rowan, 154 n.33
Williamson, Clark M., xx, 4, 33, 82 n.2, 84 n.28, 120 n.39, 162, 171 n.6

Yeats, William Butler, 153 n.25

Zimmerli, Walter, 129–130, 152 n.7

About the Author

HENRY F. KNIGHT is University Chaplain and Associate Professor of Religion at The University of Tulsa, where he teaches courses on Christian Theology, the Holocaust, and Jewish-Christian Relations. He has written several scholarly articles and coedited a book, *The Uses and Abuses of Knowledge* (with Marcia Sachs Littell, 1997).

www.ingramcontent.com/pod-product-compliance
Lightning Source LLC
Chambersburg PA
CBHW052340230426
43664CB00041B/2572